So Much for the

WHITE PICKET FENCE

A Memoir by Karen LaGraff

WALDENHOUSE PUBLISHERS, INC
WALDEN, TENNESSEE

Published by Waldenhouse Publishers, Inc.
100 Clegg Street, Signal Mountain, Tennessee, USA
888-222-8228 www.waldenhouse.com
Printed in the United States of America
Type and Design by Karen Paul Stone
ISBN: 978-1-947589-34-6
Library of Congress Control Number: 2020950319
     A woman's journey of letting go of the idealized life of the
     perfect marriage and family. It is her story of the challenges she
     faced and the lessons she learned.
BIO026000 BIOGRAPHY & AUTOBIOGRAPHY / Personal Memoirs
FAM000000 FAMILY & RELATIONSHIPS / General
SEL031000 SELF-HELP / Personal Growth / General

Dedication

To my family – the one I came from and the one I created.
And to all the families created who will come after me.

Contents

Preface

We live and learn about life within our families. This is the story of what I experienced. In sharing it, my hope is that my readers will be inspired to face their own challenges with courage and hope for a better tomorrow.

A picket fence, ideally white, has iconic status as Americana, symbolizing the ideal middle-class suburban life, with a family, children (2.5 children and a dog), a large house, and peaceful living.

It represents a relationship that is considered standard, old fashioned and idyllic.

---- Wikipedia

The fence says, "Everything is wonderful. Nothing is wrong here."

The fence is a defensive construct, a boundary, but over time, it takes a lot to maintain the fence.

---- Fr. Mark Hamlet

Foreword

"An ordinary life examined closely reveals itself to be exquisite and complicated and exceptional, somehow managing to be both heroic and plain."   Susan Orlean, *The Bullfighter Checks Her Makeup*

Attention Book Club Members: *So Much for the White Picket Fence* is going to be such a perennial favorite for all book clubs that I suggest you put it on your reading list immediately.

How do I know this? Because I read the book cover to cover in one day, then turned back to page one and read it all over again on the next. I liked it even more the second time around. What were the magic ingredients that made this happen?

First, this is really a story about how we all belong to many families that combine together to make our one true family: the families our parents were children in, the families they created where we were the children, the families of our parents' siblings, the families of those we loved as we grew up, the families created by our siblings, the families we created with our partners, the families our children created in living their lives and loving their partners... all those families that we belonged to, have belonged to and belong to now. Family is instinct, values, the place where you are loved the most and act the worst. It has a "No replace, no return" policy. Karen shows this in every word.

Second, as I write this it is June 2020, a year that has seen a pandemic sweep death throughout the world leaving a path of misery and confusion, as well as a year that has seen the United States split apart by political factions that detest each other. What we all need right now is an end to grinding one another, and a sense of grounding. And if there is one thing I can guarantee you will get from reading Karen's book, it's a sense of grounding.

So here are the facts I glean from this book: The world is not set up to make us happy. The world is not set up to make our partners perfect, our children flawless, and ourselves instruments of God's eternal peace, equanimity and bliss. We live in a messy world; we live messy lives. But when you read Karen's book, there is a deep message of acceptance, fortitude, and perseverance. As do we all, she faces a lot of confusing behaviors from loved ones around her, yet she faces their "I don't care and I won't budge" obstinacy not with punishment, but with a heartfelt curiosity to know what can be done to make their lives better. Of course, she throws up her hands more than once in a while, not in defeat, but in frustration. Karen is no saint, just a wonderful human being struggling to make a good life for her family and herself.

Third, this book plays with two senses of time: the swift passage of tick-tock time and the elephantine crawl of eternal time. In tick-tock, the narrative's sixty years go by like sixty seconds because the story is so darn entertaining. We don't so much read the book as live it. Along with Karen, we suffer and cry and lose and doubt and hurt. We also get some real chuckles, achieve grand accomplishments, and experience moments of profound love and contentment that make life glorious. In eternity, this book develops like Penelope's tapestry: a grand pageant of historic proportion that comes to life a little at a time. Each thread is woven in so skillfully that one doesn't see the entire tableau until the very last strand is in place.

Fourth, the best kind of story telling is that which makes the ordinary extraordinary not by sensationalizing, but by telling the absolute truth in such an honest, open way that its truthfulness is a beacon in the often dark tunnel of life. What are Karen's ordinary events made extraordinary? Young love snuffed out by untimely death, an infant challenged by autism, a son's addiction, and a marriage damaged by an affair are the dramatic events Karen has lived. Of course, the wonder of the book is that the darkness turns to light because tragedies are faced squarely, grieved properly, and worked on faithfully.

Fifth, this book is inspirational. I have taught memoir writing for decades, and I have seen many books transform from dreamy gleams to masterpieces. How did these transformations come about? By effort and determination, which often lead to inspiration. This is not just the secret of writing a good book but, as *So Much for the White Picket Fence* demonstrates, one secret of a happy life. It is Karen's conviction to move ahead into the unknown without a map, without a flashlight, and often without a helping hand that makes this book such a wonder.

Finally, Karen outlines a pattern for success that we would all be wise to follow:

First, begin with love. Rumi, the Whirling Dervish poet, wrote, "Your task is not to seek love, but merely to seek and find all the barriers within yourself that you have built against it."

Second, never waver from that love. Jodi Picoult, the best-selling author of many books about families, wrote, "You don't love someone because they're perfect, you love them in spite of the fact that they're not."

Third, mistakes are inevitable and forgivable. Even Madonna acknowledges that "No matter who you are, no matter what you did, no matter where you've come from, you can always change, become a better version of yourself."

Fourth, when tragedy strikes, mourn your loss fully, learn to love yourself again, and move on in a new direction. The great author and psychologist Irvin Yalom wrote, "If we climb high enough, we will reach a height from which tragedy ceases to look tragic."

Fifth, love comes to those who love. Paulo Coelho, the author of *The Alchemist*, wrote, "My heart might be bruised, but it will recover and become capable of seeing the beauty of life once more. It's happened before; it will happen again, I'm sure. When someone leaves, it's because someone else is about to arrive. I'll find love again."

Sixth, love your perfectly imperfect children with all your heart. As the writer Jhumpa Lahiri said, "Imperfection inspires invention, imagination, creativity. It stimulates. The more I experience the imperfect, the more I feel alive."

Seventh, practice self-care. As the educator and self-care advocate Parker Palmer wrote, "Self-care is never a selfish act—it is simply good stewardship of the only gift I have, the gift I was put on earth to offer to others."

Eighth, share your life with others. Finally, as the author of this Foreword and reader of this amazing book, I want to say that *So Much for the White Picket Fence* has once again convinced me that everyone should write a memoir. As I have told my memoir students again and again, in a life of many decades, if you can't come up with 300 pages—basically 15 hours of living and reading—then you haven't really lived. Live your life. Read memoirs. And, just as Karen La-Graff has, write your own. You will be giving us all the very generous gift of yourself, which is the greatest gift of all.

---- *Joe Ryan*
Ph.D Clinical Psychology,
English professor, Los Angeles City College

PART ONE

Grief is like the ocean; it comes in waves, ebbing
And flowing.
Sometimes the water is calm
And sometimes it is overwhelming.
All we can do is learn to swim.
                    -Vicki Harrison

Chapter 1

June 1959

As a child, there was a certain magic that happened every year when spring turned to summer. This particular one was especially magical for me. I loved the unstructured vacation time bringing freedom from school and the confines of sitting in a desk, having homework, and being on a schedule. It was a time for sleep-overs with friends, swimming in the local pool, going to movies, and seeing more of my family.

I loved going to my paternal grandparents' house. We lived in Tennessee, and they lived in Georgia, just over the state line, twenty minutes away. We called my grandfather, "Big Daddy," and my grandmother was "Big Mama." We always went there for holidays and sometimes for short afternoon visits on the weekends. The kids sat quietly in the living room while the adults visited. I was always enamored with my grandparents.

They had raised six children, five sons, and a daughter. My father was the oldest. Big Daddy had built a large, yellow brick house for their large family in 1930. It was a grand house with high ceilings, four large bedrooms, a large living and dining room, a piano room, and a sunroom. It had art deco lighting and built-in wooden cabinetry. It had a brown slate roof and a circular driveway leading up to the house on a slight hill. Big Daddy had done much of the work himself.

By the time I was born, Big Mama and Big Daddy were both in their late fifties. Big Mama was a large, robust woman, always in a modest, button-up dress with sturdy leather shoes, usually scurrying around her kitchen getting a meal ready. She was smart and had been valedictorian of her senior class in 1912. She wrote an impressive speech and had her picture made in a long, flowing, white dress. Her house was immaculate.

When we visited, Big Daddy could usually be found slouched in his chair watching television in their living room. Often he would be smoking a cigarette, which Big Mama always made him put out when we arrived. He was short and stout, and usually wore a dress shirt with slacks and a hat. He was involved in many businesses, from owning a restaurant to running an oil distributorship, an automobile dealership, building a hotel, and a landscaping business. His six grandchildren thought he was rich because he gave us ten silver dollars and a six-pack of Life Savers for Christmas every year.

I loved visiting them on special occasions when the house was filled with aunts, uncles, and cousins. Although their home was impressive, nothing could compare to the summer cabin Big Daddy built later. It was my favorite place. The cabin was located in the mountains of north Georgia. We called it "the Camp." The experience was rather like being at camp, but the name came from my grandfather's name, Hoyt Campbell.

As a child, nothing got me more excited than hearing my mother say, "Get your bags packed; we're going to 'the Camp'." I loved the feeling of togetherness when our family of five loaded our two-tone blue 1958 Ford station wagon with food and bathing suits and headed for the mountains.

Tall, lanky pine and birch trees lined the sides of the driveway. The cabin sat back in tranquil woods at the end of a long winding dirt road. It was thirty minutes from our home, but it seemed to take forever since several large wooden gates had to be unlocked. My brother, sister, and I often argued over who jumped out with the key to open the locks. The anticipation built as we sat in the backseat, knowing we were almost there. By the time we arrived, we were all standing behind my parents waiting to be turned loose.

A large screened-in porch lined with rocking chairs greeted you as you entered the cabin. A mountain stone fireplace occupied one end of the long narrow living room. We often used this room as a performance stage, as we danced and did what kids did to entertain themselves without TV. Plenty of floor space allowed us to practice cartwheels and splits. At night, when we tired of this, we went outside into the fresh mountain air to catch lightning bugs.

The property had a small swimming and fishing area. Although the lake looked murky, we couldn't wait to get in. Mother always reminded us, "If you eat lunch first, you'll have to wait thirty minutes before swimming," so I always skipped lunch and jumped right in. She sat on the bank in her Bermuda shorts and monitored us swimming, which made me feel safe, even though we could swim, and she couldn't. The icy, cold water felt refreshing on a hot, humid day in the south.

My sister, Diane, and I, along with any friends we brought along, danced the Shuffle and argued over what records to play. Diane was four and half years older than me and introduced me to all the popular musicians: Ricky Nelson, Bobby Darin, Frankie Avalon, and Paul Anka. I often heard them on TV when she watched *American Bandstand.*

My brother, Kimmy, was seven years older and enjoyed fishing but also spent time in the wooden boat ferrying us from the bank to the dock at the end of the lake. My first cousin, Kay, a year older than me, was often there with her parents, brother, Pete, and sister, Sandra. I was the youngest among all the cousins.

Our families gathered around a large round table for dinners. Breakfast and lunch were on the go since we were in a hurry to get outside. A single wire swing hung from the trees behind the house. The seat was a log turned horizontally, which swung you out over the trees looking down on the cabin. Being able to maneuver the swing on your own was a rite of passage for all the cousins.

At night, in the bedrooms we shared, the sound of bullfrogs croaking and the loud buzzing sounds of the cicadas, often made it hard to fall sleep. I would lie there surrounded by the musty smells that permeated the cabin. I felt deeply happy and content being surrounded by the trees and water, and my family. I look back and remember, longing to feel that way again, knowing I never will.

The summer before I turned nine, my parents asked a new young doctor and his family to join us at the cabin for a cook-out. They brought the oldest of their four children, Linda and Robert. My sister and I were already jumping off the wooden dock, doing cannonballs into the water. Diane and Linda quickly started a conversation, but Robert seemed shy and hesitant.

We spent the day eyeing each other curiously, talking only occasionally. Something about this boy, one year older than me, caught my attention. He had a sheepish smile, lacking in self-confidence, but also impish, slightly mischievous. His smile, I learned through the years, was indicative of his personality. I was smitten.

By 4th grade, it had become acceptable to be showing interest in boys, so I couldn't wait to tell my girlfriends about this cute boy.

"You wouldn't believe this boy I met last weekend. We got to swim together at Big Daddy's camp," I told my best friend, Cathi.

"Who is he? What makes him so great?"

"I don't know …. he just has a cute smile, and his father is a doctor. That's about all I know."

I asked around and found that he lived in Copperhill, another small town adjacent to Ducktown, my hometown. He was entering fifth grade. Linda was his older sister, and he had two much younger siblings, Laura and Luke. He swam on a swim team.

The first time I got sick after meeting Robert, Mother took me to Dr. Lee's office. I waited nervously in the small waiting room with a crowd of people. After being called back to the examining room, my mother and I waited for Dr. Lee to arrive.

"Well, isn't this nice? He has family pictures on the wall. Look, there's Robert, you remember him, don't you?" she asked. I could feel myself blushing just at the mention of his name.

"Yeah, I remember him." I never minded going to the doctor again since it meant I could check out all the pictures. Call it an obsession or infatuation, the feelings I felt were intense for a nine-year-old girl.

The following school year, I spent time jumping rope on the playground singing the familiar sing-along girls my age sang as they jumped rope, "Karen and Robert sitting in a tree, k-i-s-s-i-n-g, first comes love, then comes marriage, then comes Karen with a baby carriage. How many children will we have? 1, 2, 3, 4, 5 …"

Aside from my interest in Robert, I had plenty of time to still be a kid. I spent time after school playing with friends, riding my bicycle, taking ballet and piano lessons, doing homework, and reading.

My mother's sister, Aunt Geneva, helped instill a love for reading in me. She worked as a librarian at the Library of Congress in Washington DC and always gave books for Christmas presents.

As a young child, I got various Little Golden Books, later introducing me to *Nancy Drew* and *Little Women*. Mother also loved to read, so we frequented our local library often, especially in the summer. I loved checking out autobiographies at my school library, learning about interesting people. Our once weekly library time gave me a chance to expand my world, to visit other places far from Ducktown, Tennessee. I also dreamed of being a Girl Scout or a Candy Striper, but my small town didn't offer those opportunities.

My mothering instinct was strong from an early age. I cut out a picture in *Life* magazine of a family with lots of kids. I wanted twelve and picked out names for all of them. I loved playing with dolls, but this was before Barbie. All my dolls were baby dolls with blankets and bottles. My pretend play wasn't complicated by Barbie and Ken's relationship.

I had a Tiny Tears, a doll with openings on each side of her eyes that allowed her to cry. I also had a Betsey Wetsey, a doll that wet her diaper after giving her a bottle. I imagine these new features were to make little girls feel like real mothers meeting a baby's needs. Or possibly preparing them that a baby does more than just snuggle in the cradle of your arm.

Our family ate dinner together at night, often having to wait until Daddy got home from work. Afterward, he retired to the couch while my sister and I helped Mother clean the kitchen. He spent the rest of the evening stretchd out on our couch with his head on Mother's lap and watched TV. Our family's favorite was *Father Knows Best*. The family had three children, two girls, and a boy, just like ours. It revolved around family issues and depicted life in pure and uncomplicated times. There was always a happy ending. They probably had a white picket fence.

We also liked to watch, *Leave It to Beaver*, a sitcom about the adventures of a young boy at home, at school, and around his neighborhood. It was written from the perspective of the young boy called the Beaver. He had one brother named Wally. His family, the Cleavers, exemplified the idealized suburban family. June Cleaver was seen as the ideal mother, always in a dress and perfectly coiffed.

My mother was close to being a June Cleaver. She set an example of being a contented wife and devoted mother. She kept our house neat and clean, never cluttered. She also kept her appearance neat, usually wearing a dress, and never missing her weekly hair appointment. She did, however, always love to take off her bra and put on her house duster at the end of the day. It was simple and loose fitting, something between a house dress and a housecoat. She managed most details of our household without the help of my father and made it seem effortless.

～

I continued to keep my interest in Robert to myself, a few friends, and Diane. Mother frequently helped my father at his businesses, so sometimes I was left at home with only my sister. This meant I could use our phone without my mother knowing what I was doing. "Girls don't call boys" was a rule in our house my sister and I were expected to follow. Our only phone, a black rotary dial, sat on a small table in our dining room. It didn't offer much privacy.

With mother gone, a small window of opportunity presented itself. I made sure Diane wasn't within hearing distance. I found Robert's phone number in our thirty-page phonebook –5370. A four-digit phone number was typical in my hometown. I could feel my heart pounding. *Can I do this?* Finally, getting up my nerve, I dialed the number and waited. *What am I going to say?* Mrs. Lee answered the phone.

"Is Robert there?" I asked hesitantly, my voice soft and meek.

"Yes, just a minute."

I waited and waited, thinking he must be outside. *Should I hang up?*

"Hello," he said, sounding slightly out of breath.

I couldn't think of any words, so I carefully slid the phone back on the hook. I called without considering I was bothering Mrs. Lee, disrupting Robert, and most likely making him annoyed. Hearing his voice was a thrill. Since he went to a different elementary school, there weren't opportunities to see him. I would have to make do with hearing him say, "Hello." I did this more than a few times.

I hadn't seen Robert since our swim at Big Daddy's cabin three months before. I had gone out to dinner with my parents and enjoyed my time alone with them. We were on our way home, when my father turned toward my mother and asked, "Why don't we stop by and visit with Doc Lee? I'd like to talk with him about his house plans."

"Oh, they're probably not home. I don't like stopping in unannounced," my mother replied. She was always hesitant to go anywhere when we weren't invited.

"We won't stay long. I like Bill and Lorraine. We haven't seen them since we invited them to the Camp."

This got my immediate attention. I was ready to go.

"Yeah, I don't want to go home. Let's go. Please, Mother, please," I pleaded.

As my father made the turn to indicate we weren't going home, my stomach lurched into my throat – a sudden flood of butterflies filled my chest. The Lees were living in an apartment as they prepared to build a house in the next year.

Daddy parked the car, and we walked toward their modest brick apartment complex. I walked behind my parents, full of anticipation. *Will he be home? Please be home.* My father knocked. I could hear their TV from outside the door. Dr. Lee answered the door.

"Well, Kim Campbell, what do you know? Good to see you. Come on in, Edith. Oh, and Karen is here, too. It's been too long. We've been meaning to have you over."

Mrs. Lee joined in to welcome us, "Hi, we wanted to get together again since the visit to the cabin. We enjoyed it so much. I'm so glad to see you. Sit down, what can I get you to drink?"

Robert peered into the living room from the hallway to see who was there. He was home. *What do I do now? What should I say?* I could feel my face flushing and heart racing. I immediately regretted the phone calls I had made. As our parents began to make conversation, we looked awkwardly at each other.

"Robert, you remember Karen?" Mrs. Lee asked.

There was that smile.

"Yeah, I think so." He hung behind his father just as I was doing to my mother.

Dr. Lee finally broke the awkwardness.

"Do you like to play board games, Karen?"

"Yeah, I play 'Clue' and 'Monopoly' sometimes with my friends," I managed to say.

"Robert, why don't you take Karen to your room and find a game to play?"

All I heard was, "take Karen to your room." Suddenly we were sitting on his bed. I was in his apartment, in his room, on his bed. *Is this really happening?* I listened to Robert explain the rules for 'Parcheesi.' It was hard to concentrate when you were so close to your childhood obsession. He knew my name, so who knew what the future might hold.

His family soon built a new home atop a mountainous area at the foothills of the Cherokee National Forest in east Tennessee, called Cherokee Hills. Homes built there offered beautiful views and plenty of privacy. My family was in transition after living for a year in my maternal grandmother's home after her death. I knew my parents were also making plans to build a new house.

Six months later, after spending an afternoon with Big Daddy discussing building sites and floor plans, my father came home and announced at dinner, "Well, Karen, I've got some news I think you're going to like. It looks like we're buying the lot right above the Lees, and Big Daddy is going to oversee the construction of our new house."

"What? I thought we were building over near the airport?"

"Big Daddy thinks this is a better lot, and we're going to order the plans and get started. What do you think?"

I could feel myself blushing, my eyes widening. Maybe this was just a joke since by this time, everyone in my family knew of my crush on Robert and often kidded me about it.

Right next door meant on the nearest hill, so it was as close as a house could be built. This was like finding out you were going to live next to the movie star you idolized, like maybe Paul Newman or Michael Landon.

Since my birth, we had lived in five different houses, but this was to be my parent's dream home. I spent the next year wondering what it would be like to be next-door neighbors with Robert. I was ecstatic. How much luckier could a little girl get? It was going to be my dream home too.

We moved into our home in the summer of 1961. In the fall, I would turn eleven and be in 6th grade. Our house sat on either what you might call a huge hill or a small mountain. My parents picked house plans and chose a one level solid brick home. They traveled to Cleveland and Chattanooga frequently to select materials and furnishings. It was an exciting time for our family.

The view from every window was spectacular – cascading mountain ranges in the distance from the Cherokee National Forest. There were four bedrooms, two baths, a large kitchen and breakfast room. Like most new houses in the sixties, we had a formal dining and living room, reserved only for special occasions.

Our family time was spent in the den. The walls were constructed from wormy chestnut, the flooring was oak, and the focal point was a large brick fireplace. The overall ambience was warm and inviting and became the center of our family life since my parents splurged and got a color TV. My father had worked hard to provide such a home for us.

The most unique feature of our home was a bomb shelter. During the early sixties, there was talk of war with Russia. So my father decided to enclose part of our basement as a shelter to provide a safe place for our family. I worried about this sometimes, but it didn't diminish the excitement I felt about moving into a brand new house and my new neighbor.

Eventually, the bomb shelter became an office for my father and a perfect room for slumber parties. The room was built with cinder blocks and had no windows. There was no source of sunlight. Turning off the lights created pitch-black darkness. Several years later, the room became the perfect setting for various teen parties and a good game of Spin the Bottle.

Since our move, Robert and I would attend the same school and ride the same bus. I had never been so excited for school to start since this meant seeing him every day. The word had spread that the mysterious phone calls were from me, and he was not the least bit interested. I was just an annoying girl bothering him. *What can I do to turn this around?* He was known as quite a mischievous boy. He was smart, so his teachers were charmed by him, but he was always getting into some kind of trouble.

Since he was a year older, he was in class with my best friend, Darlene. Her mother, Ollie, and my mother were best friends who grew up on the same street in Ducktown. Darlene and I were especially close and spent the night with each other most weekends. We loved to watch *The Mickey Mouse Club* because the cast included both a Darlene and a Karen. We also loved *Lassie*, a series about a female Collie dog, and her adventures in a small farming community. Darlene was especially fond of the old Shirley Temple shows from the mid-30s. It was always fun at her house.

Darlene and I discussed what happened at the end of every school day. Robert was known to keep his teachers on their toes with his antics, so I looked forward to hearing what was going on in 7th grade. Because of my friendship with Darlene, Robert began seeing me in a new light. She was smart, popular, and athletic, and I was her best friend. Our school had one class for each grade, and I was in 6th-grade, but soon, because of my connections, I began to be included in all the 7th-grade social gatherings. *Maybe Robert will start noticing me now.*

Although I was certainly interested in boys, I was not physically mature, like many of the 6th-grade girls. Oh, how I longed for breasts! Maybe this would help me get noticed, but all I really wanted was to fit in. All my girlfriends were developing but not me. I was skinny but considered cute with blonde hair and freckles. Once, after spending the night with Darlene and sleeping late on a Saturday morning, Ollie came in and threw a small, brown bag on the bed in my direction.

"Open it," was all she said, as she left the room.

When I realized she was talking to me, I slowly opened the bag. There it was – my first bra – a white padded bra, the stitching in circles making it look like a bull's eye – a 28AA. It was perfect. I tried it on and looked at myself in the mirror. My feelings exploded into a huge smile as I looked at my reflection. My mother was waiting until I physically needed one, but Ollie knew I needed one for other reasons.

Robert and I started talking on the phone after school, but he didn't acknowledge me much in public. We danced at friend's birthday parties playing the latest 45 vinyl records, "Sherry" by the Four Seasons, "Soldier Boy" by the Shirelles, "The Twist," by Chubby Checker, "Breaking up Is Hard to Do" by Neil Sedaka. Everyone was beginning to have what we called boy/girl parties rather than the all-girl slumber parties.

How thrilling it was to be close to Robert, dancing hand in hand, although I had to share him with several other girls. At these parties, we learned to do the Monster Mash, the Locomotion, the Mashed Potato, and the Twist. Rather than the usual crewcuts, the boys started letting their hair grow long. We wore Madras shirts, Lee jeans, and Weejans, a type of penny loafer. These all held status in our little community.

Not wanting to forget any memorable events, I filled a scrapbook with important items, like the wrapping paper from the Christmas gift Robert gave me in 1961 and the cup that held the Coke he gave me at a basketball game. He filled my purse with trash – two Popsicle sticks, four cigarette butts, discarded chewing gum, dirty Kleenex, a broken pencil, and a few other unidentifiable items. I glued all of this onto the pages of my scrapbook.

I was sentimental at a young age. I was aware of life moving quickly and wanting to hold onto my childhood. Mother often reminded me I wouldn't be a child forever when she said, "Just wait till you have kids of your own." She made it sound a little daunting.

The summers seem endless when you're in seventh grade. Robert was on vacation with his family at Callaway Gardens, and I was missing our phone calls. His two weeks away seemed like a month. One morning Mother brought a letter to me in my bedroom. On the back of the envelope were the letters – "SWAK", "Sealed with a Kiss." The song's lyrics rang in my head. He was sending me all his dreams in a letter sealed with a kiss.

My heart soared before I even read his letter. Seeing those letters was enough for me to realize he was beginning to like me. This was the first letter I had ever gotten from a boy. Robert was left-handed with distinct handwriting. I could barely concentrate on his words, telling me about learning to water ski.

Back in school the following year, Robert and I were both playing on our school's basketball teams. It was the only extra-curriculum activity offered at our school. The Ducktown Ducklings' biggest rival was the Turtletown Turtles. Out of town games required us to take a school bus. Boys and girls were not allowed to sit beside each other, but you could sit across the aisle. Holding hands was not forbidden, and it was amazing how intimate that felt at age twelve.

Butterflies would fly around my stomach before every out-of-town game, wondering if I would be the lucky one to sit across the aisle from Robert. Sometimes I was, and sometimes I wasn't.

Robert and I got to know each other primarily through extended phone calls. But the year he was in eighth, and I was in seventh grade, we took our relationship to a new level. We became an on and off couple, doing activities together in public.

When we were off, he was involved with Jeri Gail. She was certainly more developed than me, cute and popular. This was my first introduction to female jealousy, envy, and heartbreak. When he sat beside her and not me, when he called her and not me, when he danced with her and not me, I felt miserable. The uncertainty of how he felt about me often left me anxious and crying on the phone to Darlene.

In my scrapbook dated December 16, 1962, I wrote on a Christmas themed party napkin, *Mrs. Taylor had an 8th grade Christmas party, and I was invited. We exchanged names for gifts, and Robert got Jeri Gail's name, and she got his. But he switched names with another boy in his class and Jeri Gail didn't know it until the party. He didn't get her a gift. She gave him an ID bracelet, and he's already got one. She thinks he is going to give it to her. He told Darlene he was going to give it to me.*

Another written entry from a white napkin dated August 2, 1963 – *Kay and I had a party at Big Daddy's Camp. We had a hayride up there. The boys were acting like a bunch of nuts. We danced, and nothing else. Robert and some boys put a firecracker in a frog's mouth and blew it up.* Oh, the drama of being twelve.

Robert left home for an extended trip with his family that summer. It seemed unusually long and lonely for me. Dr. Lee had volunteered to go to South America to treat villagers in rural areas. His parents were religious and also doing missionary work. The trip was an enriching cultural experience, and an article written in our local newspaper detailed their exotic and adventurous activities.

Later in life, they continued both their medical and missionary work, eventually visiting all seven continents. They had a special affinity for Native Americans, so they flew to the bottom of the Grand Canyon, living and working there for several summers with the Havasupai tribe who have inhabited the area for over eight hundred years. The Lees were an amazing couple, admired by our entire community.

Robert was finishing 8th grade, and the 8th-grade banquet was an end of year school tradition. I was already wondering who he might ask to the dance. During one of our afternoon phone calls, he surprised me.

"You want to go to the banquet with me? It's in three weeks. We'd have to get dressed up. I've heard it's pretty fun. They play records and stuff. We can dance."

Oh wow... he's asking me? He's asking me!!

"Well, yeah, sure. I'd love to go. I think my parents will let me, but I'll have to ask," I answered, trying not to sound overly excited. Four years had passed since becoming infatuated with Robert. Now my young crush was beginning to develop into a real relationship.

The banquet was a dress-up affair with dinner and dancing. Darlene's mother, Ollie, was a beautician, so I spent the morning getting my hair styled. Before leaving for the event, my mother posed Robert and me for a picture in front of our dining room table. We stood awkwardly beside each other, not touching. The yellow orchid corsage was carefully pinned to my light green organza dress. Robert towered over me in his white jacket and narrow black tie. Both of us looked uneasy as we smiled slightly. The picture doesn't begin to show how happy and excited I was.

The evening was all I had hoped for. We danced and laughed with our friends. And the best part was I had Robert all to myself.

We frequently met each other on Saturday at the movie theatre in our neighboring town. We were still paying a child's admission of thirty-five cents but soon would be paying adult admission of sixty cents. At that point, we might not be able to afford popcorn and Coke. I remember seeing Doris Day in *Pillow Talk,* Sandra Dee in *Gidget, The Headless Ghost,* and *Horrors of the Black Museum.*

I loved going to movies primarily because it opened up my sheltered and secluded world. I loved the emotions they evoked – the laughter, the tears, or the fear. My mother would drop a friend and me off, and her mother would pick us up. Robert would do the same with one of his friends. We sat side by side with his arm around my shoulder or holding my hand. *Is this what it feels like to be in love?*

I was always excited when Robert would ask me to go with him and his parents to a Saturday night horse show in small towns across Tennessee. His family owned horses, and Robert competed in barrel racing. I sat beside him in the back seat of their station wagon as they pulled their horse trailer. But I didn't share a love of horses. Big Daddy also owned horses, and I had been thrown a few times. I just liked being with Robert.

◡⌒⌐

Our worlds were soon going to change since Robert would be going to high school in the fall. Now we shared the same set of friends, but I knew he would be meeting new people and maybe leave me behind. I felt scared and uncertain. *What will this mean for us?* But I told myself we would still ride the same bus and see each other often.

Although I was still a kid, I was aware that in our community, Saturday nights were date night. So I was worried that Robert would start dating, and I would have to wait another year or so. There was pressure to have a boyfriend or girlfriend so you wouldn't be left at home with your parents watching TV, possibly still a black and white one.

My sister was already dating, and I knew couples went to the Canteen to flirt and dance to local bands or went to the local drive-in, snuggling up in the back seat. I always had an interest in boys, chasing them at recess and hoping to be noticed. But after that first encounter meeting Robert, he was my one and only.

◡⌒⌐

So I was more than excited when Robert called one day in late summer of 1963, just before he started high school. Most of our phone calls began with a short conversation about who's doing what with whom. He started this one a little differently.

"Hey, you know there's a summer fair going on up in Blue Ridge, you know, with Ferris wheels, and cotton candy and all that stuff. Maurice has his driver's license now, and he asked if we wanted to go with him and Laura. Do you think your parents would let you go?"

Is he asking me out on a real date, a double date?

The excitement was already bubbling inside me.

"Oh, wow, that sounds fun. Yeah, I'd love to go. I'll have to see what Mother and Daddy say."

Allowing me to go on a date would be a big step. I was anxious about asking them. *What if they don't let me go?* They knew Maurice and his family and also Laura and her family. But did they want me going with Robert? Was I too young to go unchaperoned?

With their approval, the four of us headed off on a hot August night. When we got there, the loud carnival music was blaring, the colorful neon signs were everywhere, and the smells of cotton candy and popcorn filled the air.

"Would you like to see if I can win a stuffed animal? Would you want one?" Robert asked, maybe thinking I thought I was too old for a stuffed bear or dog.

"I used to collect them when I was little. I'd love one."

Both Robert and Maurice tried throwing balls in hoops and darts at dartboards, but neither of them was lucky enough to win anything. We rode the bumper cars, laughing hysterically as we repeatedly ran into each other. The swings lifted us high into the air as we circled the fair over and over. The Tunnel of Love allowed us to sit close as we maneuvered our boat through a waterway. This all left me light-headed. My heart raced from being so close to Robert.

"Wanna have our picture made? We can get in the booth together."

"Oh, my hair looks terrible after riding all these rides."

"Come on, it doesn't matter. Let's do it."

We climbed into the booth together. I rested my head on his shoulder, and we leaned in for the pictures. We were a couple. I was dizzy with the unfamiliar emotions I was feeling. My heart felt full. We left with a strip of four black and white photos to remember this night forever. Afterward, we had two small medallions made that you could imprint with words. We chose *Robert and Karen, August 29, 1963.*

It was exciting to be part of the crowd of mainly teenage couples enjoying the summer fair, although I was three weeks shy of turning thirteen. It was soon time to head home. Maurice drove a little black Peugeot, and Robert and I sat in the back seat holding hands. The scent of Robert's cologne, English Leather, filled the air. *What is happening to me?* My entire body was responding. The marketing campaign for this men's cologne used this slogan, "If your grandfather hadn't worn it, you wouldn't be here." Pretty powerful stuff.

When we pulled into our driveway, the light over the porch created a golden glow onto the two sets of brick steps. My heart was pounding so loudly, I was afraid he could hear it. *Will this be the night of my first kiss?* I was as nervous as I had ever been in my life.

We stood outside the door, and he looked down at me.

"I'm glad your parents let you go. It was a lot of fun."

"Yeah, me too. Thanks for asking me. Maybe next time you'll win a stuffed animal." We both laughed nervously. Our eyes locked as if we both knew it was time. He leaned down, put both hands on my shoulders, and kissed me gently on the lips. I floated into the house, my feet seemingly not even touching the floor.

Robert started high school a few weeks later, and I was trying to make the best out of our separation. It was November and time for our school's annual football banquet. I was a cheerleader, so we were included and could ask a date. I didn't have to think twice about who I wanted to ask. Unfortunately, I woke up sick the morning of the banquet and stayed home from school. I most likely wouldn't be wearing the new pale pink sweater and skirt, but was hoping I might feel better by the end of the day, and mother would let me go.

I spent the morning on our couch going back and forth between the three channels of TV we received, while mother brought me cough and cold medicine. It was early afternoon when an announcement came on interrupting an afternoon soap opera, *As the World Turns*. It was Walter Cronkite, a CBS news anchor, with a news bulletin.

"In Dallas, Texas, three shots were fired at President Kennedy's motorcade. The first report says President Kennedy has been seriously wounded." Then it was back to the soap opera.

My heart dropped. I immediately felt apprehension and panic. My stomach was in knots as I continued to watch TV, hoping for some good news. Walter Cronkite was back on an hour later.

"From Dallas, Texas, President Kennedy died at 1 pm central time." He looked down at his papers. His lips quivered. He took off his glasses. I was frightened to see him so emotional. Even at my age, with limited experience, I felt the world change. Our president was dead.

The football banquet went on as planned, regardless of the circumstances. Mother allowed me to go, thinking being with my friends would be helpful. We all stood around, trying to have fun. No one could get into dancing. There were no sounds of laughter. While we talked, a few people broke down in tears. Everyone was in shock.

My friend, Darlene, and I spent the next four days glued to the TV. We watched the all-day coverage about the assassination and the funeral, with a box of Kleenex between us. It was all televised publicly – the national wake, the national funeral, and national burial. His flag-draped coffin was pulled through the streets of Washington by a horse-drawn caisson. The sound of the horse's hooves on the payment and the rhythmic beat of the drums in the background was dramatic and soul-stirring.

I had never experienced such strong emotions. Everyone was fond of President Kennedy, no matter their political party. He was young, enthusiastic, and passionate. It was fun watching his young family on the news. His death was devastating.

We cried and cried as we watched Mrs. Kennedy, Caroline, and John John sharing their grief with the world. We went back and forth between Darlene's house and mine. It was especially hard for Darlene since her father died when she was three, in an accident in the local mines. Ollie, her mother, was left to raise three little girls on her own.

A little over two weeks later, I experienced a more personal loss. I was on the basketball team playing out of town. We won the game, and I was thrilled because I scored nine points. This was a record for me since I wasn't particularly athletic. My parents weren't there to watch, so I was anxious to tell them my news.

I walked into a dark house, wondering why they weren't still watching TV. I went down the hall toward my bedroom. Diane was lying on the floor, talking on the phone. I stood there wondering where Mother and Daddy were.

"Where is everyone?" The house seemed usually quiet. Diane just kept talking on the phone.

"Where is everyone?" I repeated.

Diane covered the phone with her hand.

"Big Daddy died tonight. Mother and Daddy are with Big Mama at her house."

I leaned into the wall, which seemed to be closing in on me. I felt like I had been punched in the stomach.

"What happened?"

"He went to a restaurant to get dinner for the two of them and collapsed in the men's restroom. They took him to the hospital, but he didn't make it."

It was all too sudden for me. *No, please no, not Big Daddy.* I had always felt close to Big Daddy. Many family members thought I resembled him, with a round face and hazel eyes. I felt scared and alone as I waited for my parents to return. It was late when they got home. I was crying silently on the couch.

"What happened? I thought Big Daddy was okay now. He had surgery, and he was doing good. He was just here. He looked fine. It's not fair."

The grandkids thought Big Daddy had undergone serious heart surgery the previous year. He went to Memphis to a heart specialist, and we all assumed, even Big Daddy, that the problem was repaired. But it was determined to be an inoperable situation, and nothing could be done.

Big Mama was afraid he would give up on life if he knew the truth, so she and their children chose not to tell him. His sudden collapse was not unexpected for them. They knew this would happen eventually.

The next few days were emotional as my aunts, uncles, and cousins gathered to say goodbye. We spent most of our time at my grandparent's house, where friends and family came to pay respects. I stood outside their living room door and saw my father sitting in the chair where Big Daddy always sat. I didn't want him to sit there. *No, please don't sit there; that's where Big Daddy sits.* I could still see

Big Daddy slouched in his chair, smoking a cigarette. Tears stung my eyes. My father was telling a funny story about his father. Daddy's voice cracked and he stopped. I felt scared when I saw him cry for the first time.

Our family life changed after Big Daddy died. Their house seemed unusually empty without him. The large rooms and high ceilings seemed to echo with sadness. My father sold the Camp since it proved to be more than he could keep up with. My brother and sister were both gone from home now, and I was moving on to high school. My childhood days were over.

Chapter 2

September 1964

I had worried for years about being alone on the kids' side of our house, knowing my brother and sister would be gone. I would be the only child. Our house was long and narrow, and the kid's bedrooms were on one end and my parents' bedroom at the other. But instead of feeling lonely and scared, it was exciting to have the place to myself, especially the phone.

My parents frequently settled in their bedroom at night to relax and watch TV, leaving me to do as I pretty much pleased. Which meant, choose the shows I wanted to watch, eat my favorite snacks, and talk with Robert and my girlfriends on the phone. And, oh, I forgot... do homework.

My girlfriends were now a huge part of my life since we had been together since 2nd grade. We were in the same class every year and enjoyed spending the night and going to movies together. We were enjoying high school – sharing secrets, giving advice, and supporting each other through breakups with boyfriends.

Life was good. But I was slightly troubled since I was the only one in my circle of friends who hadn't started their period. Being fourteen, I felt excluded from this transition from girl to woman. My friends used code words to let each other know when they had their periods ... grandmother came to visit. "Yeah, I didn't get to go swimming, *grandmother came to visit.*" My grandmother visited often, but she never brought my period.

We were shown a film in fifth grade about menstruation. During the film, there was a list of what you could and couldn't do when having your period, the dos and don'ts. "You can bathe and shower but only with warm water and dry quickly. You should only swim after starting for two or three days. You should not skate, horseback ride, or square dance. No basketball or volleyball. You should pay extra attention to your nails and hair." Despite all these forewarnings, I was still envious of my friends.

During freshman year, at the end of a long school day, Robert and I were on the phone discussing the day's events. Needing to use the bathroom, I asked, "Can you hang on a minute?"

"Yeah, hurry, I'm going to have to hang up soon. I've got to do my homework."

"Ok, I'll be right back."

Discovering *grandmother* had arrived. I rushed back to the phone.

"Well, I'll let you go. See you tomorrow on the bus," I said, trying to control the excitement in my voice.

I wouldn't be sharing this with him. As far as he knew, I was already a woman. After telling my mother, I called my girlfriends to let them know *grandmother* was alive and well at my house.

My excitement lasted only a few short months. I was plagued with debilitating cramps. If I started at school, I would call Mother to come get me because of the excruciating pain. At home, I went to bed with a heating pad and pain pills. *So this is what women have to deal with?*

I loved high school, but there were so many social distractions making working up to my potential a low priority. I had made good grades in elementary and middle school, and it was important to me to please both my teachers and parents. I knew my parents had academic expectations for me since my brother was a pharmacist, and my sister was studying to be a teacher. But college seemed a vague distant concept.

I was more interested in getting involved in as many social opportunities as possible. I liked meeting new people. Our school's population of students came from three feeder schools, so I decided I would try out for the basketball team to increase my circle of friends.

Since I had played in middle school, I knew being part of a team was fun. I diligently practiced in our garage every day after school. The list of the selected players was posted on the gym door. I was cautiously optimistic that I would see my name.

My heart dropped. I felt tears stinging my eyes, ready to roll down my cheeks. My name wasn't on the list. I couldn't wait to get home. I held myself together at school, but after arriving safely inside my house, it all came pouring out.

"I didn't make the team," I wailed.

I threw myself on the couch. As usual, my mother had kind words to say, but I was heartbroken.

"I practiced and practiced and thought I had a chance," I said as I choked back sobs. "It's not fair!"

Mother sat next to me on the couch, gently trying to console me. "Well, Karen, you know you tried your best. That's what's most important."

"But I wanted to play so bad. Darlene and Joyce both made the team."

"Well, everyone has talents. We can't be good at everything. You're talented in lots of ways. Maybe you could be in the band like Diane was."

I had already given up on piano and flute, so I knew I wasn't musically gifted. This was the first time I had not been good enough; my first big disappointment in myself.

Although I loved playing the game, my skills were not as good as others. At our eighth-grade sports banquet, the previous year, awards were given out for "Best Forward," "Best Defensive Player" and "Best All-Around Player," and I was excited for my friends as their names were called.

Then the coach said, "And for one of the most important awards, "Best Sportsmanship," the player who took all our losses in stride and never stomped off in anger, this goes to Karen Campbell."

Who? Me? I wasn't expecting to get any awards, so I was shocked but proud. The truth was, I just didn't have much of a competitive spirit. I tried my best, but it was never my goal to be *the best.*

Freshman year went by fast. I was happy that Robert and I were attending the same school again. Robert had made a name for himself at Copper Basin High School. He made friends easily, had a good sense of humor, and was good looking. Not a bad combination for high school. He was voted *Most Popular* his sophomore year, and I was one of several girls he was interested in. At the end of the year, he wrote this in my yearbook.

Dear Karen,

I sure do appreciate what you wrote in my annual, although the part about you making me "sick" was pretty bad. Anyway, you make me something far different from "sick" (not worse) I keep saying to myself that I don't like you and then I think I wouldn't want to see you, be with you, or talk with you but I want to do all of those. I've been thinking about it, and it must mean I like you. (really) You may not think so by some of the ways I have treated you, but I say now that I am very sorry. Forgive me, please. We have had some pretty good times together, and I hope they will continue. About your figure? Well, I think it is just fine. I like it the way it is. Don't ever worry about that.

> *Love ya,*
> *Robert*

At the end of the school year, I decided to try out for cheerleader since basketball didn't work out. Cheerleading in high school was quite different than in middle school. My nervous anxiety almost got the best of me when trying out in front of the coach and other cheerleaders. My stomach was churning. *Will I be able to remember the cheers?* I didn't like being the center of attention.

After being chosen, I wasn't sure what I had gotten myself into. This required more commitment and talent than I thought I had. We spent a week on a college campus at cheerleading camp. This was an eye-opening experience since we were there with girls from across the state of Tennessee. We came home armed with fancy new cheers and uniforms. I was ready for my sophomore year.

Every Friday was game day, and the cheerleaders held a pep rally, so I had to get over my lack of confidence. Not growing up in a family interested in sports, there were embarrassing moments when I chose the wrong cheer for the wrong play during an important football game, "Push 'em back, push 'em back, waaaaaaaaay back," when we had the ball.

Robert was on the team, so I was thinking about him during most games, anxiously awaiting the sock hop after the game in the school cafeteria where we played the top hits on a record player. The girls, in their Ladybug or Villager sweaters and saddle oxford shoes, waited on the sidelines to be asked to dance. It was hard having to watch Robert dance with other girls. I wanted him all to myself.

When Robert and I were not getting along, I went out with different boys rather than stay home alone on Saturday night. None of them appealed to me as Robert did. He was a James Dean type, a non-conforming rebel. He wasn't particularly tall, maybe five-nine, with light brown hair and emerald green eyes, twinkling with mischief. He had a thin body with narrow hips and broad shoulders. I loved the way he walked. *Why am I so attracted to his bad guy persona?*

When Robert and I did have a date on Saturday night, we always had to wait until after *The Porter Wagoner Show* because he was enamored with Dolly Parton, the young country music singer on his show. He liked the way she sang and loved the way she looked. So when Robert was turning sixteen, he asked his parents for tickets to the Grand Ole Opry. He asked me to go with them even though I wasn't much of a country music fan. However, Robert thought going to Nashville to see Dolly in person would be the ultimate birthday gift.

As we entered the auditorium, the loud hum of the crowd was energizing. We found our seats which were toward the back, which was disappointing to Robert. We listened to several singers since Dolly had not yet achieved her superstar status. As soon as Dolly appeared, Robert was captivated. She was wearing one of her skin-tight outfits, showing off her voluptuous hour-glass figure, wearing high heels and lots of makeup.

"Come on, let's go up front so we can see better," he said, without taking his eyes off the stage.

"You go and enjoy the view," I replied, giving him a smile and a look that said, "I know what you're going to check out."

Her voice was angelic, pure, and soulful. Robert couldn't stop smiling. Typically, he was emotionally restrained, but now he was completely immersed in the moment. Nothing I could have given him could have compared to Dolly as a birthday present.

He also loved Elvis Presley. On Saturday nights, we often went to the drive-in to watch an Elvis Presley movie, *Viva Las Vegas* and *Blue Hawaii* were favorites. Robert let his sideburns grow down the side of his cheek, just like the *King*. I was slightly embarrassed by this since Elvis was *out* at the time, and the long hair associated with the British invasion music scene was *in*.

My cousin, Kay, had introduced me to the Beatles. Living in Dallas, she was always on top of what was cool. I was into Paul the way Robert was Dolly. I bought many of their 45 records and loved their *Rubber Soul* album. I watched them perform on the *Ed Sullivan Show* in 1964 for their United States debut, along with 73 million other people in the United States. One of the most-watched shows in US history. Beatlemania had arrived, even in Ducktown.

During the mid-sixties, many young musicians were trying to become famous. Even in my small town, there were two bands, The Twilights, and The Blazers. They performed at the Canteen, one in Copperhill and one in Blue Ridge. They got the crowd energized with "Wild Thing" by the Troggs and "Wipe Out" by the Surfaris.

I had a crush on one of the drummers who was seen somewhat like Ringo Starr in our community. He asked me to dance one Saturday night, and I was so intimidated by him. He said, "Why are you shaking? I'm only the drummer." I wasn't so impressed with him after that. He was full of bravado.

At home, my girlfriends and I spent time listening to "Louie, Louie" by the Kingsmen. It was a controversial song supposedly having explicit sexual lyrics. The words were muffled and caused mixed interpretation. So we listened to it repeatedly, trying to decipher the lyrics. It was an exciting time for music since new groups were emerging all the time: The Monkees, The Lovin Spoonful, The Mamas and the Papas, The Supremes, The Byrds, The Temptations, and of course, the irreverent Rolling Stones.

If you didn't have a date, you could still go to the Canteen with friends and dance. Afterward, we spent an hour or so sitting in the parking lot of the Tastee-Freeze, checking out who had a date with whom. We parked our cars along the back wall and waited for the server to take our orders. We visited each other's cars while we waited for our French fries, onion rings, or chocolate sundaes.

As the summer continued, I got an unexpected phone call from my cousin, Kay, in Dallas. Long-distance phone calls were usually an indication something significant had happened.

"Hello."

"Hey, I've got news you're not going to believe."

Thinking I would hear about her latest adventure sneaking her parent's car out late at night, I wasn't ready for what she said.

"Sandra called, and she got us tickets to a concert in Atlanta."

Sandra was Kay's older sister, who was already married with children, living in Atlanta.

"What concert?"

"*The BEATLES!*"

"What? Are you kidding? We're going to see *The Beatles*?"

"Yes, it's in August. She's going with us. It's at the Atlanta Stadium."

"I can't believe it."

I spent the remainder of the summer looking forward to this event, trying to imagine seeing the Beatles in person. Kay was a huge John Lennon fan, and I was all about Paul. We counted down the days.

August finally arrived, and I met Kay at Sandra's house. She was as excited as we were, driving us around Atlanta the day of the concert, hoping we might see them somewhere. The Beatles were considered the phenomenon of the century. They had just begun performing at large stadiums to accommodate the thousands of crazed fans. We arrived ready to listen to our favorite Beatles songs.

"Oh my, look at this crowd!" I had never seen so many people in one place.

"I hope we have good seats," Sandra said.

"Well, I'm just glad we're here. This is the best day ever." I shouted above the roar.

We showed our tickets to the ushers, and to our dismay, we were a very, very, very long way from the stage. The concert was at the new outdoor Atlanta Stadium, and the band was on a plain stage near what would be second base during a baseball game. Atlanta was the third stop on their North American tour.

Then the radio station sponsoring the event made an announcement. "I would like to remind you to please take care of yourself and remain in your seat. Make all the noise that you like. Wave all the banners that you have. But please take good care of yourself here and on the way home. We love every one of you. Give *The Beatles* the greatest welcome I've ever heard for them. Show them they are loved when we bring them on. Okay, *The Beatles!*"

What I thought was loud noise now became a rumble of shrieking screams. The girls all around us were crying and screaming, holding their heads in disbelief, flailing their arms as if possessed. There was mass hysteria. Although I had seen this on TV, it was bizarre to witness in person, to be in the middle of it. At a previous concert, two hundred and forty people were hospitalized.

"I can't even hear them," Kay yelled.

"I know. This is crazy!"

"I can't see them either," she added. From where we were sitting, they didn't look much larger than actual beetles!

They were dressed in blue suits, white shirts, and ties, looking incredibly cool as they performed on this hot summer night. They played ten songs and two more during the encore. Most of their song choices were the high energy songs such as "Twist and Shout," "Help," and "Can't Buy Me Love." I was slightly disappointed they didn't play my two favorites, "Yesterday" and "I Want to Hold Your Hand." It was a total physical experience. Taking it all in left me exhilarated. I had never been a part of anything so large and powerful. We stood for the entire music set.

Did it matter we could barely see or hear them? We were at a *Beatles* concert. It was a dream come true for a fifteen and sixteen-year-old in 1965.

As the concert wound down, Sandra shouted, "Let's leave early and see if we can get a look at them when they leave."

"What? Leave early? I don't want to miss anything. I want to stay."

"Don't you want to see Paul up close?" she asked, knowing that was all she needed to say.

Sandra was older and in charge, so we followed her down the aisle and to an outside exit. I could still hear the music and wishing I was back inside. We were missing the encore. We stood along the ramp, and soon the police lined the driveway. *Are they going to drive right in front of us?*

As a much larger crowd gathered, we held our places, and soon a large, black limousine emerged. We could still hear the screaming from inside the stadium. *Oh, my God, it's them!!*

Ringo and George were on the side of the car nearest us, but I was looking for Paul. There was no one but Paul with his long, silky, brown hair and his bedroom eyes. I got a brief glimpse of him, from across the limo, but they were whisked away, and the policemen were pushing the crowd back with their arms so they could escape. Days later, it all seemed like a dream. A perfect dream. And I kept my $4.50 ticket stub to remind me it was all real.

Kay and I loved sharing this experience and telling our friends all the details. I was especially close to Kay. Her mother and my father were brother and sister and the two oldest of Big Mama and Big Daddy's six children. She was often with me when we visited our grandfather's cabin, where I first met Robert. She loved coming to visit Ducktown and, at one point, decided she wanted to move there. After Big Daddy died, she wrote Big Mama a letter asking if she could live with her. Since Big Mama had already raised six children, she wasn't interested in raising any more.

Kay and I frequently wrote long letters between Ducktown and Dallas, worlds apart in every way. We only saw each other in the summer and at Christmas. So letters kept us in touch. I used the letter as an ongoing diary and sent it when it was almost too big to fit in an envelope.

I used it like a "little black book," like a journal full of secrets and potentially shameful indiscretions. So I decided it was the perfect way to let Kay know what had happened when I was grounded for being on the phone too late. Robert and I had gotten frustrated at not being able to see each other, other than at school, so we came up with a plan.

Late at night, Robert would sneak out of his bedroom window, walk up his driveway, over our fence, up the hill, and into my bedroom window. There wasn't anything too serious going on, but we did lie in my bed, talk quietly, laugh, and have a few passionate kisses. It was easy to get away with this since my bedroom was at the opposite end of our house as my parent's bedroom. In my letter, I went into great detail about what went on during these late-night dates in my bedroom, often embellishing this risky behavior.

After my grounding was over and before I mailed Kay the letter, I was at the local Canteen to be with my friends and dance. When the dance was over, we came out the front door, and I noticed my parents' car sitting in front of the entrance. They weren't going to miss seeing me. I wanted to hide but knew I couldn't.

What in the world are they doing here? I imagined there was some tragic news for them to be at the Canteen in Blue Ridge.

"Get in the car," my father said.

I got into the backseat, and I knew I was in serious trouble. They had found my letter to Kay.

"How could you be doing this right in our own home? You're humiliating us."

This got my attention. My mother was usually the one who did the disciplining. It was a twenty-minute ride home, and my mother cried quietly in the front seat. I felt terrible. I didn't like hurting my parents. If only I had hidden the letter in a better place.

When we got home, my father sat down across from me at the kitchen table. My heart was pounding. I wanted to run to my room, lock the door, and tear the letter up. But it was too late for that.

"If everything you wrote in this letter is true, then we are ashamed of you. You need to understand that men don't want a woman who has been with other men."

I didn't know how to respond to this, so I said nothing. *This is not going to work on me. I'm not going to be with any other men. Robert is the one. We didn't do anything bad.*

I stared at the floor. Mother sat quietly on the other side of the table. She said I was going to have to "pay my dues" this time. I felt small and ashamed. I was embarrassed they'd read this personal letter, which was about half true, regretting all I had embellished.

"You're grounded again for a month with no phone privileges, and we might just have to tell the Lees about this," my father said. This bothered me as much as my parents knowing what we had done. *What will they think of me?*

I felt terrible that I had hurt my parents. I felt terrible that the Lees might find out. I felt terrible that I was grounded again. I got up from the table and went to my room. I cried and cried, feeling sorry for myself and my parents.

My parents didn't share my opinion that nothing too serious was going on in my bedroom. They were shocked. I tried convincing them that much of the story was embellished, but just knowing he was in my bed was enough for them to be mortified.

Eventually, my grounding was over, and Robert and I resumed our secretive, late-night phone calls. This soon came to an end when Mother caught me again on the phone exceptionally late. This was the "final straw" as she put it. The next day I came home from school. Mother was waiting at the door.

"Well, you did it this time. You won't be making any more phone calls from your bedroom. You'll be sitting right here," she said, pointing to the small stool in the kitchen where there was another phone.

"What do you mean?"

"We had your phone taken out today, that's what I mean."

"What?" *How can I live without my phone?*

I walked down the hall to my room, and it was gone. I was frantic. I slammed the door, falling onto my bed, convulsing into sobs. I knew my parents had every reason to take it away, but I didn't like it. I didn't yell or beg to get it back. I knew it wouldn't do any good. This felt like the worse punishment I had ever received.

We felt lost without our late-night phone marathons. I drew closer to my girlfriends, spending more time with them and catching up on their lives. Robert developed a new interest in motorcycles. Since he could get a license at fifteen, he talked his parents into a small bike. He had always been a dare-devil and pulling pranks that got him in trouble – firecrackers in a locker, stealing other students lunches, driving around without a driver's license. The freedom of riding a motorcycle gave him a sense of exhilaration that he seemed to crave.

But soon his inexperience and cockiness caught up with him when he had an accident and broke his leg. This didn't stop him long, and he was back on the motorcycle before the cast was off. This became a way of life for him. He had accident after accident, always breaking the same leg. He never seemed to consider giving up this dangerous sport.

He eventually replaced his small bike with a large Harley. I rode with him a few times on the Honda, but the Harley was intimidating. I didn't have the free spirit that Robert had and wasn't sure he would be mindful of my fear.

I finally agreed to go on a short ride, holding tightly to Robert's waist. As we were returning home, he did a wheelie up a long sloping hill for what seemed like forever. I was furious he had taken advantage of my attempt at being somewhat adventurous. I never rode with him again.

Robert's interest in motorcycles soon took over his life. He took a welding class and started rebuilding motorcycles, opening a business he named, "Lee's Cycle-delic Shop." His choppers were impressive, full of chrome and metallic paint with long extended handlebars. They were exactly like the bikes in the movie, *Easy Rider*. He took pride in his work, working long hours, and keeping his customers happy.

Although Robert was now spending much of his time working on and riding motorcycles, he still found time to date. We both dated other people from time to time, and he had been spending time with a girl named Althea. She attended another local high school. I didn't know her but had heard she was cute and popular. Robert mentioned we might go to the drive-in on Friday night, but then told me he had to go out of town to pick up some motorcycle parts so we wouldn't be able to go. I was suspicious, especially after I found out Althea was up for homecoming queen at her school's Friday night football game.

So with my parent's car and no driver's license, I set out with my friends, Cathi and Carolyn, to find out for myself. The car was near empty, and her high school was thirty minutes away. I solved this problem by stopping at my father's gas station and filling up the car, not thinking about the consequences.

When we got there, we found Robert inside a long hallway, standing with her, waiting to go out on the football field. She looked beautiful in her long evening dress and corsage. We knocked on the glass window of the door to get his attention. He turned to see us peering through the glass. He smiled, turned back around, put his arms behind his back, and shot us a bird.

My face flushed with anger. I wanted to go in and jerk her arm out of his. I wanted to scream at Robert for not telling the truth. I wanted to tell her he was leaving with me and she would have to find another escort. My feelings of jealousy were intense. I found out later she was crowned queen which only made me more miserable. To make matters worse, my parents found out I had taken the car, leaving me grounded again.

Several weeks later, I realized our basketball team was playing Althea's school team, and she was a cheerleader. I could feel the jealousy bubble up in me thinking about seeing her again. *Will Robert be waiting for her after the game?* Later that week, Robert called me.

"Do you want to go to the East Fannin basketball game on Friday?"

I couldn't believe he was asking me to this game. We didn't mention the fact this was where Althea went to school or the incident at her homecoming.

My heart lurched. *Is he joking? Is he finally realizing I am the one he really likes?*

"Well, yeah, sure," I managed to answer, thinking this was just what I had in mind to get revenge. Now, Althea could see us together.

I was thrilled and picked out the perfect outfit – plaid skirt, white shirt, and navy blue V-necked sweater. I teased, styled, and sprayed my hair until it looked perfect. Walking into the game on Robert's arm was going to feel amazing. Now she could be the jealous one. Since Althea was a cheerleader, she would be along the sidelines of the basketball court. If I was lucky, we might get to walk right past her.

I was ready thirty minutes before Robert said he would pick me up. I paced and paced, stopping every few minutes to look in the mirror. There was a moment of fear when he wasn't there on time, which was going to make us a little late for the beginning of the game. But I decided this would make for a more noticeable entrance.

I worried all week that he might change his mind, so when I heard his truck in the driveway, I was relieved. When we neared the entrance of the gym, my heart was pounding. I was thinking about walking into the gym with Robert and how good this was going to feel. Robert pulled up to the door and stopped. I waited, with thoughts about what was going to happen filling my head. Suddenly, my attention was back in the car.

"Aren't you going to park the car?"

He turned and looked at me with a slight smirk on his face.

"No, I asked you if you wanted to go to the game, but I didn't say I was going to go with you."

I sat and stared at him, thinking he must be kidding. He wasn't. He thought this was funny. I was humiliated, disappointed, and furious all at the same time. The tears were already clouding my vision. I looked away. If this was a joke, it wasn't funny. It was my first time being betrayed. My heart was broken. He started to laugh. *What are my friends going to think? They are all inside, waiting to watch this drama unfold.*

"Take me home," was all I could manage to say. We rode home in silence.

I was finally sixteen and a legal driver. I had been driving my parents' Ford Mercury Montclair, but my brother had left his 1965 Ford Mustang at home while he completed boot camp, so I was allowed to drive it for the summer. It was dark blue with a stick shift. I loved driving it around as if it was mine. I was good at screeching out of the Tastee-Freeze parking lot when I saw Robert with someone else. We were still in an on-again, off-again relationship.

Robert drove a black Ford pick-up truck and used it to store saddles and various horse grooming supplies and motorcycle parts. For special occasions, he would borrow his parents' car. But we liked the truck because I could sit beside him without a console between us, especially when we went parking.

Parking was the time when couples found a secluded spot to park their car to have intimate time together. It was easy to find a place with a national forest nearby. It was always interesting to find out on Monday mornings how intimate all my friend's Saturday nights had been.

Since Robert had become so preoccupied with motorcycles, he began to make friends with people who his parents felt were questionable. He was not focusing on school and continued to get into trouble around town. So it was time for them to get strict and turn their son around. They chose a school called Farragut Military Academy in St. Petersburg, Florida. *Military Academy?? How is this ever going to help?*

This meant I would not see him for months, and life as I knew it was over. No more Saturday night dates to the drive-in, no more parking along the side of a mountain road. He was gone before I knew it. There were no phone calls since long-distance calling was restricted to more important issues. We wrote long letters to each other, and I counted down the days until I could see him again.

⌒⌐

It was May, and I hadn't seen Robert since January. I was home doing homework when Mother called me to the phone.

"Karen, it's Lorraine Lee. How are you? Is school going okay?" I wondered why she would be calling me.

"I'm fine, and school is okay," I answered. If I had told the truth, I would have said, "I'm miserable and lonely. When is Robert coming home?"

"Well, I'm calling to see if you might want to go with me to Florida. The Academy is having a special weekend for Mother's Day, and I'm planning on flying down to see Robert."

"Well, yeah, I would love to. How long will you be there?" I asked, knowing my parents would be less likely to let me go if I had to miss much school.

"We would fly out of Atlanta on Friday night and come back on Sunday afternoon," she said.

Perfect. My parents agreed to let me go. I hadn't felt this excited in a long time. Maybe since I thought I was going to that East Fannin ballgame with Robert.

It was startling to see him in his military uniform among all the other cadets. He looked handsome in the white pants, white double-breasted jacket with gold buttons, and the white cadet hat. But he looked completely out of character. His hair was shaved close to his head. At least his eyes and smile were the same.

We attended a fancy reception with his mother. We never had any time alone, but just being next to him was enough. His arm around my shoulder and his hand holding mine were enough to let me know he was longing for me just as much as I was for him.

But before the school year was over, he was back in Ducktown, riding a motorcycle again. He had gotten a bike in need of repair in Florida, worked on it, and rode back to Tennessee. His parents were as surprised as I was to see him. His military career was over. He never went back to school in Florida. His grades were high, even making the dean's list, so it wasn't because he didn't apply himself and flunked out. I never knew whether he was asked to leave, or his parents made the decision. It didn't matter to me. I was just happy he was home.

Now Robert was back at our high school, and we picked up where we left off. We were spending most of our weekends together again, but he was going to be out of town for homecoming weekend, so I made plans of my own. I was going to the big game, and the sock hop afterward. My friends and I planned a slumber party at my friend Wanda's house. Her mother was going to be out of town. At the sock hop, we asked some of the Twilights band members to come to her house afterward. We felt flattered that they were paying attention to us.

It got a little crowded at Wanda's house, so we decided to join them for a kind of joy ride into the Cherokee National Forest. It all felt so daring. We weren't into drinking, but they brought along a 12-pack of Budweiser, so why not? I drank a few sips, never to have a Budweiser again. We hung out in the woods for several hours, talking and laughing. A few people paired off into couples, leaving me feeling lonely and miserable. *Wonder what Robert is doing?* It began to rain, so I climbed into the trunk of a car. My legs dangled out the back as I sat and felt sorry for myself.

The following week the news of our wild night in the woods made its way around school. The story was so exaggerated that it sounded like a boisterous, out of control, drunken brawl. Several teachers heard about it and felt it was their responsibility to let our parents know. One teacher called my mother.

"Karen, I need to talk to you." Mother said, soon after receiving the call.

It had been over a week since the sleepover at Wanda's, so I wasn't expecting that this had anything to do with "The Party," as it came to be known.

"I just got a phone call. Everyone at school and all over town are talking about this party you and your friends had after the homecoming game."

I could feel the rush of adrenaline as she continued. My stomach rolled. My heart raced.

"You were out in the middle of the night with boys you hardly knew. Riding in their cars? And there was drinking. Is this true?"

"Well, sort of. They just came over after the dance and asked us to go for a ride. Bobby got a new car, so we rode down to the river road. There was beer, but I didn't drink any," I said, knowing I was in big trouble.

"How could you do this to us? Everyone in town knows about this. I'm ashamed of you."

There was that word again, …ashamed. This was the most hurtful word to hear. I loved my parents and had no intention of hurting them. It was all so innocent, and at sixteen, it was hard to see it from their perspective.

"We didn't do anything bad. We just took a ride and came home," I tried to explain. "It wasn't a wild party or anything like that."

"It sure sounded that way…. going out in the middle of the night and drinking. You know better than that. You have certainly embarrassed us this time." She started to cry.

To me, it still seemed it wasn't the big deal it had turned into. But I hated seeing my mother cry over what I had done.

"I'm going to have to let the other parents know. So you and all your friends will be grounded. You won't be seeing them for a while."

Oh no, my friends are going to hate me. Friend's opinions held a lot of weight.

All the parents were called, and once again, I was spending Saturday nights at home.

Since Robert was a year older, he had started making college plans. His parents were encouraging him to think about veterinary school and focus on large animals. He had always worked with horses, riding them in barrel racing competition as a young teen and eventually going to farrier school to learn horseshoeing. So he made plans to attend a state college three hours away to take his basic courses and later try to get into Auburn for veterinary school. I was wondering if our relationship would last with him away at college.

I was starting senior year, and Robert left for college in the fall. We missed each other. Neither of us was dating anyone else. Our relationship had become more serious. He drove home every weekend, and we wrote letters to each other every day. Cathi picked me up every morning for school, and we stopped at our post office so I could get my love letter from Robert. It helped the week go faster.

Robert was soon home from college for Christmas vacation, and we were enjoying our time together. He was reconnecting with some of his motorcycle buddies, and they planned a campout along the river road. They were meeting there on their cycles.

Unfortunately, the camping trip came to a quick end when some friends were going down the mountain road and some up the mountain road, and they collided. Three of the boys had injuries, and Roberts' was the most severe. He broke the same leg again. By this time, his leg was so mangled he needed an orthopedic surgeon. The hospital in Ducktown wasn't equipped to handle the seriousness of his injuries, so he was transported to Chattanooga, and in a body cast for three months.

He was completely immobilized in his parents' house, and since I lived next door, my evenings were spent by his bedside. We watched TV, played cards and some board games with his younger sister. We discussed what was going on with all our friends. I was missing socializing with my friends since it was my senior year, but I loved seeing Robert again every day, even under the circumstances. We grew closer and longed for time alone. It was rare we could even steal a kiss. We did the best we could.

As he recovered and regained his strength, he renewed his love for motorcycles. There was no stopping him. He continued his education, but rather than going back to the large state college, he started commuting to a small community college. He spent his spare time rebuilding motorcycles and was living at home. We settled into our lives again, going to movies and meeting friends at the Tastee-Freeze. But as life goes, everything soon changed.

Chapter 3

May 1968

My graduation from high school was soon approaching. I wasn't prepared for college in any way, not academically, emotionally, or socially. The year, 1968, saw the world in turmoil. It was easy to feel removed from all that was happening living in such a small town. It has been recalled as "the year of tragedy and change between generations." During that year, there were deaths of heroes, uprisings over the Vietnam War, and suppression among blacks. The death of Martin Luther King and Robert Kennedy happened within nine weeks at the end of my senior year.

The world felt like a scary place. Two men who promoted harmony and peace and inspired hope had been gunned down. There was rebellion and disorder. It was also the beginning of both the women's movement and the environmental crusade. I watched all this playing out on the evening news, but being the teenager I was, soon realized it was time to watch *Peyton Place*, a popular evening soap opera,

I chose to attend college at the University of Chattanooga, later changed to the University of Tennessee at Chattanooga, only an hour and a half away. It was a big move for me, leaving for the unknown. My generation of girls looked forward to getting married and having children, not necessarily having a career. Choices were limited in the sixties, and women often chose to be stay-at-home mothers, although some became secretaries, nurses, or teachers.

I had always thought I would go to college, so I was excited about this next part of life. But I also felt nervous and apprehensive. I had never had to make new friends since I had the same friends since second grade. I was concerned about how prepared I was for college work. I was going to find out that my *just enough to get by* attitude in high school, was going to catch up with me.

As a graduation gift, Kay and her parents, my Aunt Helen and Uncle Bryon, invited me on a road trip to California to visit our uncle Lynn, one of my father's brothers. I flew to Dallas, and we drove on

to San Francisco, which seemed to take forever. I had never spent so much time in a car. But this was the only negative aspect of the trip. I loved staying in hotels and eating in restaurants. My aunt and uncle got annoyed with me for not being very open to unfamiliar food. I was a very picky eater.

Seeing the Pacific Ocean left me in awe. The steep cliffs and rocks along the water were beautiful, so different from anything I had ever seen. We toured Hollywood and walked through Haight-Ashbury. This was during the hippie movement, and it was fascinating observing all the flower children on the streets. The girls and guys were both in bell-bottomed jeans with long flowing shirts and hair, making it hard to tell who was female and who was male. They were standing around the streets and in the park, making me feel uncomfortable. I wasn't sure why. The trip opened my world a little bit more as we saw unfamiliar scenery and people as we drove across the country.

After flying back into Atlanta from Dallas, I was excited that Robert was picking me up at the airport. After departing the plane, I walked through the waiting area, eager to be reunited. I scanned the crowd and finally saw him. Wearing a pair of tight jeans, a black tee-shirt, and his cowboy hat, he looked especially sexy as he leaned against the wall, hands in his pockets. I had missed him terribly. Two weeks is a long time when you're seventeen.

Then he took off the hat. *What the hell??* A huge grin spread across his face. His hair was shaved bare on the sides, and a long narrow piece was left down the middle. A Mohawk.

"So what do you think?"

I sort of wanted to keep walking and pretend I didn't know who he was.

"Oh, NO, I think it looks terrible. Why did you do this?" I asked, a little too loudly.

I was always more into appearances than he ever was, so I was embarrassed for him. Thinking it would be fun to see my reaction, he planned this reveal around my trip. Normally, his thick, light brown hair had a slight curl to it. The night before my senior prom, he came to my house, and we used a straighter on it. He wanted it long and silky. Now he didn't have any curls to worry about. What was left was not appealing.

All the way home, he kept laughing and checking it out in the mirror, then looking at me to see my expression.

"Aw Karen, it's just hair. It'll grow back."

That was true. There wasn't much he could do that would change my feelings for him. He had a free spirit that I loved but was always trying to rein in.

In late August, Mother helped me pack for the move to college. I called Diane and asked for suggestions for my dorm room. Mother was sad over her last child leaving home and having an empty nest, but I was oblivious to what her feelings might be. I found out later she called Diane in tears when she returned home. Only seventeen, I was still a self-absorbed teenager and only aware of what was happening in my own world.

I had decided I wanted to become an interior decorator. I was very visual and noticed details others often missed. On shopping trips to Chattanooga, the window displays fascinated me. During her spring cleaning, Mother would sometimes rearrange our den or bedroom furniture while we were at school. I loved how it made the room look so different. Decorating my bedroom as a child had allowed me to express myself, so it was a priority in my dorm room to surround myself with what I loved – pictures, posters, and various meaningful souvenirs.

Soon after declaring a major, I realized that majoring in Interior Design required a semester of chemistry. I had taken chemistry in high school, and the teacher gave passing grades to myself and my good friend, Wanda, only because we were the only girls in class planning to attend college. I didn't earn a passing grade. When I found I needed chemistry, I felt totally unprepared and foolishly changed my major to elementary education. I could always decorate my classroom. I would regret later that I didn't follow my passion.

After settling into my classes, I fell into the same routine as Robert and came home every weekend. Robert drove to Chattanooga to pick me up every Friday afternoon. He was always sitting on the small brick wall beside the sidewalk outside my dorm. His legs dangled over the side as he patiently waited for me to finish my last class.

As soon as we saw each other, we would break into a mutual smile in anticipation of spending the weekend together. My heart always felt full seeing him again. He would load my suitcase in his truck so we could leave for Ducktown, bringing me back on Sunday night.

Sometimes the four days between Sunday and Friday seemed too long, and he would visit during the week. We would go out to eat or to an early movie but were always aware of my curfew in the dorm, which was 8:30 pm during the week. I was required to sign in and out, and demerits were given when rules were broken.

Our relationship had deepened, and we started talking about getting married. Neither of us had any interest in dating anyone else. But I felt the pressure of other people thinking we were too young to be so serious, especially from my parents.

Our interest in getting married was mainly because we were trying to wait to have sex until after marriage. It was driving us both mad since there were such strong feelings of passion between us. *The pill* had become popular on college campuses, and I was considering checking into getting a prescription. But I just couldn't bring myself to go to a doctor and ask for this *pill*, allowing me to have sex outside of marriage and not worry about pregnancy.

This was a huge fear since I couldn't imagine disappointing my parents in such a way. I did have trouble believing it would be morally wrong because it seemed like a manifestation of the love we felt for each other. But I was trying to be strong and wait. Such longing just added to our sexual chemistry.

As my freshman year progressed, I made friends easily in the dorm but didn't join any clubs or participate in any social activities. My parents weren't at all excited seeing me come home every weekend. They had hoped I would get more involved in college life.

Since Robert and I were spending most of our free time together, our relationship grew stronger. In October, Robert was in Chattanooga for a mid-week visit, and we made plans for dinner at

Shoneys. After dinner, while we were waiting for our chocolate sundaes, Robert seemed unusually nervous and smiling for what seemed like no reason.

"What are you so happy about?" I asked.

"Well, we've been talking about getting engaged, and I was wondering if you'd like to go look at rings?"

I was both excited and hesitant. *What will my parents think? And his parents? And our friends? When will we get married?* This was a big next step.

All these thoughts didn't stop me.

"Oh, wow, tonight? Yes, yes, of course, I'd love to."

From across the table, Robert was grinning at me, his eyes twinkling. I could still see the little boy I fell for when I was eight.

It didn't take long to find just what I wanted – a small, single diamond, half encircled with a band of yellow gold, the wedding band would complete the circle with a band in the other direction. It was simple and elegant, not excessive in any way. It felt perfect as I repeatedly held up my hand to check it out, first with just the engagement ring and then with the wedding band. My thoughts were already racing ahead to the dress and wedding. All my dreams were coming true. Well, almost.

Another question I should have considered was, "How are you going to pay for the ring?" He was still going to a community college, doing work on motorcycles, and living at home, so he didn't have the money. Maybe this was another one of his pranks, "Do you want to go look at rings?" And then saying, "I didn't say I was going to buy you one."

He didn't buy it that night, saying he wanted to surprise me later. Anticipating it might be my Christmas present, it was hard not to feel disappointed when he gave me a pantsuit instead.

But finally, two months later, when I was home for the weekend, he surprised me by giving me the ring in the front seat of his pickup truck. And it was the one I picked out. There are a dozen clichés to describe my feelings, but none of them would be adequate … *on cloud nine, tickled pink, over the moon, in seventh heaven.*

We celebrated by going out for pizza. I could hardly take my eyes off the ring. It was strange seeing an engagement ring on my hand. Now I was the one who couldn't stop smiling.

My parents were asleep when I got back home. For me, getting to sleep was difficult with so many thoughts racing through my head. The next morning, Mother came into my room to wake me for church.

"Robert gave me something last night you might want to see," I said, half-asleep. I pulled my hand out from under the covers to show her.

There was a long silence.

"Well, I knew it was going to happen, but I was hoping you'd wait a while." She looked at me with regret. She didn't like hearing this news.

Trying to make her feel a little better, I said, "Well, we aren't getting married now, but we are getting married."

She was still holding onto the idea we would date other people and explore other relationships. It was too late now. I knew she was shocked and worried, but she didn't say much. I let her break the news to my father. They weren't convinced Robert was the one for me. We were young and in love, and in their eyes, this was a scary combination.

Back in my dorm on Sunday night, I got plenty of attention showing off my new engagement ring. I was only eighteen, and he was nineteen, so we decided we would wait until after my sophomore year to marry. Waiting until I was almost twenty seemed respectable. We chose August 29 for the wedding date, the date I had gotten my first kiss.

Freshman year was challenging for me for many reasons. I made myself known in many classes by being perpetually late. Mother had given me a radio alarm clock as a graduation gift with a note, "Good Luck Next Year." She was turning the responsibility over to me. She was finished with her job of trying to pry me out of my bed in the mornings. My sister and I were notorious for not being able to get up and ruining my mother's start to her day. My tendency for being late did not help my success in college.

I was looking forward to the end of the school year. I had struggled academically and wanted to be out from under all the pressure. I had failed World History. I was humiliated when I saw the F I had earned. Mrs. Waller, my history teacher, had a reputation and expected you to know all the details about every historical event. I was unprepared for such rigorous expectations. My high school had not prepared me to take notes, study, and pace myself to be a successful student. Being named *Best Dressed* and *Most Popular* in high school didn't help much in college.

I finished my freshmen year with a 2.3-grade point average. I was certainly not on the dean's list but was relieved to know I could go back the next year. I was looking forward to the summer at home, away from school responsibilities, and being with Robert.

I was planning on working at my father's tourist shop and saving lots of money, maybe for our honeymoon. During senior year, a friend had brought a magazine to school with an advertisement for "Honeymoon in the Poconos Mountains," showing a couple in a heart-shaped bathtub. I had daydreamed about this a few times.

It was not unusual for couples to marry right out of high school. Our senior play was called *Headin' for a Weddin'*. All my close friends were cast members, and it seemed to predict the future for many of them. Out of six of my closest girlfriends, four were married soon after graduation.

As my summer progressed at home, Robert and I began to doubt we were ready to marry. Robert spent much of his time with his motorcycle buddies, and I was left at home. All my high school friends had moved on and no longer lived there. Life in Ducktown no longer held much excitement. At some point, it became too much, and I gave the ring back to him. We weren't actually breaking up, but we had both become more aware of how young and unprepared we were to be thinking about getting married. How we planned on supporting ourselves wasn't even a consideration.

So I went back to college in the fall without the ring. I decided to branch out and try to get more involved in college life. My freshmen roommate and I hadn't had much in common, and I always felt lonely coming back to my dorm room on Sunday nights. But there was a girl down the hall who always made me laugh, and our personalities seemed more in sync. So we signed up to be roommates my sophomore year.

Margie was from New Jersey – cute, funny, popular, artistic, and fun to be around. She had beautiful long strawberry blonde hair and cool glasses. She was confident around everyone, which gave me confidence when I was with her. We had fun decorating our dorm room and being silly, sharing clothes, and stories about our past. She belonged to a sorority, so I decided to join to meet more people. If I was going to get married, I wanted to have as many experiences as possible before that happened.

Although I no longer had the engagement ring, Robert was still coming to Chattanooga every Friday, and we drove home to spend the weekend together. Neither of us was dating other people. He had changed a lot since high school, no longer seeking out the attention he got from the pranks he was notorious for. He was attentive to me, and I felt loved.

Homecoming weekend was soon approaching, and I was determined to go and be a part of the festivities. The girls, especially the sorority girls, always wore a dress and heels, and the guys wore a sport coat and tie. I wanted to go but wasn't sure how Robert would feel about going. He was unsure of himself in social situations, particularly since he wouldn't know anyone. I knew he would feel like he didn't fit in. To ask him to dress up for the occasion would make him even more uncomfortable. He was usually in jeans and a tee-shirt. I wanted to go to the game. It wasn't the game I was interested in, but rather being involved in this big social event on campus. So I decided to ask.

"I was wondering if you might want to go to a football game with me?

"Well, maybe. Who are they playing?"

"It's the homecoming game at UC. I don't even know who they're playing. But lots of my friends are going. It's next Saturday.

You could come down in the morning, and we could eat lunch and then go to the game. You'd have to kind of get dressed up a little."

"Like how much?"

"Just some nice dress pants and a shirt. And maybe a tie and sports coat."

"A tie? I'll do the dress pants and shirt but not a tie. I don't even have a tie or a sports coat."

"Ok, that's fine. You'll look okay. We can go home after the game if you want."

I was torn between wanting to go but not sure it was a good idea. I wasn't sure I could enjoy myself for worrying about whether he was enjoying himself.

As the weekend approached, my parents called to tell me my sister-in-law, Donna, stationed in Germany with my brother who was in the military, had just found out that her sister died suddenly of a brain hemorrhage. This meant Donna was flying back to the United States with their two young children, one of whom I hadn't seen. My nephew, Jeff, was two, but my niece, Lisa, only six months old, was born in Germany. They would be staying with my parents the same weekend as homecoming, My sister and her husband were also coming in from Florida. So this set off a change of plans.

Since I wanted to meet my new niece and visit with other family members, we wouldn't be able to attend the game on Saturday. So I decided to cancel the plans for homecoming, Robert would pick me up as usual on Friday.

It was mid-October in the South, and there was just beginning to be a feeling of fall in the air. The leaves were turning brilliant shades of red, yellow, and orange, signaling the change of seasons. There was a slight coolness in the air, enough to make you eager for "sweater weather," as we called it.

Robert picked me up in his parents'new green GTO. He was usually in his pick-up truck, so this was a surprise. I resigned myself to the fact the homecoming experience would have to wait another year. As he drove the hour and a half trip home, a Beatles song, "Get Back," played on the radio, He turned toward me and grinned, playfully bobbing his head to the beat. We shared a quick mutual look of love, and then he turned his attention back to driving.

When we arrived at my parents' house, he came in to see the kids and visit with Mother. Robert was somewhat uncomfortable around my parents, but on this day, he seemed more at ease. She asked him about school and his plans for the weekend. Since I was going to be spending most of my time with my family, he had made plans of his own. He was going on a motorcycle trip to the Smoky Mountains with a friend from Chattanooga. They were leaving the next morning.

We were still in the process of examining our relationship to determine how much freedom a couple has when they are either engaged or dating someone exclusively. This freedom was more about time spent with friends rather than being with another person. When Mother left us alone, we sat on the couch and discussed our dating situation. The kids soon awoke from their naps and were playing around us. We would have to continue our discussion later. This left me feeling uneasy. I spent the remainder of the afternoon playing with my new niece and nephew.

Later, my mother needed groceries, and I offered to get what she needed. I bought the groceries, but on the way home, unsettled feelings made me decide to stop by Robert's house. We were able to talk some more.

"Karen, we can work this out. I like spending time with you, but I also like hanging out with my friends. And you know how much I like working on my motorcycles. That doesn't mean I don't want to be with you."

"I know. I just feel left out sometimes. I like being with my friends too, but I'd rather be with you."

We smiled at each other.

"I've just been busy lately trying to get some work done for some friends and school and everything. You know I like being with you. We always have fun together." He was sweet and loving.

As our conversation continued, it cleared the uneasiness I was feeling. We were alone in his family's den, and he followed me to my car since I needed to get home to take my mother her groceries. He stood outside the car window, and when I was ready to leave, he leaned in and kissed me.

"I love you."

"I love you, too." I responded softly as we stared into each other's eyes.

The following morning, I awoke when Mother came into my bedroom, abruptly opening the door. Her voice was alarming, and I knew something was wrong.

"Karen, you need to wake up. Robert has had another accident."

Coming out of a deep sleep, I jumped out of bed feeling disoriented.

"What? How do you know? What happened?" Suddenly I was wide awake.

"I don't know what happened. I just got a phone call, and that's all they knew."

I tried to make sense of the words. My heart was pounding. I looked out the window and down the hill to Robert's house but saw nothing unusual. I seemed to remember faintly hearing the sound of motorcycles outside earlier that morning.

After I left Robert's house the night before, he worked most of the night on his motorcycle. But he did leave for a while to attend our local high school's football game. His mother recalled he came to bed unusually late. His friend from Chattanooga drove to their house early Saturday morning to leave on their trip. They left together on their motorcycles and began a long descent down the hill below our houses.

According to the other boy, Robert accelerated down the hill, going across the road, head-on into an embankment. The friend rushed back to Robert's parents' house to get help. Since it was Saturday, Dr. Lee was home, and he gave Robert a tracheotomy at the scene of the accident. He was rushed to a large intensive care unit in

Chattanooga. As the news began to sink in, I was numb. *Oh, God, another accident... no, no, please no.*

My father drove Robert's mother and me to Chattanooga. Dr. Lee had gone with him in the ambulance. There was little conversation since we were all lost in our thoughts and fears. *God, please, please let him be okay.* The lump in my throat and the knot in my stomach was making me nauseous.

We arrived at the intensive care unit, and a nurse took us to his room. The sight of him was the first indication this was not like his other accidents where he would sheepishly smile at me, and make an excuse for his latest mistake. His face was gray. He was being monitored by several machines, his eyes were closed, and no response came from any tactile stimulation. Dr. Lee took a fingernail file and ran it under Robert's fingernail to check for any reflexive action. Nothing.

I was only allowed in the room for 10 minutes, twice a day. Dr. Lee would gently open Robert's eyes, only to see they were fixed and dilated. It was easy to imagine he was only asleep. I stood beside his bed and held his hand. I kissed his cheek and talked to him. I told him I loved him. But he didn't talk back. He was in a deep coma.

The days were endless. I often sat in the stairwell away from anyone and sobbed. I wasn't able to make casual conversation as a way to distract myself, as others seemed able to do. I prayed for signs of improvement, but after the third day, a brain scan was done that revealed a severe brain injury. His brain was swelling. I wanted to bargain with God, try anything to turn this around. I would promise anything. *Please, God, this can't be happening. What will I ever do without Robert?*

During one of my brief visitations, I started feeling light-headed. All of the emotions I was feeling were too much. Like I just couldn't take anymore. The room began to spin and suddenly darkened.

"Are you okay, Karen?" Dr. Lee saw me holding on to the side of the bed. I felt the room closing in as if I was suddenly in a dark tunnel.

"I don't feel too well. I just...."

I felt myself collapsing onto a cold tile floor.

Dr. Lee left the room to find a nurse to bring smelling salts, which quickly brought me around. I sat up, confused, not knowing where I was or what had happened. For those few brief moments, all the pain I was feeling both physically and emotionally drifted away with my consciousness. But the strong hospital smells quickly reminded me where I was, as did seeing Robert lying unmoving in the bed, the breathing tube in his neck, the sounds of the heart rate machine beside him.

Dr. Lee helped me to a chair. I looked around the room, feeling disoriented. *Where am I?*

"I think you should go back to your dorm and get some rest."

He got me some orange juice and told me to take my time. I pulled myself together. I just wanted to get to my dorm room and go to bed.

The next day Robert's father called me into the hall. He looked tired and distraught.

"I need to ask you something important," he said, looking down at the floor.

"Did Robert ever say anything to you about his feelings concerning organ donation?"

It took a minute before I could process what he was asking.

Does this mean Robert is dying? Are they thinking about donating his organs? Oh, my God, no."

"No, we've never talked about that."

"Ok, I just … we just thought we should ask you. Organ donations help so many people, and Lorraine and I, well, we would want to do that if it would help someone else."

I didn't ask any questions because I didn't want to know the answers.

I knew Robert's injuries were life-threatening, but I hadn't let myself think too much about *what if he dies*. I was scared that Dr. Lee was preparing me for Robert's death. *Do I give up my hope for a miracle? Miracles happen, don't they?*

It had been four days since the accident, and since my dorm was near the hospital, I was trying to maintain a sense of normalcy by going back to class. I woke up early and was thinking ahead to when I would go to the hospital to see Robert later in the day. I was already dressed when Robert's grandmother suddenly appeared at my door. I knew this was a sign something significant had happened. *Maybe he has regained consciousness.*

But then I just stood and stared at her. The look on her face told me everything. As she walked toward me, I felt an immediate sense of doom, like I was watching a glass fall in slow motion, waiting for it to break into sharp, jagged, raw pieces. This was going to be me.

"He's gone," she said.

The words reverberated in my head … "He's gone, He's gone, He's gone."

I put both hands in front of me as if to shield myself against the truth. I didn't want to hear any details. My heart raced. The room began to spin. I closed my eyes and found my way to a chair. I was trying to remember to breathe. There were no tears yet.

His grandmother was crying and becoming hysterical. *Why did she come? Who sent her to deliver this news? What do I do now? Just please tell me what to do now.* Margie stood beside me, with her hand on my shoulder, almost as shocked as I was. The worst possible thing had happened, and my life had suddenly changed forever.

I sat for what felt like forever… Racing thoughts bouncing around my head. Panic setting in. I felt her words move through my entire body. *Oh, God, please, no, no no.* I couldn't move. Time had stopped. I finally looked around the room, feeling disoriented and light-headed, trying to determine if this was real.

I closed my eyes and put my head in my hands. Margie offered me a glass of water and a cold cloth for my face. "Just sit here, Karen, as long as you need to."

I could already feel the weight of the news on my chest, as if suddenly my breathe had been knocked out. Margie knew we needed to move on to the next step, which was getting me home to my parents.

"Do you want to call your parents?'

I couldn't talk. My heart pounded and my hands shook but no words would come out of my mouth. I tried standing up and needed help walking into the hall. Margie dialed the number and handed the phone to me. The emotion hit me as soon as I heard my mother's voice.

"Robert died. Robert died." I sobbed into the phone. As soon as I said the words, I knew it was true.

"I know, we just found out ourselves. I'm so sorry, Karen. I know you're heart-broken. This is going to be hard. We're coming to bring you home."

I couldn't answer any of her questions so Margie took the phone and explained how I found out and made plans with my parents to take me to the airport where they would meet us. My father owned a small plane, so he was flying to Chattanooga to pick me up. Margie helped me pack a suitcase, along with her own. She was going with me. I was so thankful.

We left with Robert's grandmother for what should have been a fifteen-minute drive to the airport. But as could be expected, Robert's grandmother was not handling this well. She insisted we stop at one of her friends to tell her the news. Margie and I were left to sit in the car for what seemed like forever. *Can this situation get any worse?* I felt more and more panicky.

When we finally got to the airport, my parents had already landed. Mother gently embraced me. Her eyes were swollen and puffy.

"Oh, Karen, I'm so sorry. We were all praying for a miracle," she said. I just wanted her to keep holding onto me and make this all go away. But she couldn't make everything better this time. I felt fragile and weak, struggling to walk.

My father was all business trying to get our bags in the plane and preparing to take off again. Although my parents were not crazy about the idea of us marrying young, they knew how much I loved Robert. They knew this was life-changing for me. I would need their support to get through this. There weren't any words or actions that could make me feel any better. We flew home in silence.

As we left Chattanooga and headed toward the mountainous area of home, a brief sense of calm came over me. Looking out the window, I felt God's presence. I could see all the houses, buildings, and the people driving around as we flew above the city. Life would keep going, no matter what had happened. *This is not part of God's plan or God's will.* I didn't want to hear this from anyone.

Sitting quietly in the backseat of the plane, with Margie's hand resting on my arm, I quickly decided I could never accept that Robert's death was part of God's master plan. "Everything happens for a reason" was not going to work for me. I found no comfort in that. I could not accept a God who could let Robert die in a motorcycle accident before his life had even begun.

I didn't ask, "Why?" I wasn't angry at God because of what happened. It was purely an accident, a terrible set of circumstances with a tragic end. I was already feeling the loss, not only of Robert, but of my innocence, my sense of security, and the world as I had known it.

I asked God for courage and strength. Flying through the clouds and seeing the majestic mountains, seeing the world from above, left me feeling maybe I wasn't completely alone.

The following days were full of feelings I had never experienced. I felt like a piece of glass, as if anyone who hugged me a little too hard would cause me to break into pieces. I couldn't eat or sleep. While I dressed for the visitation at the funeral home, I couldn't imagine what this was going to be like. *How do I say goodbye forever?* As we neared the front door, I couldn't move. I stopped and felt frozen. I wanted to stop what was about to happen. Mother took one arm and Daddy the other.

"Are you going to be okay, Karen? We can wait a while if you want."

Tears rolled down my cheeks. *Can I do this?*

When I walked into the funeral home, the whole room fell silent. The scent of all the many flower arrangements swept over me, the combination of roses, gladiolas, and carnations. It reminded me of walking through this same door after the deaths of my mother's mother, Mama Chancey, and Big Daddy. At ages nine and thirteen, their deaths were the only ones I had experienced. The smell of the flowers represented death. It was strong, and I wasn't.

All eyes were on me. Dr. Lee came and held me for a long time. He and Mrs. Lee walked me over to the casket. *Do I want to see him?* He was dressed in a dark blue pinstriped suit. One his mother had purchased for him only a few months back for a family picture. The suit didn't seem appropriate for Robert. He would have preferred his black leather motorcycle jacket with his motorcycle club insignia on the back. He no longer had the smile I was so accustomed to seeing. His skin was chalky white. His eyes no longer twinkling.

His father escorted me to a seat at the end of the casket. Lines of people snaked through the funeral home – family friends, relatives, friends of Robert's older sister, Linda, but few of Robert's motorcycle friends. They were in shock over his sudden death.

One of Robert's old girlfriends came through the line. We had squared off one time over whether he was staying with her or going with me. He stayed with her. You didn't fool around with her. She was much older and had been around. She was now married to one of Robert's motorcycle buddies. She walked straight up to me.

"Robert really loved you." I stared at her. What could I say?

Yes, I did believe he loved me, but now it was love that could never be reciprocated or consummated. *What am I going to do with all the deeply felt feelings I have for Robert? Will they just go away now that he will no longer be here?*

I sat at the end of the casket until the last person came through the line and gave their condolences. Lots of platitudes that only made me angry: "It was his time to go;" "He's in a better place;" "God never gives you more than you can handle." I cringed inside every time anyone said words like this. "God had other plans for him." *But what about our plans?* I didn't make conversation with anyone. I was weak with fear and anguish. I knew they meant well, but I didn't find any comfort in their words. The sliver of hope I had managed to hold onto was slipping away.

I asked Robert's parents if I could put something in the casket with him. I still had the little silver medallion engraved with our names and the date when we went to the county fair, and I received my first kiss. This was the date we had chosen for our wedding. They placed it in the breast pocket of his suit. It gave me comfort knowing I left something with him, part of us. Then hundreds of people passed by in a blur. I needed help getting back to the car. I was drained.

The funeral was the following morning. I looked at myself in the mirror after dressing. I felt disconnected from myself. *Will I ever smile again?* The ride to the church was silent, just as the trip home from Chattanooga had been. I walked into the foyer of the church on the arms of my parents. Two of my childhood friends who had experienced my obsession with Robert stood waiting at the door. We hugged, and it helped to know they were there. My parents and Margie helped me to a seat behind Robert's extended family. Margie was on one side and my mother on the other. Although these were the people I needed the most, I had never felt so alone.

The minister began the service with the question, "What Is Your Life?" His eulogy began with several quotes about life.....Every man's life is a fairy tale written by God's fingers.... From Hans Christian Andersen. Another unknown quote, "Life is a jigsaw puzzle with most of the pieces missing." Carlye said, "One life…a little gleam of time between two eternities." He quoted the book of John, "Life is even a vapor that appeareth for a little time, and then vanisheth away."

He continued with an emphasis on the frailty of life. "Life is uncertain, one moment we enjoy it, and the next moment we do not. This was true of Robert Lee. One moment he was experiencing the height of ecstasy, riding his motorcycle, his favorite hobby. The next moment, he was in agony. Robert would soon have been twenty years old. He was a person who loved adventure and the excitement of life. But he chose to endure suffering and sacrifice, if necessary, to satisfy his ambition. He was not a quitter."

His words were uplifting. I felt a slight sense of calm. I had been afraid the minister would try to save people with his words, or possibly I would have to hear more spiritual platitudes.

He finished with these words, "God will strengthen you for every crisis you face and every decision you have to make. God is love. During the days when the sky is beautiful, the sun is warm and bright, and everything is fine and also when there are dark black clouds on the horizon, when the storms of life come, when heartbreak and heartaches also come." I needed something to hold onto, an incentive to keep living, and I found solace in his words. *I will try to channel the love I feel into strength.* If I didn't have hope for the future, I would have nothing.

The procession to the cemetery wound its way along a country road, just like out of a movie. The white hearse was followed by many familiar cars. It was a beautiful fall day, sunny but slightly brisk. As family and friends gathered around the gravesite, Dr. Lee brought me into the crowd and provided a seat beside the casket. It all felt like a bad dream. How can I face a future without Robert? I was nineteen and had been involved with him since I was eight. My heart was broken. So many emotions and so little life experience to process them. *How can I go on?*

My parents helped me back to the car. Margie got a ride back to Chattanooga with a friend, and I was left alone for the first time. Looking out my bedroom window as I had a thousand times before, I could barely see the Lee's house since cars lined the driveway and into the road. Had I been the wife or fiancé, I would have been included in the family gathering.

But no one could make this any easier for me. I prayed for strength and courage. I made phone calls to several old friends to let them know what had happened, thinking maybe telling the details out loud would make it seem real.

Alone in my bedroom, thoughts raced through my mind. If my sister-in-law's sister hadn't died, Donna wouldn't have come home from Germany with my new niece and nephew. I wouldn't have come home, and Robert and I would have gone to the homecoming game. The circumstances were like dominos falling, leading to this moment. God's will? God's plan? No, I still couldn't go there. Things happen. People make choices, and God helps us deal with the consequences. This was the only way of thinking that was going to get me through this.

As the weekend came to an end, it was time for me to go back to school. Trying to study and take tests seemed like an impossibility. My mind constantly raced with thoughts of the past and fear of the future. I didn't want to go, but staying in Ducktown with my parents would be even harder. I couldn't even imagine what my life was going to be like now.

As some of the shock began to wear off, the emotions washed over me. They were powerful and overwhelming, causing deep sobs, coming from a place I had never been before. The pain inside was real physical pain, tearing me apart. I felt directionless, not knowing what to do with myself.

As a child, I had been shocked to learn the soul wasn't actually a body part, like a kidney or a liver. Now, it felt like a body part had been extracted. There was a huge, ugly, gaping hole inside. *Is it my missing soul?*

When I did sleep, it was even harder when I woke and was faced with my life now. I would vacillate between numbness and pure panic. Thinking about going back to college, to continue my education … for what? My life, as I knew it, was over.

Mother had made arrangements for me to ride back to Chattanooga with four girls who also attended my college. As I sat at the kitchen table, my mother was encouraging me to try to finish a sandwich before I left. The anxiety had taken away my appetite. I stood and kissed my mother goodbye. She hugged me tightly and helped me to the car. I felt weak and vulnerable, unsteady and unstable, miserable and hopeless, despondent and directionless, a whole world of new emotions for a young girl only nineteen.

On the ride back to school, I sat silently in the backseat as the girls made conversation around me. I stared out the window. It was dark and rainy. I watched the patterns the rain made on the windshield. The whole world felt different. My stomach churned. I felt invisible.

The accident happened on Saturday. He died on Wednesday. The funeral was on Friday. I was back in my dorm room on Sunday night.

PART TWO

Accept what is,
Let go of what was,
And have faith in what will be.

-Sonia Ricotti

Chapter 4

October 1969

Every step down the long hallway to my dorm room felt like a mile. I was full of anxiety. *I don't want to be here. I can't do this.* Margie was waiting for me. She hugged me a long time. She had taken down all signs of my life with Robert. His senior picture on my desk, our prom picture, a bulletin board full of photos, sayings, and mementos of our lives together … gone. It was all replaced with inspirational quotes, flowery images, and positive thoughts on posters. This was my first realization I was going to be expected to *move on.* I stared at it all. Then I had to sit down, putting my head in my hands. *God, please … this is awful.*

"I know this must be terrible, but you didn't need to come back to all those pictures. I didn't know what else to do." Margie explained.

There was nothing to say. I was numb. I couldn't even cry since it seemed to take more energy than I had. There was an emptiness I couldn't escape. My feelings, other than sadness and intense anxiety, had flat lined.

As I tried to begin some sort of adjustment, life felt surreal. Nothing about it felt familiar. My body seemed disconnected from my mind, which was reeling with thoughts. Just doing the necessities in life, like eating and showering, took effort. I just wanted to sit and stare. I felt I was under a weighted blanket, not being able to find my way out from the heaviness. I was being pushed down, down, down by the grief. I couldn't even look up when I walked.

Late at night, when I couldn't sleep, I would get up and go down the hall to stare out the window. There was a church across the street from my dorm with a tall narrow steeple with a cross on the top. It reached into the sky, and I could see the mountains surrounding the city behind it. Something about it gave me hope. *Is the steeple pointing toward God?* I needed to trust God and feel his compassion for me. I prayed for strength to keep going. Sometimes the hopefulness was strong, and sometimes I thought it too had died. Then total despair set in.

I constantly went through the "if only's" and the "what ifs" in my head. My scattered thoughts were of memories and worries about my future. I wanted there to be a reason for Robert's accident – *did his brakes fail? did he fall asleep?* A cause for the accident was never determined. But what difference did it make? It wasn't going to change anything. He was gone forever.

Going to class and completing school assignments was almost more than I could manage. I would venture out, only to see couples on campus holding hands, laughing together, looking so happy. I often returned to my room when the panic was more than I could handle. I called my parents one desperate night.

"I don't think I can do this. I can't concentrate on school. My mind is reeling, and I'm having trouble sleeping and eating. I'd like to just drop out for this semester." My voice quivered. I was trying to be strong and not worry my parents.

"I know this is hard, Karen. But what would you do? I don't think it's a good idea. Don't worry about school too much. Just do the best you can."

"I'm just so miserable."

"If you came home, I think it would be harder for you. You wouldn't have any girlfriends here. Get out and just try to stay busy," Mother advised. I felt like I was trapped in a maze with no way out. But I was beginning to realize there wasn't anything that was going to make my life any easier. Nothing.

I used sleep as an escape and frequently to avoid my responsibilities as a student and cut class. I met with each of my professors and explained what had happened. They were understanding and allowed me to turn in assignments as I was able to finish them. I just couldn't concentrate on economics, history, math, or anything.

During the early months back in school, Margie was my rock. She made me laugh when I didn't think I could. She encouraged me when I wanted to give up. She often cried with me when I was overwhelmed with grief. She was letting me grieve as I needed to, never being judgmental. When the numbness wore off, there were plenty of tears. I never had to hide them from her.

I received many sympathy cards, but the words of one in particular resonated with me, "To be forever remembered is one of life's truly everlasting gifts." The words spoke to me in a way the others didn't. This would be my inspiration. I would hold onto my memories as if they were a gift. I would always remember Robert. I could enjoy this gift without feeling guilt or sorrow. It would be a gift I would have for the rest of my life, and nothing could take it away.

This brought me a sense of control and solace. I cut the phrase from the card and decoupaged it onto a small piece of wood, placing it on a picture stand. I read it often when I felt I couldn't keep going. Its simple message gave me strength.

Five weeks passed, and it was time for Thanksgiving vacation. This would be my first weekend home since the accident. I was full of dread thinking about going back. The Lees' invited my parents and me to join them at their church for a Thanksgiving service. I sure wasn't in the mood to express gratitude for all my blessings in life. I wasn't feeling any gratitude. I was feeling cheated.

The service was at the church where Robert's funeral had been. I couldn't focus on the words. All that had occurred was roaming around my head. I spent the entire time holding back tears. Afterward, the Lees suggested we join them at their home for refreshments. *How can I go back to their house without Robert being there?* So many memories of time spent together. So many dreams that would never come true.

As we walked into their den, I noticed a picture of Robert I hadn't seen before, sitting on a table between two of their large lounge chairs. I stopped and couldn't go any further. He was wearing the dark blue suit he was buried in. It was as if he was looking back at me.

"You haven't seen the picture, have you, Karen. Doesn't he look handsome?" Mrs. Lee asked. "I have small pictures if you'd like one."

I couldn't talk. My throat tightened, and I started to cry. I couldn't hold the tears in any longer. I went to the bathroom to try to compose myself. I couldn't stop sobbing. Looking in the mirror,

I could only see a face I didn't recognize. *How am I ever going to get through this?*

Back at school, I struggled with panic attacks. I could barely go out. My heart pounded. My palms would sweat. I was light-headed. *You have to do this.* Everyone was going about their normal routine, and I was struggling to breathe. I was seeing all the familiar buildings and people but with a different perspective.

I had to talk myself into going forward and pushing myself to continue. Sometimes I would find myself able to work through the feelings, but other times I would go back to bed and stay there.

Sleeping helped me cope. I didn't want to be awake. Sleeping gave me a way not to feel anything. The less number of hours I had to deal with this the better. My dreams were a way to be with Robert again. He came alive again. Being awake and having a constant stream of memories running through my head left me drained.

I was struggling in many ways, but there was no mention of counseling by family or friends since this wasn't common in 1969. I was not the wife, nor was I the fiancé, since I had given the ring back. I was only the girlfriend. Most people didn't want to talk about it or didn't know what to say, but I needed to talk. People kept saying, "You'll find someone else." *But I don't want someone else.* Part of me knew this is what I would eventually want, but I couldn't stand to hear those words.

The days seemed like weeks. The weight on my chest felt heavier and heavier, a dull, empty ache, A piece of myself was missing. I bought a book called *Grief's Slow Wisdom*. Maybe at the end of all this, I would feel smarter. But would there be an end? I was searching for answers.

Friends and family often told me, "Life goes on." It was going on for me but not for Robert. It wasn't fair. His life was over. I just couldn't wrap my head around this. There was a massive crater inside me. A hole so big I was sinking into it. Pain like I had never experienced before. I couldn't get away from it. I was shattered.

Friday afternoons filled me with anxiety since I had always gone home for the weekend. Now the thought of being at home terrified me. Staying in the dorm was my only other option. I was so thankful to have Margie there with me.

Some of the worst loneliness and despair occurred as the afternoon turned into night. I would think about taking all the sleeping pills my uncle prescribed, getting them out, and lining them up. But underneath my despair there was usually a glimmer of hope. I wanted to live through this. I wanted to get past this. I wanted to feel alive again. Did my faith help me through this? Not the kind of faith that said, "Everything happens for a reason" or "This was God's plan," but the kind of faith that said, "God will help you through this."

One weekend in early January, Margie and I were sitting in our dorm room, trying to decide what we might find to do. Margie didn't have a boyfriend, so she often made weekend plans with girl-friends and usually included me.

On this particular lonely Friday night, a girl we didn't know was going up and down the hallway of our dorm yelling, "Anyone want to go with me to Memphis State? I need someone to ride with me."

Margie and I looked at each other. *Hmmm…. This might be a possibility.*

"Hey, we might want to go with you. What are you going for?" Margie asked.

"My boyfriend goes to school there, and I gotta get there to see him."

Margie and I looked at each other and were both thinking, *"What the hell … why not?"*

"Yeah, we'll go," we said simultaneously. We were looking for some excitement to relieve our boredom and put a little adventure into the weekend.

"How long does it take?" I asked.

"We should be there in about five hours. Hurry, let's get on the road."

We now had plans for the weekend. We quickly packed our bags and were out the door with a stranger. We didn't know where we would stay or what we would be doing, but it seemed better than our weekend sitting in the dorm. We would figure that out when we got there.

We soon realized what a mistake we'd made. Margie was looking at me, and I was looking at her. *What the hell are we doing with this girl?* She drove like a maniac, careless, and fast as if she were running from the police. We couldn't figure out why she wanted anyone to ride with her. She hardly talked to us. She just wanted to get there as fast as possible. It took only four hours, and we couldn't wait to get out of her car.

We quickly made plans to crash for the night at a sorority house on campus. The next day we checked out the university and spent most of our time wondering, *What the hell are we doing here?* Trying to make the best out of a bad decision, we went to a fraternity party and danced with a few drunk guys doing the gator. This was our attempt at salvaging the weekend with a little fun. Another what the hell?

The thought of riding back to Chattanooga with the crazy girl, who thought she was driving in the Daytona 500, was terrifying. We had no choice but to get back in her car and hold hands in the back seat. At one point, the song "Spirit in the Sky" by Norman Greenbaum played on the radio, and she turned up the volume. His words of dying and being laid to rest seemed a real possibility at this point. We just might be *goin' up to the spirit in the sky.*

Margie and I looked at each other and laughed hysterically. I hadn't laughed like that in a long time. It felt amazing.

As the months passed, I began to go out more often with Margie and other girlfriends to get pizza or go shopping. After four months, the panic attacks were beginning to subside. With lots of gentle persuasion from family and friends, I finally agreed to go on a date. *Who is going to want to go out with a girl who is still grieving over her old boyfriend?* To my surprise, there were quite a few who didn't seem to mind.

I never neglected my physical appearance during this time of intense grief. My hair was long and blonde, and I had gotten quite thin. Continuing to take pride in my appearance gave me a sense of control over my life. I could make my outward appearance appear normal. No one could see what devastation there was on the inside.

Later, in the process of dealing with all my emotions, I began to try to fill the emptiness with food. The pounds started to creep up on me. Dieting became a way of life. I was obsessed with every calorie, fantasizing about foods to eat after ending the diet – cookies, ice cream, pie, bread, etc. The diets would last a few weeks, followed by a food binge. Eating until I was miserable, hoping to fill the enormous void, left me even more depressed.

I never considered making myself throw up. I'd always hated that part of any stomach virus. My stress also began to show up with episodes of stomach pain and diarrhea, which lead me to several doctors. My periods stopped, and I was a physical and emotional mess.

After I shared what was going on in my life with my doctors, they felt it was all stress-related. I became more conscious of the reasons for my destructive binging, realizing it was all about the hole I was trying to fill. I managed to work through this on my own, and my weight stabilized.

I was still struggling to manage my day-to-day life, so thinking about dating and having a social life didn't hold much interest for me. But Margie and my suitemate, Jody, felt it would be cathartic, encouraging me to at least give it a try. It was uncomfortable in so many ways. I had such limited dating experience, and I felt I was being watched for any signs of breaking down.

Everyone on campus seemed to know I was the girl whose boyfriend died, or maybe I just felt they did. The dates were painfully awkward. I was not a fun date. Not having much confidence, I could always feel myself blushing in difficult social situations. I was self-conscious about what I said and did. I often doubted myself and worried about whether the guy might try to kiss me. I wasn't ready to be touched.

Jody was dating a good looking fraternity guy and wanted to fix me up with one of his two roommates, either Skip or Dan. They were living off-campus in an apartment. The two roommates tossed a coin to decide who would ask me out. Dan would be the one who asked. He was tall with long brown hair, sky blue eyes, broad shoulders, and muscular arms. He carried himself with complete confidence. He was good looking, but all this was lost on me.

It was March, five months after Robert died when Dan called and I accepted his invitation to go to a concert to hear a band called Strawberry Alarm Clock. The concert was held at our college gym, so there wasn't a huge crowd. We sat in the stands and talked, even carrying on a conversation during the performance. He was easy to talk to. He was funny and made me laugh. I enjoyed his sense of humor.

In May, he asked me to attend his fraternity's end of the year dance called the Sweetheart Ball. I had gained weight and looked quite pudgy in the short pink dress I wore with a string of pearls around my neck, looking a little like Miss Piggy with her pearls. *What was I thinking?* We sat at tables with other couples and enjoyed dancing. Dan knew everyone and was introducing me throughout the night. We laughed a lot. I was still emotionally numb, and when Jody asked me if I had fun, I didn't even know what to say.

We continued to see each other until school ended for the year. We were just getting to know each other. Dan was a northern Catholic and a big party guy. He was popular, socially confident, and seemed to know everyone on campus. He didn't seem intimidated by my circumstances, and it was never mentioned. I was okay with this since I just wanted to escape what was going on in my head. It was a little like *the elephant in the room*, but all I was concerned about was temporarily forgetting my issues when we were together. I could enjoy his sense of humor and, for a few hours, pretend I was okay.

I soon learned Dan didn't judge his drinking limits very well. It was not unusual to find him at a party enjoying the crowd, being the life of the party, and me in the bathroom crying, trying to have the courage to go back out and join the so-called *fun* everyone else seemed to be having.

And if I had a few drinks, the tears started flowing. The alcohol stirred up the emotions I was trying to suppress. Alone in the bathroom, I would stare at my image in the mirror and wonder who

I was. Dan was unaware of what I was going through. This would be a pattern for us in the initial stages of our relationship. Certainly not *love at first sight*.

Dan left for the summer to go to his hometown in upstate New York. He would be working as a flagman on road construction projects making a good hourly wage for a college student. No matter what this summer held for him, it would be hard to compare to his previous summer. While I was home spending my last summer with Robert, he had gone to Woodstock.

It was advertised as *Three Days of Peace and Music*. He purchased tickets for himself and three friends for the three days, spending a total of eighteen dollars for each ticket, six dollars a day. He rode from Lockport, New York, to Max Yasgur's dairy farm with a couple of friends, planning to meet the others once they arrived. They avoided the massive traffic jams by taking a detour and settled in for the weekend in an old abandoned house. Dan, being eager to "get this party started," soon lost track of the friends he rode with and never saw the other friends at all.

Never one to be uncomfortable around strangers, Dan managed to enjoy the weekend on his own. Members from the band Wavy Gravy announced over the loudspeakers the next day, "Good morning, what we have in mind is breakfast in bed for 400,000 people." Only 186,000 original tickets were sold, but so many people showed up, it became impossible to police the crowd, so they spread out across a few acres of land, sharing this monumental experience amid the rain and mud.

There were thirty-two acts over the three days: Joan Baez; Richie Havens; Arlo Guthrie; Crosby, Stills and Nash; The Who; Country Joe McDonald; Santana; Grateful Dead; Janis Joplin; Sly and the Family Stone; Joe Cocker; and Jefferson Airplane, were the featured acts Dan remembers. He missed the 9 am performance by Jimi Hendrix singing the National Anthem on Monday morning that came to symbolize the event. The Vietnam War was at its height, and many performers voiced their opposition through music.

Dan met a girl and went swimming nude, even thinking his butt may have been the one pictured in a popular national magazine as they frolicked in a large muddy pond. When it was over, he hitchhiked to Albany, NY, and flew home to Buffalo. He can still get immediate attention from almost anyone when he says, "I went to Woodstock."

Years later, Dan left his wallet at a grocery store in Chattanooga after being asked for his proof of ID. They called to tell him they found his wallet and then turned it over to the police. After getting it from the police station, Dan found the entire contents were intact except for his Woodstock ticket. He always carried it with him in case he had to prove he was there. Now, all he had left were his memories.

So the following summer of 1970 was not nearly as eventful for Dan. He was headed back to his hometown to work as a laborer and flagman on road construction again. I left to go home to Ducktown.

I was a Southern Baptist, and Dan, a northern Catholic. My parents didn't drink. They were solid, hard-working people, and alcohol was never a part of their social life. They had a limited social life. Church and family gatherings were their primary outlets for being with other people. Dan's parents' lives revolved around social drinking and was a large part of their lives.

My parents held the traditional roles of husband and wife. My father owned several businesses, requiring him to go to work early and come home late. In the mornings, he left after giving Mother a loving good-bye kiss. He was out the door in his dress pants and shirt, his salt and pepper hair in a crew cut, always in a hurry to get his day started. His work ethic was just as much a part of him as his hair and eye color. He was ambitious and determined, but he did sometimes make business decisions without thinking them through. He was always willing to jump into a new business venture.

As a child, I was fascinated by his large watch and the bulging wallet in his back pocket that seemed full of hundreds of dollars. He liked to pay for everything with cash, so his wallet was several inches thick, later causing him back issues from sitting at an angle.

My parents provided a strong sense of security and continuity in our lives. We had meals most evenings around 6, did our homework, showered, watched a little TV, and off to bed. Sunday school and church were rituals, sitting on the right side of the small Baptist church in the fourth pew from the back. There were never any volatile situations at our house, and everyone was even-tempered and restrained. I never heard any words of disrespect between my parents.

However, there was never any discussion of feelings or emotions. Being stoic was expected. We were rarely criticized but also rarely praised. Neither of my parents was very physically affectionate, except with each other. Even without this, I felt loved and respected. They provided stability and consistency that I took for granted. *Doesn't everyone live like this?*

My parents began their married life in March, 1942, with a unique and humorous wedding story. My mother was twenty-one, and my dad, twenty-five. He was home on leave from the Royal Canadian Air Force since joining the forces in Canada because the United States required two years of college to attend flight school, which my father didn't have. He was between pre-flight training and flight school in Canada and briefly spending time at home.

They were on a date, parked on the dirt airstrip at the airport in Ducktown, when my father, being the impulsive person he was, proposed.

"Let's just go ahead and get married and get it over with."

Knowing they would need witnesses, they found two of my father's friends coming out of a late movie in McCaysville, Georgia. He called them over to the car.

"Hey, you guys wanna go to a wedding?" my father asked.

"Whose wedding?"

"Ours," he replied, laughing with excitement.

They jumped in the back seat, and the four of them headed off to Ellijay, Georgia. It was another thirty minutes away, so now it was near midnight. The town was deserted except for the local policeman and his sidekick.

"Where can we find a minister? My girl and I want to get married tonight."

"Don't think you'll find anyone this late."

"Just tell us where there might be one," my father pleaded.

"Follow me."

My father was dressed in his full military uniform, and after arriving at the Methodist church a short distance away, he felt confident he could convince the minister. He knocked on the door of the Methodist parsonage where the minister lived with his family.

After he repeatedly knocked on the door, a woman finally answered the door in her bathrobe. She was not welcoming in any way.

"We're looking for a minister to marry us tonight. The policeman there in his car told us this is where he lives. I'm in the service and only have a few days left in the states. I'll be heading back to Canada."

"Well, I don't think my husband can marry you tonight. He's been sick in bed with the flu for a week, and he's asleep now. So I'm sorry, but he can't do it tonight."

My father was not going to take no for an answer.

"Could you please just ask him? I would appreciate it if you would just ask. We won't have another chance before I leave," my father begged.

She left my father standing at the door and went to ask.

He waited impatiently.

"Well, he said he would do it, but he's not getting out of bed," she insisted.

My father motioned for my mother and the witnesses to "come on in." The policeman and his partner also joined the wedding party. They all followed the woman into the bedroom. There were three metal beds lined along one wall, one for the minister and his wife and two children in each of the other two beds. Everyone was now awake and wondering what was going on.

My father noticed the policeman's partner smelled strongly of alcohol. As they exchanged their vows, the partner slowly slid down the wall and onto the floor. The half-asleep children, all in their pajamas, sat in bed and watched as my parents pledged to love "until death do us part."

"A wedding does not make a marriage" was certainly true in their case. Their wedding would not be considered beautiful in terms of the dress, the flowers, the ceremony, or the setting, but it was beautiful in its example that you don't need all of that to have a beautiful marriage. They were married for sixty-one years, full of love and commitment.

I often wondered if Mother ever had regrets about their unique but rather bizarre elopement. She would have been stunning in a wedding dress, with her flawless skin, hazel eyes, dark brown hair and voluptuous figure. I don't think my father ever had any regrets since he derived so much pleasure telling their wedding story through the years.

It was unclear whether it was March 9th or 10th, since it was so close to midnight. My father remembered it as a brutally cold March night. They went back to tell their parents they were married and spent the night in my grandfather's rustic cabin on a small lake. They pulled a mattress off a bed and slept in front of the open fireplace. My father returned three days late to his post in Canada. He had to appear before his commanding officer.

"Why are you three days late?"

"I got married," my father proudly announced.

Without even congratulations, he responded, "No excuse." My father was confined to his post for a month and had to wash stones along a pathway for several days.

After completing flight school in Canada, he returned to the states where he enlisted in the Army Air Force. After completing fifty missions, flying both B 17's and B 26's during the remainder of World War II, he returned to civilian life where my mother had been eagerly awaiting his safe return.

Both my parents grew up in the area around or near Ducktown. Both were from well-established families who were successful business owners. My mother's father, who died the year before I was born, owned a general store, rather like a small Walmart, selling a little bit of everything. Big Daddy was a Gulf Oil distributor and owned several businesses over the years. It made sense that my parents would choose to raise their family in the same area.

When I grew up in Ducktown, the population was near a thousand. Located in the foothills of the Great Smoky Mountains, in eastern Tennessee, on the border of Georgia and North Carolina. Ducktown first appeared in a list of Cherokee Indian towns in 1799. Local legend said the name originated from Cherokee Chief Duck.

We had two grocery stores, a pharmacy, a doctor's office (Robert's father), a bank, a furniture store, a small department store, a YMCA (where I took ballet and tap lessons) a small library, a post office, two churches (Baptist and Methodist) and an elementary school. It was more of a community, not large enough even to be called a town, but it was on the map. All of these businesses, except for the school, were along one main street. There were no red lights and only a couple of stop signs. It was my whole world but one lacking in any kind of diversity and secluded from the rest of the world.

Thousands of tourists came every summer to enjoy our mountains and scenery. Ducktown was at the end or beginning of the Cherokee National Forest, depending on which direction you were traveling. The Ocoee River meanders through the forest as you travel along the highway. Huge boulders and rushing white water are bordered by the many varieties of trees in various shades of green in the spring and summer and vibrant reds, yellows, and oranges in the fall. There is a unique beauty, even in the winter, when the leaves are gone. The Ocoee River was also the site of the whitewater competition in the 1996 summer Olympics. Kayakers and rafters still go there during the summer months to enjoy this beautiful natural setting.

As tourists started or ended their drive through the national forest, my father's businesses awaited them like an oasis. He had a gas station, a small snack bar he later renovated into a full-scale restaurant, restrooms, and a souvenir shop. The shop sold Indian moccasins, turquoise jewelry, copper jewelry, pottery, stuffed black bears, tomahawks, Indian dolls, and hundreds of other souvenirs. My father named it *The Three Bears Tradin' Post* – in the foothills of the Great Smoky Mountains.

Outside each entrance were twelve-foot tall totem poles. The inside walls were covered in tree bark, making it feel like an authentic Indian trading post. One summer, he hired an Indian chief to live on the premises to lure tourists off the highway and into his businesses. Another summer, he bought a small live black bear. Our family went to get the bear near the Smoky Mountains in our station wagon with a cage in the third seat. We felt like we were getting a new family pet. My father would go to any lengths to muster up business.

The souvenir shop provided my first work experience, starting around seventh or eighth grade, through high school, and working a few summers in college. One summer, I worked and saved sixty dollars, which seemed like a lot then. Mother and I planned a trip to Chattanooga to shop, and since she didn't drive in the city, we took a bus. It was rewarding to spend my own money, and the sixty dollars went a long way toward buying clothes and shoes for the next school year.

Working there gave me valuable experience in dealing with the public and seeing how hard my father worked. He kept his businesses open seven days a week. He always felt he needed to be there, never feeling comfortable letting anyone else be the boss. So not only did we not see much of him daily, but he didn't understand the purpose of a vacation. He loved what he did.

My father was a true entrepreneur. Throughout his career, he owned both an automobile and airplane dealership. He ran a full-service gas station when he had to hire people to pump the gas. The small snack bar only had stools for the customers. It served delicious hamburgers, French fries, and milkshakes. It was a rare treat when Mother didn't cook, and we got to go there for dinner. Tourists stopped for cherry and apple cider, and another big draw was three rolls of film for $1.00. All of his income was dependent on the tourists traveling through the area.

My father's businesses were at a crossroads of two highways, so all the traffic passed right beside them. Eventually, new highway construction led to his businesses being bypassed. But it didn't take long for him to figure out what he needed to do. He built a motel called *The Ole Copper Inn*. He was an incredible businessman without any business degree, just a lot of on the job experience. Besides providing a good income for his family, these businesses also provided the financial resources for his flying hobby.

He had always been fascinated with airplanes. His first memory was at age four when he was taking a bath and heard an airplane flying over his house. He ran out to see this object flying through the air and was mesmerized. His love of flying continued his entire life. He flew airplanes during World War II, and when I was eleven, he was able to purchase a four-seater private plane, a Beechcraft Bonanza, for his personal use.

My father did not follow the usual career path of many young men his age who grew up in the Great Copper Basin area, as it was called. There were mines in the area that contained copper ore and sulfuric acid. So the majority of men went to work in the mines after high school. They employed tens of thousands of people throughout its sixty years of operation, from 1899 until 1987.

The ore brought both devastation and prosperity. The timber-fueled operations resulted in logging all the trees. The tree harvesting and the sulfuric acid pollution left more than 32,000 acres eroded and devoid of life. Forty square miles were stripped bare. The rains depleted the topsoil and poured acid into the streams. All of this caused the hills to be as red as the copper itself.

When NASA took the first satellite photos from space, the only identifiable place in the southeastern United States was the Copper Basin area. When I worked at my father's gift shop, the tourists always asked the same questions, "Why are the hills so red? What happened to the trees?" It was unique, with a certain beauty. The area was in stark contrast to the nearby forests.

Reclamation efforts began as early as the 1930s. The land was treated, and trees were planted, which transformed the area back to forests from the barren "moonscape," as it was often called. This took years, and not until the nineteen-eighties, did the pine trees grow enough to make a difference. Eventually, with global competition being an issue, the mines closed, and the area has struggled ever since.

Although this did not directly affect my father's work, it left the area with high unemployment rates and a depressed economy. With my father running his businesses, he was pulled in many different directions. He took all his responsibilities seriously. My mother, however, wanted him to spend more time with us so we could be a family. But he always reminded her, "Well, someone around here has to make money. It doesn't grow on trees, you know."

Sunday was a day when we attended church together and shared Sunday dinner, even though it was lunch. Mother always prepared a large meal, cooking either a beef or pork roast, or fried chicken and sides of mashed potatoes, green beans, and my favorite salad, fruit cocktail frozen with whipping cream. She wasn't a fancy cook, usually just basic southern dishes, possibly a recipe from her Betty Crocker cookbook or one from a friend in her church circle group. On Sundays, she always went out of her way to make the food we all liked. We would eat together, lingering at the table to talk. Daddy had a good sense of humor and loved to joke with his kids. We cherished this time with him.

After one particular Sunday dinner when I was nine, Daddy surprised us when he said, "Why don't we just take off and go to Florida for a few days?"

He was impulsive. This was not expected, even by Mother. We didn't give him a chance to change his mind. We immediately jumped up to pack our bags. It was early spring, and tourist season was several months away. Daddy was leaving his work behind. I was in fourth grade and filled with excitement. *Are we going on a real vacation?* I had only heard about other people's vacations.

It seemed to take forever since our car was not air-conditioned, and there were three kids in the backseat of a 1958 Ford station wagon. My father had little patience for whining kids, so we knew better. We arrived in Daytona Beach, a town that allowed cars to drive on its beaches. We stopped to take pictures before even checking into our hotel.

Daddy and I stood beside our blue two-toned station wagon, me in my plaid Sunday dress, holding both shoes in one hand and

Daddy's hand in the other. Daddy was still in his black dress pants, white starched shirt, and narrow gold tie, with a cigar in his mouth. We hadn't even taken the time to change our clothes from church. I looked down, digging my toes into the cold, wet sand. I took it all in as I looked out onto the Atlantic Ocean for the first time.

We checked into a new hotel right on the beach. It was pink. We were all in one room. I couldn't have been happier. We went to Marineland and watched the porpoises doing tricks. We rented a boat, so my brother and father could go deep-sea fishing, but this didn't last long because Mother, Diane, and I were all getting seasick. Doing activities so new and different was exhilarating. Staying in a hotel, eating all our meals together, walking along the beach.... I loved it all! I would have remembered more of the details if I had known this was to be our one and only vacation.

Although we were slightly isolated from the rest of the world, my parents saw to it that we were exposed to the world outside of Ducktown, as much as possible. They encouraged us to take any travel opportunities we might be offered, usually with another family. They had subscriptions to *Life* magazine and *Readers Digest*, always read the Sunday newspaper, and the evening news was a nightly ritual. With my father's stories from the war, I was also aware of his world travel before marriage and kids. My father was the one expecting us to get out and experience the world while my mother was the more cautious one.

I distinctly remember watching the race riots in the early to mid-sixties and my father being appalled at what was happening.

"It doesn't matter what color their skin is. They deserve to be served just like everyone else," he said, as we watched TV when the young black people were refused service at a restaurant. Although we had no people of color anywhere near Ducktown, he thankfully set an example for his children that prejudice was wrong.

We were considered well off in Ducktown and lived comfortably in our large brick house. I had a pink bedroom with white furniture and a canopy bed, any little girl's dream. The lamps were dolls with lace skirts. My mother always complained about me lying on the white eyelet bedspread. It wasn't necessarily kid-friendly but was a lovely bedroom for an eleven-year-old. I loved my room, but because of my fear of the dark and being anxious at bedtime, I frequently snuck into my sister's bedroom down the hall and slept in her other twin bed.

My mother was the one who attended to her children's emotional needs and was always there for us. Kind, caring, patient, loving, gentle, soft-hearted are words to describe my mother. I have fond memories of being sick and staying home from school. Mother would attend to my every need as I lay on the sofa watching *I Love Lucy* and *The Price is Right*. When I had a sore throat, she had an old-timey medical treatment involving rubbing Vicks Vapor Rub on an old sock, heating it in the oven, then wrapping it around your neck. The combination smells of camphor, menthol, and eucalyptus and the warmth made it incredibly soothing. Her loving treatment almost made me want to stay sick.

We always laughed when Mother watched *Queen for a Day* because she was so tender-hearted she cried after hearing all the stories. It was a popular daytime show featuring four women, each telling their personal bad luck story, and the one chosen was "Queen" and lavished with prizes and gifts. She thought they all deserved to be queen.

After being a stay-at-home mother for years, she eventually got more involved in helping my father with his businesses when we got older. But she always felt her most important job was being a mother. She saw it as being just as important as a career outside the home. However, both of my parents talked frequently to us about what we were going to do "when you grow up."

Diane and I thought we wanted to be airline hostesses, which my father described as "glorified waitresses." He wanted us to choose a career in the medical field and was not impressed when both my sister and I became teachers. Early in their marriage, my mother taught school for several years. At the time, she was able to do this with only two years of college. My father knew it took a lot of time outside regular work hours, and the pay wasn't great. So he wanted some-thing more for us.

My parents fit the images of husband and wife, as seen on all the sitcoms during the late fifties and early sixties. We watched TV at night after homework and dinner was finished. My father was not always able to join us for dinner, but my mother always had a hot well-prepared meal for us.

She belonged to a women's Circle group at church, and one night a month, she had a meeting. This was the night we got TV din-ners. We thought those were the coolest. I always wanted the fried chicken dinner, and although it didn't compare to my mother's, I loved it anyway. It was just the novelty of a little dinner all prepared made it seem special.

She cooked chicken for us but disliked doing it because of her memories as a child when her father raised chickens. When it was time to make a chicken dinner, my mother remembered her father chasing the chickens around their backyard and wringing their necks. It left her with a strong aversion for chicken. I was glad we didn't raise chickens.

Although we lived comfortably, with all of our needs met, I was aware of others who weren't so lucky, although it wasn't luck in my family since my father worked exceptionally hard for all he acquired in life. But on my mother's side of the family, my great aunt Lula lived quite modestly. She was my maternal grandmother's sis-ter, who never married and had no children and worked years earlier in my grandfather's general store as a clerk. After my grandfather's death, she moved what merchandise she could into her small base-ment, and continued to try to support herself.

Lula was short and round with a lively spirit and infectious laugh. She always wore a dress and had her pocketbook at her side. She often had on a simple necklace or colorful scarf around her neck. She lived in Ducktown, near several of the homes we lived in before building our house. She lived alone in a small white clapboard house. I loved visiting her, and it was even more special to spend the night.

When my parents had to be out of town, they usually made arrangements for me to stay with Lula. I packed my small brown overnight bag and eagerly looked forward to sleeping over at Aunt Lula's house.

Lula heated only her small kitchen and living area with a big black iron pot-bellied stove, continually adding more coal to the fire throughout the evening. She kept the door shut to the rest of the house, making it extremely cold, more like freezing, especially in the winter. I loved sleeping on her feather bed, piled high with hand quilted blankets to keep us warm. There was an outhouse beyond the small porch into her house, but in the winter, she only used a big bucket under the bed.

Before we settled down to sleep, I asked her to tell me stories about when she was a little girl.

"Well, we didn't have all the things you do. We played outside a lot, and we helped Mama around the house and with my brothers and sisters." Lula came from a family of six and was a faithful churchgoer.

"What do you think heaven will be like?" I asked. She giggled.

"Well, no one knows for sure, but I think I'll see all my family again. You know, Minnie died at nineteen. I haven't seen her in a long time. I'll see Tom, and I believe he'll be able to see again. He lost his sight when he was a young man. I think there are streets of gold, and we'll all be happy with God. But I'm not ready to go yet," she added with another laugh.

At some point during the night, she would shake me awake,

"Karen, wake up now, I want you to use the pot. We can't have a wet bed."

Having found a warm spot in the bed next to Lula, it was incredibly hard to pull myself out into the cold room. In the morning, Lula would rise early to add more coal to the fire. Putting on her apron, she made eggs, bacon, and biscuits, along with her coffee, the whistling of the kettle interrupting the silence.

"Can I help with breakfast?" I asked, knowing she liked to do the cooking.

"How about setting the table? That'd be a big help," she offered.

Lula only had a few plates but lots of shelves with interesting glasses. She collected them from the boxes of laundry detergent she bought that included a small juice or milk glass for free. I always had trouble deciding which ones to use. We sat across from each other at her white enamel topped table.

"Mmmm, this tastes great." And it always did. Afterward, we would settle in her small sitting room and talk. She was quick to smile and laugh.

Lula had a small black and white TV that she only turned on for specific shows. She loved watching live wrestling. She was also a collector of what she called "whatnots" or "knickknacks." She had a glass curio cabinet in her living room full of exciting things.

"This came from Tom's trip to South Florida when he was a boy."

"This was Minnie's glass bowl she used to put her rings in."

I was fascinated by it all. I loved hearing the story behind every "knick-knack," most being from other people's travels. But Lula seemed content with her life as it was. I never heard her complain. She was always included in our family holiday dinners. One of us would pick her up and take her home since she never drove or owned a car. When we drove her home, I would carefully walk her up the steps to her side porch, open the screen door for her, as she looked for the skeleton key in her purse that opened the door.

"Good night, Lula. It was so good to see you. See you soon." Our family rarely said, "I love you," so that would have been uncomfortable for both of us. But I did love her and wish I had told her so.

She lived independently until she was ninety-five when my mother had to make a hard decision to move her to a nursing home. Lula lived to be ninety-eight. Her happiness seemed rooted in her ability to be happy with what she had, a simple life. One not rich in money or things but rich in gratitude for just being alive.

There were many lessons to learn from Lula. One, in particular, was how to be happy without a partner. She lived alone her entire life. The summer after Robert died, I looked at Lula differently. *Is she lonely? How has she managed on her own all these years? Did she ever fall in love? Had she ever had her heart broken?* I was still feeling like half a person without Robert.

Seven months had now passed since Robert died, and my sophomore year had ended. I was able to make it through the school year, but the thought of being home for the summer terrified me. I was thankful that my parents were still there for me, but it wasn't enough. I couldn't imagine what I would do at home without Robert. It was also going to be uncomfortable being at home after leaving for college and being independent. I knew it would be better not to be back in the place full of memories with Robert, but I didn't see any other options. His absence was felt in everything I did. I longed for him back in my life. I also longed for an end to despair and sadness.

I frequently visited the cemetery. His gravesite was on a small hill with a view of both the sun rising and setting. The Lees' had a unique headstone made with the Harley Davidson wings in the center, a hammer and anvil, to represent his horseshoeing career, and another symbol to represent his welding certification. He was only nineteen, but he had accomplished quite a bit.

I often visited the local florist and took two roses intertwined, placing them on his grave. I wasn't trying to be dramatic. I still needed a feeling of connection. I thought about the suit he was buried in. I thought about the metal medallion inscribed with our names in his breast pocket. I thought about death. I wasn't making much progress toward "moving on" as everyone kept reminding me I should be doing.

Working in my father's tourist shop kept me busy during the day. The nights were the hardest. As the day began to end, the anxiety would increase, and I was increasingly restless. My life felt as if I had to function in a world I didn't recognize.

I made frequent visits to the Lees' that first summer. They were welcoming and upbeat. At one visit, Mrs. Lee surprised me.

"Karen, there are some things in Robert's room that I thought you might be interested in. I've been meaning to ask you if you'd like to see if there's anything you might want to keep."

"Yeah, well, I guess so." I hadn't been in his room since he died. I wanted to go, and I didn't want to go.

As we walked down the long hall toward his room, I wasn't sure this was going to be helpful in my attempts to move on with my life. It felt so intimate. I could feel his presence.

"Robert kept all the letters you wrote to him through the years, and I thought you might want them back."

As she opened the drawer, it felt like we were intruding.

"I didn't want to just throw them away before I asked you first."

"I kept all mine from him, too. Thank you. I'll take them." I said as I put them in my lap.

"Also, the monogrammed jacket you gave him for Christmas is here. Would you like it?"

His last Christmas, he wore the jacket in front of their Christmas tree when Mrs. Lee took our picture. I stood beside him in my gold monogrammed jumper with a long-sleeved white shirt. We both looked so happy, his arm around my waist, me holding a large Christmas gift. I recalled how handsome he looked in the blue, London Fog, zip-up jacket with his initials -REL- on the front. I sat on his bed and stared at the jacket. I pulled it to my face. It still had his faint smell. This was painful in so many ways.

Mrs. Lee noticed me struggling. She sat down on the bed beside me, resting a hand on my leg.

"Oh, Karen, I'm so sorry. This is upsetting you. I'm saving some of his clothes for his brother when he gets older, but the jacket was a gift I knew you gave him."

So many emotions were flooding in as I looked around his room. I held the jacket close. All my feelings of loss were fresh again. I'm sure Mrs. Lee thought by waiting this long, I would be more able to handle this, but it was traumatic.

I knew I needed to try to emulate the Lees' ability to move forward with my life. They had two younger children, Luke and Laura, who kept them busy and engaged. I always left their house with an increased sense of loss, but at the same time, it helped to be with his family. This night I left with the grief raw and exposed. I had not only lost Robert but knew I was also expected to let go of his family.

That summer, I made myself go out on a few dates with some of Robert's old friends. It felt strange and uncomfortable. There were no feelings there and no fun either, just a reminder of what I had lost. I knew I needed a change of environment with new people and new scenery, a fresh start to jolt me out of myself and my feelings.

After a lot of back and forth, wondering if it was the right decision, I decided to transfer to the University of Tennessee at Knoxville, a much larger college for my junior year. I wanted to try to have a new beginning and meet people who didn't know my sad story. I was tired of people staring at me. I was tired of feeling so broken. I enrolled in late summer school classes in Knoxville so that I could acclimate myself to a new school and city.

Chapter 5

August 1970

I was starting over in a new city and new school. I had to work on a new me. I decided not to join the sorority, so I was on my own without any connections. This university was much bigger than the Chattanooga campus. *Maybe I can just get lost in the crowd.* I was open to a new beginning even though I was nervous. Leaving Margie behind was hard. She had helped me in so many ways. I missed her terribly. My new roommate was never around, and when she was, she showered obsessively. We had nothing in common. I felt so alone, but I knew I needed to do this.

Dan and I had written an occasional letter during the summer. So one lonely night I decided to call him in Lockport. He was living there with his parents until school started in the fall. Two of his brothers were serving in Vietnam, and any late-night phone calls were not appreciated. This didn't cross my mind. I was missing his ability to make me laugh. I wasn't doing any laughing these days, and it was good to hear his voice.

That fall when Dan went back to Chattanooga for his senior year, we started seeing each other on the weekends. We were two hours apart so he would catch a ride to see me, or I would drive down to see him. I liked the way I felt when I was with him as we began to get to know each other better. Dan wasn't into talking about feelings, so I opted to write him a letter explaining I was still in the process of grieving over my lost love and not ready to get serious with anyone. He never put any pressure on me. He was patient in giving me time to figure out my feelings. I was feeling weary from the constant battle in my head over what had happened and what would never happen. Dating Dan was a distraction from my grief.

I found myself looking forward to the weekends. Dan was upbeat and full of life, always in a good mood. We planned picnics, went to football games, concerts and laughed a lot. There was nothing serious going on, just a mutual enjoyment of each other. He was a gentleman in not expecting anything from me very romantic. I continued to struggle with depression, my emotions still on a roller coaster. There were good days and very bad days.

Dan and I continued our back and forth visits between Knoxville and Chattanooga. We went to fraternity parties, movies, and dinners out with friends. We were a little more than friends but not by much. Emotionally I was still fragile and wasn't ready for a serious relationship.

As the school year came to an end, I was faced again with what to do during the summer. Since my future had changed so drastically, I felt I was continually asking myself. *What do I do now?* I knew going home to Ducktown wasn't going to happen this year. I wasn't going to put myself through that again.

Margie was finishing another school year in Chattanooga, and we had continued being best friends.

In early spring, she called with a suggestion.

"Hey, I've got a plan for you. Why don't you join me this summer at the shore? You would love it. It would be good for you."

She had worked along the Jersey shore for several summers and shared fun stories about her waitressing jobs and hanging with a much older crowd at the beach.

"Wow, really? I guess I could be a waitress. But I don't have any experience. Where are you going to live?"

"I haven't got it all worked out yet. But that's not a problem. We'll figure it out after we get there."

I suddenly felt a sense of possibility, a spark of hopefulness. Even the name of the seaside town, Avon-by-the-Sea sounded inviting.

"I'm sure your parents will let you go. They don't want you to have to go back to Ducktown again this summer."

"Yeah, you're right. It sounds like fun. I don't have any reasons not to go. Are you sure you want to be my roommate again?"

"What? Of course, it'll be great. We'll have a blast."

The more I thought about it, the more excited I became. I hadn't felt this way in a long time, looking toward my future with possibilities. It seemed like a good chance to branch out from being a sheltered southern girl. My parents agreed and paid for my flight to New Jersey.

Margie and I spent several days at her parents' home in New Jersey, going shopping and swimming in their above ground pool. A trip into the city, meaning New York City, was planned before we left for the shore. It was quite the adventure for a girl from Ducktown, Tennessee. Margie had been there many times, so we got around easily and could have been twins in our matching bell-bottom pants, mine in yellow and brown, hers in red and blue.

It was my first experience riding in a taxi, on a train, and a subway. The constant sounds of car horns and the whine of police sirens were overwhelming. All my senses were engaged. So many people. So many nationalities. I had never heard another language spoken other than in my French class in high school.

Besides being amazed by so many people, I was even more astonished by the skyscrapers. I spent much of the day looking up at the massive buildings. This felt like another world and made me realize how secluded my life had been. We spent one day at the Guggenheim Museum. Margie shared information about the various artists since she was an art major. In Greenwich Village, we found ourselves trying to become part of the cool crowd of artists, writers, and students as we smoked cigarettes trying to look like we belonged.

We had dinner at Mama Leone's, an Italian restaurant, where we were able to order drinks since the drinking age in New York was eighteen. Feeling mature and sophisticated, we left the city for our adventure at the shore.

Margie and I rented a room in a boarding house. During the week, we had the place to ourselves, but on the weekend, sorority girls from a local college occupied all the other rooms. Our room was on the top floor, with twin beds and no air conditioning. Since we were only blocks from the ocean, we bought used bicycles to ride around the small beach town. We went to Carvel to eat ice cream in binges and found a great little diner where Margie introduced me to tuna fish and bacon sandwiches on rye bread. Our days were spent lying on the beach, and we waited tables at night. Our social life started after work.

I got a waitress job at one of the best seafood restaurants in town. The one that had a waiting line out the door and down the sidewalk on Saturday nights. Nearly all the waitresses were older women who waited tables as a career. The restaurant hired two extra people for the summer, and I was one of them. I had no idea what a steamer was, the difference in crab legs and crab cakes, a flounder, and a perch. I could barely identify the shrimp. They hired me because I was this little Southern girl, and they liked my accent.

I became quite the darling of the restaurant and even had guests asking for me. I also managed to survive the Saturday nights when the cook came in drunk, and all hell broke loose in the kitchen. Making good tip money gave me the freedom to play at the beach during the day, work on my tan, and talk with friends. College students were working in all the local restaurants, new and interesting people. Many were friends Margie knew from previous summers, but some were ones I made on my own. I lost some of my shyness and self-consciousness, which gave me strength and confidence.

I was enjoying this transition period into being a young adult. I had all the independence involved in being away from home on my own for the first time. I mostly managed to put the grief and sadness out of my mind, although I still found myself in tears sometimes. But for the most part, I was doing a good job of *not dwelling in the past,* as many people advised me to do.

The environment was a kind of therapy for me since it involved new people, new places, and new experiences. It also helped that there was a lifeguard, who Margie knew from years past, who started to show interest in me. Stevie was at the beach every day. He was easy to talk to, tall and thin with curly brown hair and a huge smile. *Maybe he can make me laugh.* At first, we were going places together in a group, but eventually, we were going out to dinner and taking walks along the beach alone.

Dan and I had continued to stay in touch with letters and occasional phone calls throughout the summer. When I started having feelings for Stevie and still cared about Dan, I was confused. I had limited experience in relationships, and I wasn't sure how to handle my conflicting feelings. I had been numb for so long.

At least I was feeling alive again. *I'm not damaged for life. I can still have feelings.* The feeling of the sun on my skin, the sounds of the waves crashing on the beach, the fantastic ice cream at Carvel, the sunsets over the ocean, the friendships I was making, all of this was cracking open my hardened heart.

Dan was working again in his hometown for the summer. We decided it would be fun for him to come for a weekend visit at the shore. I was excited but also nervous about seeing him. I met him at the train station. As I saw him coming toward me, I noticed his strong presence – tall, with broad shoulders and muscular arms. He was wearing a pink shirt and jeans, his hair was long, and he had a dark tan. I was now in a better place to appreciate his good looks. It felt good to be with him again. We went out for drinks with my fake id. I wouldn't be twenty-one until September.

I managed to avoid seeing Stevie during Dan's visit. I was trying to keep from having to tell either of them that there was someone else. Getting attention from two different guys was a new experience for me. As the summer progressed, I continued to juggle both relationships, Dan with phone calls and letters, and Stevie kept me busy after work.

As I became more aware of the summer coming to an end, I was full of melancholy. It was a summer I knew I would always remember, a turning point for me. All my new northern Jersey friends gave me a going-away party before I left to go home. We went out in the ocean in a rubber dingy and partied in someone's rented room. They made a big sign "Goodbye, Karen We'll miss you'all" – a little play on my Southern accent which they seemed to enjoy. I never saw any of them again.

When the summer ended, I faced a dilemma. Stevie wanted me to meet his parents who lived in another part of New Jersey and go into New York City again with him before going back to Tennessee. The only problem was I had already made plans earlier in the summer to fly to Buffalo to spend time with Dan at his parents' home. *Now, what do I do?* I had never been in a situation like this before.

I was still unsure about my feelings for both of them. I wanted to keep them both happy until I could make a decision, so I made a plan. I spent several days at Stevie's house, meeting his parents and going on a day trip into the city. Stevie took me to the airport, where we said good-bye for the summer. I didn't know if I would ever see him again, and I wasn't sure how I felt about this.

However, I didn't fly back to Tennessee, but to Buffalo, where Dan met me at the airport. The other passengers were giving me second looks since I had hugged and kissed Stevie goodbye and then ran into Dan's arms, also hugging and kissing him. Dan didn't know about my summer romance with Stevie, but Stevie was aware there was someone else. I was wavering in my commitment to either relationship. I was just ecstatic that I was feeling emotions. I finally felt I was alive again and not living in the past.

The visit with Dan was all I expected it to be. His vigor for life made everything exciting. We visited with his many friends and partied until the wee hours of the morning. During his childhood, his family spent their summers at a cottage on Lake Ontario. We spent time alone there, swimming in the lake, having intimate candlelight dinners, and drinking wine.

There were definitely feelings of romance between us. Both of us were easy going and flexible, and we got along easily. Dan's exuberance for life was balanced by my being more reserved. He was confident, and this made me feel safe. He seemed to be able to handle any situation with ease. My feelings for him were deepening.

During this visit with Dan, I stayed at his parents' home in Lockport. It was interesting to learn its long family history. Dan's grandfather had owned land in the country and farmed but unfortunately had five daughters. He needed sons to do the manual labor required to run his farm. He was struggling to manage and then died suddenly. His wife had to sell the farm and move to the "city."

So Dan's grandmother and her five daughters moved to the house in Lockport in the early 1900s. As time went by, the grandmother died, and several of the daughters began to marry and move out. Dan's mother, Rita, was the youngest of the five daughters, and she married Jack LaGraff in 1940. Because of financial concerns, they decided to temporarily move into the house until they could find a place of their own.

Being the good Catholics that they were, after five months of marriage, they discovered Rita was pregnant. This pregnancy was soon followed, within a year and a half to two years, by four other children. Dan was the fourth son, followed by a daughter. They never moved out of this house. Dan's parents, their five children, and two aunts, who never married, lived as an extended family for years. So Dan, in essence, had three mothers.

By the time I was visiting in the early seventies, his mother, Rita, and the two aunts, Flo and Mary T, had all retired from teaching, but his father still worked as a Niagara County road inspector. He had never been able to fulfill his dream of becoming a doctor. Early in his college career, he was asked to leave Northwestern University for gambling. His dreams were lost in the reality of supporting a wife and five children.

All of them smoked heavily. Dan's mother, Rita, was struggling with emphysema. She was frail and couldn't handle any type of physical exertion. The house had steep steps to the bedrooms upstairs, so she would carefully hold onto the rail as she slowly made her way to bed at night. They had to repaint the living room ceiling every summer since it would turn yellow from the smoke. But the house was kept immaculate. The three women shared the chores, and all knew their place. Flo was a meticulous house cleaner and cleaned the ashtrays almost as soon as the ashes fell.

Being in a small town in the north had a whole different feeling than one in the south. The houses were built close together with small family grocery stores every few blocks. Anytime we visited a friend's home, the first question asked was, "Would you like a drink?" And they weren't referring to ice tea or Coca-Cola. This was also new to me. Although I enjoyed a few drinks with a meal or at a party, I didn't drink just any old time. Lockport seemed to have a bar and a Catholic church on almost every block. Religion and drinking went hand in hand. The Irish Catholics knew how to drink, and not always responsibly.

Although I was fond of Dan's mother and aunts, Dan's father was especially endearing. He made me feel like I was the best thing to happen to Dan, always full of compliments. It was obvious where Dan got his sense of humor. Jack reminded everyone of Jack Benny, both in looks and mannerisms. He made you laugh when you were around him.

Unfortunately, Jack had spent many years drinking in the bars around town. Dan remembers being left in the car with his siblings while his father went in to "talk to a man about buying a horse." Jack attended Mass religiously and sang in the choir. He was never quite able to recover from never having a place of his own and living with three women. He escaped to the closest bar as often as possible. The stress of having five children to support, living in a small house with his wife's two sisters, and never quite fulfilling his dreams, contributed to his alcoholism.

Dan was the fourth son and never the center of attention at home. His three older brothers excelled academically, but good grades were not a priority for Dan during high school. It took him five years to get out of high school because of school missed when he had mono, but he graduated from college with a business degree in four years. Just like me, he had been more into his social life during high school. He was well-liked by his peers and known for his irreverent sense of humor.

He enjoyed admiration and thrived on the affirmation given to him by his friends. He could talk to anyone and never was intimidated. He was completely charming and comfortable when he met Big Mama and my great Aunt Lula for the first time. So different from Robert, who didn't have the self-confidence to interact easily with others.

When I left Lockport at the end of my summer visit, I knew it was time to send Stevie a "Dear John" letter. The feelings I was having for Dan were much deeper and felt like more than a summer romance. When I arrived back at school, I mailed the letter and didn't expect a reply.

⮂

Dan and I were more involved during the next school year. Although we were two hours apart, seeing each other most weekends became routine. I never knew what to expect, but we always had fun together. He sent me romantic cards in the mail. I got a candy gram on Valentine's Day and a dozen red roses for my 21st birthday. He was doing all the right things to convince me I had made the right decision.

Being apart during the week made our time together on the weekends even more special. It was spring, and we planned a weekend getaway to the Smoky Mountains. The dogwoods were blooming, and all the trees in southeast Tennessee were various shades of green. We headed off in my car with no particular plans in mind. We took a cooler and made several stops to indulge in what we named "summer delights" – vodka and lime juice.

We kept passing cars with *Just Married* written on the windows or sides of the vehicle. The couples sat side by side, exuding happiness. "Ohhh, look at them," I exclaimed. We saw more and more newlyweds, and suddenly we looked at each other.

"Are you thinking what I'm thinking?" I asked.

"Yeah, let's do it," Dan smiled and pulled me over next to him.

We continued on our way until we found a gas station/grocery store. I was able to buy the white shoe polish needed to make ourselves "newly-weds."

We pulled into the parking lot beside the store, taking turns choosing what seemed like funny phrases to write on my car. It felt intoxicating … or was that the *summer delights*? After a fall picnic last year, we had given ourselves nicknames of Jack and Viola. Jack came from Dan's dad, who was called Jack, even though his name was John. And Viola was the name from the label on the cheese we were eating on the picnic.

"Just Married. Jack and Viola. Tonight's the Night"

"We Did It"

"Love and Piece" – a little play on words.

We broke down laughing, oblivious to anyone watching who might be questioning our sanity. As we pulled away, we waved and began to enjoy all the attention we were getting. Now we were husband and wife. *Well, this was easy.* Cars honked, and people waved as we continued to enjoy our prank as we drove through the mountains. We laughed and laughed.

As the day wore on, it lost its humor. We didn't have reservations, and we soon found there was no room in any inn, even for the newlyweds. We drove out of the way to try to find a place to stay. It was getting close to dark, and Dan went in to check on yet another room. I decided to wait in the car.

Suddenly I heard a voice say, "That's Karen Campbell." *Oh, damn, they know me.* I didn't know what to do but knew I had to do something. I slithered to the floorboard of the car. I wanted to disappear.

Dan came back to tell me we finally had a room. I was still on the floorboard.

"Let's get out of here, someone knows me here, and we have to leave NOW."

"What?? What are you talking about? We can't leave. Why are you on the floor?"

"Just go. We have to leave. The guys in that car parked next to us know me."

He pulled away, and we disappeared into the night. *Now, what do I do? Who could that have been?* A million different possibilities went through my mind. All I knew was it could be someone from my home town, and I needed an explanation for my parents.

As for now, it was dark, we were in the middle of the mountains with no room, and our prank was no longer funny. We finally made our way back to Gatlinburg and managed to find a place. Cars were still honking at us, people waving, and when we stopped, the typical round of "congratulations." I know they had never seen newlyweds looking so haggard and miserable.

The next morning Dan headed to a car wash, and I had to call my parents and come up with a story that might explain our foolishness. I practiced beforehand to make sure it made sense.

"We went to the mountains with a few other couples. As a prank, the couples decorated my car with "Just Married." We thought it was funny for a while, but when we were out someone saw the car and called out my name. I don't know who it was, so I just wanted to let you know. In case you hear around town that I got married, it was all just a joke,"

No problem, they laughed nervously and never questioned me any further. *Whew! ... that was crazy!*

Before we knew it, another school year was ending, and Dan's college graduation was approaching. His parents made plans to attend. Out of their five children, four of them had graduations that year, so they were busy traveling to different cities. Dan's older brother, Mike, and his wife, Susan, and their baby, Kristen, were able to join us in Chattanooga.

Everyone was staying at the Holiday Inn which provided a fun atmosphere with its pool and party room. Dan's father liked to entertain in style, so there was plenty of beer, champagne, and food. We spent time by the pool, went out to eat, and did some sightseeing. Dan's father insisted we call friends to come party after the ceremony. What would graduation be without a party? It was fun being part of this celebration.

A few days before graduation, Dan and I had a private party of our own. I planned a picnic at a local park and brought a bottle of champagne. I had spent several days clipping phrases out of magazines reflective of our relationship. I collaged them around the bottle... *Life is beautiful...watching the sun go down...a roaring fire...a walk through nature...big weekends...greet the dawn together... the beautiful world of Tennessee...facing the cold cruel world.*

We drank the champagne. There was both an air of happiness and sadness in our togetherness. I felt we were both wondering, *Where is this relationship going from here? When will we see each other again?* He was going back home for the summer.

Dan was going back to wait for an important phone call. Before I met Dan, he had damaged his left eye during the early part of his junior year by over-wearing his contact lenses and getting an abrasion. The situation got worse when he got herpes virus in this eye from a cold sore, which destroyed his cornea. He was on a transplant list and was waiting on the call telling him there was a donor.

He had worn a patch over this eye for over a year. His eye was continually draining. The first time I met Dan, I went with my suite-mate, Jody, to visit her boyfriend who was one of Dan's roommates. Dan came to the door and we were introduced. He had a black patch over this eye and was wearing a white terrycloth bathrobe with *La-Graff Sucks* written in black magic marker across the back. He looked a little like a pirate. *Who's this guy?*

Dan knew he would need a cornea transplant to restore his vision. The best doctor was located in New York City. So after his graduation, he returned home to wait for the phone call telling him a cornea was available. Any career plans were put on hold.

This was a stressful time for us as a couple since we had become accustomed to seeing each other on the weekends. He was much more than two hours away, and I was missing him. The summer and fall seemed to last forever. We planned to spend our first holiday together after I scheduled a flight to Buffalo for Thanksgiving. I was excited to feel his arms around me again.

It was my first holiday away from my own family, but I was looking forward to some northern hospitality. The weather change was drastic. It was still relatively warm in Knoxville, so I was excited to see snow showers in Buffalo. We stopped at a local bar to have a whiskey sour, which I soon learned was the favorite mixed drink at the LaGraff house. The combination of falling snow and the drinks left me feeling slightly giddy.

There was a tremendous amount of excitement in the air as we spent our first holiday together. I was glad I had already met Dan's parents, but I was anxious about meeting his two aunts and Dan's sister, Susie. We all enjoyed a formal Thanksgiving dinner with all the trimmings, no southern casseroles, but they did have dressing and apple pie. No one drank ice tea.

His family was easy to be around. There was constant laughter when we played charades. They told family stories from the past and seemed to enjoy each other's company. I felt Mary T and Flo, Dan's aunts, were checking me out – this Southerner among all the Northerners. But I felt comfortable enough just to be myself.

The holiday was soon over. Dan took me to the airport, and we lingered together in the terminal lobby as long as we could. I looked back at him with tears in my eyes when it was time for me to board. Our goodbyes were getting harder to get through. I quickly found myself back in school, counting down the days until we could be together again.

Dan soon got the phone call to report for surgery. Although he lived near Buffalo, he had never been to New York City. Even I, the little southern girl from Ducktown, had been there twice. He went to New York City alone and rented a small efficiency, where he was going to recuperate after the operation. In the early seventies, this was major surgery, and he was supposed to take it easy for three months. We talked on the phone and wrote long love letters to each other, but not seeing him was hard. The absence was making my heart grow fonder.

One of my roommates in Knoxville had just started design school in New York City, so we hatched a plan. I would tell my parents I was going to see Dan and stay with my roommate. We did just the opposite. We went to see her, but I stayed with Dan.

I took a cab from the airport to his place. I was feeling a mixture of emotions – some guilt over not telling my parents the truth, and some fear that I was alone in New York City in the back of a cab, and excitement that I was going to spend four days with Dan. He was staying in an old hotel converted into efficiencies, somewhat dark and gloomy.

When he came downstairs to meet me, all my worries disappeared. He looked so sexy in his jeans and tee-shirt; his hair was long, and he no longer had the patch over his eye. We were back together, and that was all we needed. We went out to a small diner near his room to eat our meals, and the rest of the time we were holed up in his bedroom.

"I know you're not supposed to be very active, so I brought a book to read," I told him as I unzipped my suitcase. He gave me a rather disappointing look, but it quickly changed to anticipation as I showed him my book, *Everything You Wanted to Know About Sex but Were Afraid to Ask.* We read passages together and laughed hysterically at the names given to various sex acts.

The surgery left two small black spots on his cornea, but Dan thought there was supposed to be only one. One morning, after a little too much activity the night before, he panicked when he noticed the other spot. He was afraid he had jolted something, and his surgery was now a bust. He called his surgeon and asked for an emergency appointment. As I sat there alone, I felt so guilty.

He returned home with the news, "Everything is okay. The two black spots are normal after cornea surgery." Ahhhhh…. back to the book, there were a few things we hadn't tried.

It was February in New York and bitterly cold. We bundled up in our heavy coats and hats and took short walks. There was snow on the ground as we walked hand in hand. It all felt terribly romantic. I was in love.

Dan recovered, and the operation was a success. He regained his eye-sight and could now make plans for his future. His previous plans included joining the military after college. He was in ROTC during college to prepare for serving his country. All three of his brothers joined a branch of the service after college, two of them going to Vietnam. The first step in signing up required him to take both a physical and mental exam. He was still holding out hope his aspiration to become a soldier might be possible.

After the exam, the doctor declared emphatically, "Well, you aren't going to Vietnam for two reasons. First, the damage to your eye physically disqualifies you, and secondly, anyone who wants to go to Vietnam is crazy, so that mentally disqualifies you." This became one of Dan's biggest disappointments in life. He wanted to go and liked to tell people, "If I'd gone, we would have won the war."

I wasn't happy that he had to have a cornea transplant, but I was happy that he wasn't going into the military. Because of this turn of events, he had to change his post-college plans completely. He found a job in Chattanooga, using his business degree to work for an insurance company. The timing was perfect since I was finishing my senior year in education and would be doing my student teaching there in the fall. For the first time, we would now be living in the same city.

Chapter 6

January 1973

Dan found an apartment and began his 9 to 5 job in the insurance business. I soon followed him to Chattanooga. His place was in a large historic house converted into apartments. There just happened to be a loft apartment available. Perfect.

Skip, Dan's college roommate, who he tossed the coin with deciding who was going to ask me out, was also living there. He was dating Lee Ann, and we became fast friends and decided to share the loft apartment. Dan and Skip lived in the two downstairs apartments, and we had the one upstairs.

The house was on the outskirts of the university, and many of the renters were students. It was known to the college kids as "the green ghetto," so this told us the level of luxury it provided. There were no amenities – no laundry room, no fitness room, no pool. Painted an ugly shade of green made it an easy landmark. Or maybe it was called "the green ghetto" because of the smell of marijuana that often flowed out from under many of the apartment doors.

I started my student teaching assignment. My three-month placement was in a first-grade class in a city school. I was prepared for planning lessons and teaching, but the discipline techniques needed to hold their attention weren't my strongest attributes as a teacher. I loved the kids, but they took advantage of my inexperience. The teacher I was working under was patient with me and provided support when I felt defeated at the end of the day. Teaching was going to be challenging in more ways than I had anticipated. *Why didn't I stick with interior decorating?*

My college graduation followed my completion of student teaching. It was March, so I wouldn't be looking for a full-time job until school started again in September. I fell back on my waitressing experience and found a job waiting tables at the Chattanooga Choo-Choo. It was always busy with tourists, but it was easy in comparison to dealing with the needs of children all day. I could go to work, do my job, walk out the door, and I was finished. With teaching, the work was never finished.

I felt new freedom after completing college and not having many other responsibilities. Dan and I had never been together daily, so we took advantage of the summer months, partying with our friends, going out to eat, swimming at the lake, entertaining at the ghetto. Although we had separate apartments, we spent most of our time together. I felt lucky to have Dan in my life, who continued to make me feel safe and always made me laugh. We shared the same sense of humor, and our personalities complemented each other.

In mid-summer, we spent a Sunday afternoon with Skip and his now fiancé, Lee Ann. Dan and I had been dating for three years. It was hot and muggy, so we all decided to head to the lake to swim. After a long day of sun and fun, we went back to Dan's apartment and drank a considerable number of the infamous *summer delights* – vodka and lime juice. Dan always loved his music loud, so the stereo was blaring. The four of us danced unrestrained to "Ramblin Man" by the Allman Brothers Band.

Dan suddenly pulled away from me.

"Will you marry me?"

What? Did I hear him right? I was stunned. This was completely unexpected. Suddenly our party of four turned quiet and serious.

Although I felt this was in our future, we had never actually discussed marriage. Our relationship was all about having fun, and this was one of those decisions you make once in a lifetime, a serious commitment. *Where was the ring? Did he plan this?*

I knew Dan had an impulsive side … not always thinking through his decisions. As I had found out through the years, he didn't have much of a filter – he would think it and then say it. *Could this be the summer delights talking??* Although this wasn't the kind of engagement I had in mind, I had an answer.

"Well, gosh Dan, yes, I guess so… yeah, I'll marry you."

Regardless of the circumstances, I was thrilled. *I don't really need a ring, do I?* The party ended with us calling our parents to give them the news. Although Skip and Lee Ann were already engaged, they hadn't set a date, so we pulled out a calendar and decided we needed at least four months to plan a wedding. It was June, so we chose October. Theirs would be two weeks before ours, to give them time for their wedding and honeymoon, followed by our marriage. Our wedding date was set for October 20, 1973.

As we put together wedding plans, I became increasingly nervous. Our parents had never met, and I wasn't sure how the Northern Irish Catholics and the Scottish Southern Baptists were going to hit it off. Being from the north, Dan was accustomed to a large sit-down dinner reception with a band, with guests enjoying an open bar. Being from the South, I was more familiar with a traditional simple wedding, the reception in the church basement with nuts, mints, and punch.

This was going to be interesting. And there was the added problem of where we were going to get married – Catholic church? Baptist church? Minister? Priest? Alcohol or punch? Lots of decisions to make. Even though there were lots of differences, we managed to work it out.

We decided the marriage ceremony would take place in the Baptist church I attended as a child. I had fond memories growing up there and felt it helped shape the person I had become. But we would have two Catholic priests officiating. *Hummmm? How's this going to work?* First, I had to call the minister of the Baptist church and ask for permission. I didn't know him since I had been away from my hometown for five years.

He was not at all excited about two Catholic priests in his church, even though they wouldn't be saying mass. His immediate response was, "You know those Catholics, they don't know the Lord." This was not going well. He said he would have to talk to the elders of the church.

Although I wouldn't have called my father an overly religious man, more of a righteous man, he still attended our church and always gave a generous donation at Christmas. I'm sure this influenced the minister since he finally gave permission for us to be married in the Baptist church.

We decided to hold the reception at my parents' house. The views from their home would be the perfect backdrop for an outside reception. In October, weather in the South can either be stunningly beautiful or wet and cold, but that was something I couldn't control.

The next hurdle was the question of alcohol. I knew my parents would never agree to beer, which would be totally unacceptable. Liquor would be even worse. So we thought champagne would be respectable and festive. They agreed. The food would be a buffet of heavy hors d'oeuvres in the dining room.

Mrs. Lee, Robert's mother, offered to have a wedding brunch for all the women in the wedding party and out of town family members. She was gracious and showed nothing but love and happiness for me. All the bridesmaids, Dan's mother and aunt, my mother, and aunt were all sitting around the room where Robert's picture in his suit still sat on the table. It felt slightly wrong for this wedding event to be happening in his house. *I wonder who knows my history here?* I couldn't help but look at his picture. He was smiling back at me. I felt confident Robert would be happy for me. I had found love again.

I had many concerns about the rehearsal dinner, the wedding, and reception. I wanted everything to be perfect, like most brides on their wedding day. Using several books for inspiration, we wrote our wedding vows, wanting them to reflect our special relationship. We planned to use wine in our ceremony – real wine, in a Baptist church. We were breaking all the rules. The wine would be in two individual wine goblets, and after some poignant words, we would pour the wine into the same goblet and both drink from it.

Dan went to a family friend's house to get a special homemade wine to use in the ceremony. He took it to the church earlier in the day, but the door was locked, so he hid it in the bushes outside the church. Unfortunately, when he got back to the church, the wine was gone. We decided one of the southern Baptists heard we were using wine and stole it from under the bush. They were probably at home having a drink themselves! Dan hurried back for more wine, but none of this special wine was left, so we had to use a cheap substitute.

Our hopes for the perfect wedding day started with plenty of sunshine and the feel of fall in the air. All the Catholics and Bap-

tists gathered to witness our wedding vows. There were no traditional vows, "for richer, for poorer, in sickness and in health, till death
do us part," this was too old-fashioned for us. Taking a considerable
risk, we both memorized our vows, faced each other, and recited the
words we had carefully chosen.

"Karen, I take you as my wife. I pledge to share my life openly
with you and to speak the truth to you in love. I promise to honor and
tenderly care for you, to cherish and encourage your fulfillment as an
individual throughout all the changes of our lives."

"Dan, I take you as my husband. I pledge to share my life
openly with you and to speak the truth to you in love. I promise to
honor and tenderly care for you, to cherish and encourage your fulfillment as an individual throughout all the changes of our lives."

Although they were only words, I made a commitment to Dan
and our marriage. Although we didn't say "until death do us part," I
felt it in my heart. Life seemed full of promise as we walked down the
aisle to Karen Carpenter's song "We've Only Just Begun."

The reception was especially meaningful since it was at my
parents' home. People sat around on the porches outside and min-
gled around the food inside. The only problem was the champagne.
Somehow, everyone seemed to end up with their own bottle. The ca-
terers kept bringing out cases of champagne from their car, and people just kept drinking. Our friends didn't seem to miss the beer and
liquor and enjoyed this abundance of champagne.

My brother, who was normally not a drinker, was celebrating
the marriage of his little sister. My mother was embarrassed for him,
saying, "He's like three sheets to the wind." Dan's father, Jack, also
had a few too many glasses and kept everyone entertained doing his
unintentional Jack Benny imitation. After the wedding and reception,
he insisted on going to Mass at the one and only Catholic Church in
a nearby town. My brother-in-law took him and dropped him off. No
one remembers how he got back to the house.

The wedding was at two o'clock, and Dan and I left around six.
We drove to Atlanta, spending our first night there before going on to
Miami, where we caught a flight to Jamaica for our honeymoon. Big
Mama was unable to attend our wedding due to her declining health,

but her house was on our way out of town. Dan made the suggestion we stop to see her and tell her good-bye. *What a thoughtful gesture.* We stopped and spent a few minutes with her. She was surprised and happy to see us. I was glad we took the time and was sad that Big Daddy wasn't still there with her.

Due to our limited income, we made plans to stay in a small bungalow across the street from the Holiday Inn in Montego Bay. It was perfect since its décor gave an authentic feeling for the island. We took advantage of the proximity of the Holiday Inn and used their swimming and dining facilities. We rented a car and went into the hills and thoroughly loved every minute of our week in paradise.

Soon it was back to reality. Both of us had difficulty ending the celebration of our marriage. We had taken a week off from work for the honeymoon and continued to celebrate well into two weeks after we returned. Skip and Lee Ann had postponed their wedding plans but were still a couple, so when we arrived home, they were ready to party. We finally settled into our apartment as Mr. and Mrs. Dan La-Graff, anxious to live our happily ever after.

We continued to live in *the green ghetto*, which was located less than a block from Dan's fraternity house. He was still involved as an alumnus, and there always seemed to be guys coming and going from our apartment.

We decorated our living room by hanging small, wooden shingles along the bottom half of the room and painting the top a bright red. The bathroom had antique fixtures, a claw-foot tub, and a round porcelain sink. We added to the uniqueness of this room by wallpapering with comic strips from our Sunday paper. A large water bed took most of the space in our only bedroom, which opened onto a small side porch overlooking the side street from the second floor. We added pets to our home, a beautiful tabby cat named Morris, and a Chesapeake Bay retriever named Dylan. Life was good.

But some adjustments came with the responsibilities of having a home and being the wife. Without any discussion, we pretty much divided our chores along gender lines we had witnessed from our parents. I did the grocery shopping, the majority of the cooking, and most of the cleaning. Dan took care of paying the bills, cleaned up after dinner, and took care of anything that needed fixing. For the most part, we were comfortable in our roles.

I also had to get used to a side of Dan I wasn't familiar with, the all-business serious side. I was only familiar with the weekend, *life of the party* guy, so I often felt like I was living with two different people. He handled both roles well, always saying, "I work hard, and I play hard."

Teaching was an incredibly time-consuming career. I felt like I never had any time for myself. It was demanding and didn't fit well into our party lifestyle. I was teaching in Georgia, and we lived in Tennessee, a forty-five-minute drive. Never being a morning person, getting up at six o'clock was a problem for me.

One morning as I stumbled into the bathroom, I longed for a pleasant wake-up shower. Since we didn't have a shower, I had to stretch out in our big, claw-foot bathtub in warm, soothing water every morning. One particular morning proved to be too relaxing when I woke to the sound of a car honking. It was my friend, Kathy, who I carpooled with to our teaching jobs. After sending her on her way, I called my school, telling them I would be late. *If only I could just go back to bed. Being an adult is hard.*

My evenings and weekends seemed to be taken up more and more with school work. Grading papers and developing lesson plans had to be completed after my regular school hours. Coming home from a long and exhaustive school day and traveling 45 minutes, I could barely face the chore of cooking dinner at night. Getting used to the grind of a daily demanding job and dealing with the household responsibilities was another huge adjustment.

We had lived in the ghetto for two years when Dan woke on a Saturday morning and said, "Get up, we're going to look at a house."

"What for?" Although I knew it was in our future plans, we hadn't discussed buying a house. Dan had seen a *For Sale by Owner* sign at his job with a picture of a home in North Chattanooga and called about it. So we went to look at two houses. The second house proved to be the one we couldn't resist. The owner was friendly and warm. She met us at the door and immediately pointed out the glowing fire in the fireplace. This was our only specification for any potential house. It had to have a fireplace. It was easy to envision ourselves having romantic dinners and evenings in front of this fireplace.

The house was an older home, built in 1927, in an established neighborhood with lots of character and potential. There were three bedrooms, a kitchen, a living and dining room, one bathroom, and a playroom downstairs. The owner walked us through each room, describing why it was special and how much she enjoyed raising her children there. I was already thinking, *Two kids in this room and two kids in this one.* It was easy to picture our future family in this house. Dogwoods in full bloom surrounded it, and the woods behind the house were another reason to love this house and neighborhood.

There was only one problem. We hadn't saved any money toward a deposit. Both of us wanted this house, so Dan called his two aunts, still unmarried and living with Dan's parents, to ask if they might be willing to loan us the money. They each gave us 1,500 dollars for the three thousand dollar deposit. Now we were going to be homeowners over the span of one weekend.

We couldn't help but feel sad over leaving our first apartment. It felt as if we were leaving behind our youth and becoming more responsible adults. We were grateful Dan's aunts made this possible but still had some worry over this major move. Are we ready for this? Moving day soon arrived, and we left the ghetto behind.

We couldn't have been happier in our new home. I loved to decorate, and Dan was quite the handyman, so we were both able to do what we enjoyed. There were always things we wanted to update or change, and the house became a mutual hobby. We added a large screened porch and deck, with Dan doing most of the work. It looked out onto the woods behind our house and felt secluded, considering we lived only a few miles from downtown. It offered a perfect place to entertain. Although we were now homeowners, we still enjoyed entertaining our friends.

Dan's parents, Jack and Rita, were eager to see our new home, so they made a trip from Lockport to Chattanooga, a year after we bought the house. We planned a family dinner with both sets of parents. As I began to prepare the meal, Jack snuck into the kitchen several times for a quick shot of Peppermint Schnapps. He was hiding the bottle in a kitchen cabinet. He would never sit down with a drink. I imagined it was a form of denial, as if no one would notice. Oh my … This is not good. Should I say something to him? I was getting more and more anxious about how this dinner was going to go.

By the time my parents arrived, he was loaded. He walked around the dinner table with my green Playtex rubber gloves on his hands, making everyone laugh. He was entertaining us with his antics; however, Rita was not amused. She seemed embarrassed, shaking her head but not saying anything. My parents were laughing nervously. The alcohol took away his appetite, so he just picked around on his food. He was quite funny when he drank, never mean and insulting. We finished the meal, but everyone continued to be a little uncomfortable.

⤳

Rita had also had issues with alcohol earlier in her life. When she was raising five children and living with her two sisters, plus teaching school full time, she had used alcohol to deal with the pressures of life.

I was never able to become close to Rita. Even when I did see her, we rarely had any chances to talk when there weren't other people around. Sadly, she was a smoker, and it was killing her. She became seriously ill after Dan's sister's wedding in October of 1976.

We had plans to go to Lockport for Christmas and hoped she would still be alive. She had been hospitalized for several weeks. The emphysema was getting worse and worse. We were at the airport waiting for our plane when Dan was paged for a phone call. A co-worker gave him the news on the phone. His mother had passed away. I knew when I saw Dan walking back to the table, looking down at the floor, deep in thought, that it was bad news. Knowing we did not get to say good-bye was heartbreaking. We barely even noticed it was Christmas. We were involved in making funeral arrangements.

Dan's father was now left to live with his two sisters-in-law, Mary T and Flo.

Later that same year, Rita's death was followed by Flo's death. Flo seemed to be partial to Dan. He may have been closer to her than his mother. Her illness and death came quickly from kidney cancer. Dan went to the funeral in Lockport. Now Dan's Dad would be living alone with his sister-in-law, Mary T. I was worried about Jack. There had always been so much activity in their house, and now there would only be the two of them. *Is this going to cause him to drink more?*

Even after four years, I was still adjusting to my teaching career. I was finding it harder and harder commuting to Georgia. I decided to look for a job closer to home and managed to get a third-grade position at a private Catholic school in Chattanooga. There were thirteen children enrolled in my class. It was a more manageable teaching situation after three years of commuting and much larger class sizes.

I was now really enjoying teaching. Since I was taking my class to mass on Wednesdays, I became interested in learning more about the Catholic faith. Even though I had been to church with Dan many times, I had still held onto my Baptist faith though I didn't attend regularly.

I knew we would be having children soon and wasn't sure how we would handle the area of religion. Dan would never be anything but a Catholic. He was a cradle Catholic, and even on Saturday nights when he partied a little too much, he still went to Mass on Sunday mornings.

After considering it for a while, I began classes with a priest to better understand the Catholic church history and traditions. For eight weeks, Dan and I met weekly with a priest to discuss a chapter from a book I was asked to read. At the end of the book, I was confirmed as a Catholic. *Wow, that was easy! From Baptist to Catholic in eight easy lessons.* So on paper, I was no longer a Baptist but now a Catholic. I was still questioning parts of both religions. I felt like I was a Christian, trying to live by the most basic tenet of both faiths, *Do unto others, as you would have them do unto you.*

I became a Catholic because I didn't want Dan to go with our children to one church on Sunday and me go with them the next week to another. Despite my Baptist upbringing, I had decided God meets the needs of all people through different religions. But in the end, there is only one God. This made sense to me. I decided I could worship God in the Catholic Church and be with my husband and children. My belief was that no matter what church I attended on Sunday, I tried to live my religion everyday in the way I lived my life.

Dan continued to work in the insurance business, and we had settled into married life. We loved our home and spent most of our free time finishing projects. Many of our friends were now young married couples who were also new homeowners. Rather than going out to party, as we did when we were younger, we now loved entertaining at home.

We knew our home would only be complete with a dog to love. We had lost our first dog, Dylan, during one of our parties at the ghetto. He got lost in the crowd coming and going and disappeared into the night. He was a Chesapeake Bay retriever who needed lots of outdoor activity, which we didn't always provide. One day he must have been bored and ate off one side of our oriental rug. Sometime later, when a friend was visiting, he asked, "What kind of dog is Dylan?"

"An oriental rug eater!" Dan replied.

Now, living in our home surrounded by trees, we had plenty of room for dogs, so we decided to get two. I wanted a golden retriever, and Dan wanted another Chesapeake Bay retriever, so we decided to get one of each. Both were large breeds requiring lots of exercise and food. The golden we named Amber because of the color of her fur. With friends and family starting to frequently ask us, "When are you two going to start a family?" we named the Chesapeake, Familee. Now we were a family of four.

Soon, a home next door was for sale and we asked Skip and Lee Ann if they might be ready to become homeowners. Even though we had a mutual engagement party, they had postponed their wed-

ding for two more years as they had somewhat of a tumultuous relationship. They were now married and living in an apartment, so they
were interested in the house. It wasn't long before we were helping
them move in.

PART THREE

Being a mother is learning about strengths
You didn't know you had
And dealing with fears you didn't know existed.

--Linda Wooten

Chapter 7

July 1977

After living as neighbors at the green ghetto, we were excited Skip and Lee Ann bought the house next door. There was always someone around to talk to and on most weekends we were cooking out at either their house or ours. Lee Ann and I were good friends and were alike in being more reserved than either Skip or Dan. They often regressed to their college days in their approach to life with Lee Ann and I trying to rein them in. But we all got along and enjoyed working on our houses, going out to eat, and often weekend trips out of town.

After two years, we had finished many improvements to our home and decided it was time for a real family. I always knew I wanted children and thought I wanted lots of them. Dan was from a large family and was looking forward to this next phase of our life together. Our lovemaking was different when we were trying to conceive. It seemed alive with feeling and intensity. We were doing this to try to make a baby, another human being. *Amazing... this is going to be fun.*

Three months later, I was suspicious I was already pregnant. My period was three weeks late. I was visiting my parents in Ducktown and didn't want to wait any longer to find out, so I called Darlene, my childhood friend who was a nurse. She offered to give me a pregnancy test. I had already started being sensitive to tastes and smells so I was pretty sure the test would be positive. Even with these symptoms and wanting to have a baby, it was still a little unsettling to hear her say,

"Yep, you're pregnant."

Dan planned to join me at my parents for the weekend and I wanted to give him the news in a special way. Big Mama had a high chair she had used for all seven of her grandchildren. When she died, I asked my parents to store the high chair in their basement. I had plans for using it someday. Now was the time to bring it out. I wrote a note, "Congratulations, you are going to be a father!" and put it on the tray.

"Come downstairs, I want to show you this piece of furniture that was Big Mama's. Daddy saved it for me." It was hard trying not to give the news away with too much enthusiasm. When we walked in and he saw the chair, he looked confused.

"Well, what do you think?" I asked. A big smile spread across his face.

"You're pregnant?" he asked. "Do you know for sure?"

"Yes, just found out today. We're having a baby."

"A baby. Oh, man. This is great." He took me in his arms. My heart was full. We shared the news with my parents and went out to celebrate, getting pizza and ice cream. *I can justify this now. I'm eating for two.*

Soon I was dealing with morning sickness, which took the edge off my excitement for a while. I had a carsick feeling, not only in the morning but all day. It reminded me of being so excited about starting my period but then dealing with cramps. Now, I was pregnant and having to deal with morning sickness. Both experiences were lessons in living with the good along with the bad. After the fourth month, the nausea ended and I was energized by this new life growing inside.

I was in my old childhood bedroom when I first felt the baby moving. We were home for Christmas and had just gone to bed on Christmas Eve after opening gifts. I was lying on my back and trying to get to sleep after a busy day. Suddenly I was wide awake after I felt a stirring. A flutter of movement.

"Dan, it's the baby! I can feel it moving."

I carefully placed his hand over my abdomen, but it was too soon for him to feel anything. I had just been given the most amazing Christmas present ever! Throughout the next five months, the movements of the baby were a constant source of amazement.

My interest in decorating kept me busy painting the nursery, buying colorful curtains, cross-stitching wall sayings, and buying the perfect baby bed and rocking chair. The focal point of the room was a handmade baby quilt I made to hang over the bed.

I had seen a picture of it in a magazine which included a pattern you could order. I spent weeks finding just the right pastel colors of gingham. Each block was a different size and color of gingham with large flowers in solid shades hand sewn on top. The words "Our Baby Is Here" was quilted onto the middle section. It was perfect. I anxiously awaited April 30th, the due date.

I was soon full of baby. I had gained forty pounds. April 30th came and went and every day seemed a little longer than the one before. I was having trouble sleeping since I was going to the bathroom throughout the night. Two weeks past the due date, the doctor ordered a stress test to check on the baby. The test showed no signs of stress, so I was sent home. *This baby may not be under stress but I sure am.*

Now it was May, and I had daydreamed about celebrating my first Mother's Day with my new baby. But it came and went without me. I was still waiting, getting bigger, and feeling depressed. Even though I was scared about going through childbirth, I was ready to get it over with. Every day more and more people were calling to see if we had had the baby. It was hard to do anything or go anywhere when you knew your water could break and contractions start at any time. I hated this feeling. *Why is this baby not ready to come out?*

Finally, I got up to go to the bathroom early on a Sunday morning around 1 am and saw the blood that let me know I had lost the mucus plug. The contractions started soon afterward. They felt like mild menstrual cramps but were soon more painful than any cramps I had ever had. We called our doctor and were advised to stay home until the contractions were closer to five minutes apart. We got to the hospital around four am.

We had taken Lamaze classes and I felt as prepared as I could for this unknown experience. Dan was beside me, being my coach, as we took the breathing techniques seriously. At one low point, a nurse said to me, "Is this what they taught you in those Lamaze classes?" She seemed threatened and didn't approve of what we were doing. *Hey, lady...I'm doing the best I can here.* I wanted to strangle her. I needed all the support I could get, and I wasn't getting any from her.

I didn't get an epidural but did ask for a shot for pain relief. It didn't help much. It only gave me a vague feeling of being out of it. The contractions were excruciating but I was trying to focus on the result of the pain. I would have a baby.

After many hours of contractions, the doctor finally said it was time to push. *Whoaaaa.... something has taken over my body.* The strength it took to push the baby out into the world was incredible. It was a force of nature, a true animal instinct with guttural sounds coming from me that I didn't recognize. I could feel it all. I knew then why it's called labor. The hardest work I had ever done.

Our son arrived at 12:39 pm after twelve hours of labor, nine pounds, six ounces, twenty-one inches long. He had a head full of red hair. *Who is this little stranger??* The red hair took us completely by surprise. Dan's mother, Rita, and Big Mama both had red hair, but with neither of us being redheads, we hadn't thought of this possibility. This was the first of many surprises about this new little person.

Our paper had recently run an article about a new program that would soon be starting at our hospital called *rooming-in.* This allowed babies to spend most of their time in the mother's room rather than in the hospital nursery. It was innovative and quite liberal for our hospital to be implementing this new concept. And this happened to be the best advantage of being three weeks late. I was the first mother to try *rooming-in,* and we were featured in our local paper with pictures.

It was time to put a name on the birth certificate. We had chosen Tyler Madsen or Lauren Elizabeth, but at the last minute changed the boy name to Luke John. Skip had always said he wanted to use the name Luke for his son's name. So we sort of stole the name. Something about his red hair made him seem more like a Luke than a Tyler. John was Dan's father's official name although everyone called him Jack.

We didn't realize until later what a religious name we had chosen for our firstborn. The birth of Jesus is written in the book of Luke and the story of his resurrection in the book of John. A hard name to live up to. *What should we expect from this new person in our lives?*

Our baby was rooming-in with us, only rarely having to go to the nursery. Lying in bed with my baby, I had never felt so complete. But along with the happiness was a lot of anxiety. Being responsible for another person in every way was daunting. I had never done much babysitting and had limited experience with nieces and nephews.

This was going to be different. I was breastfeeding and this little person was completely dependent on me. My body was still exhausted from the birth but my mind was racing. I couldn't sleep well as I was always waiting for the little whimpers telling me I was needed again.

After I settled into my room, I made a phone call to my parents. My father answered the phone.

"Hello,"

"I just wanted you to know you have a new grandchild, another grandson."

"We do? That's great!"

"He was born just a few hours ago, nine pounds, six ounces."

"Oh… a big baby."

"And he has red hair!"

"Really? That's great."

Then after a long pause, my father asked "Who is this?"

"Who is this?? This is Karen, your daughter. Didn't you know it was me?"

"Well, no, I didn't think you'd be calling this soon after having a baby."

We had a good laugh. He then gave the phone to Mother so I could share more of the details.

Luke was their sixth grandchild but they were just as excited as if he was their first. Mother came to stay a few days to help with the adjustment. Although I had not spent much time around babies, I was surprisingly feeling confident, instinctively knowing what to do.

I left Luke with Mother one afternoon while I went to get thank you notes to send to the many friends and neighbors who sent food and gifts. As I tried to make a decision, wondering why I was feeling so uneasy, I was overcome with a powerful sense of panic. I was away from my baby for the first time. I stood there with my milk coming down, crying, and worrying about getting back to him safely.

At that moment, I knew my life had changed forever. There would always be another person more important than me.

As we settled into being parents, we struggled along and had everything we needed, maybe not everything we wanted. Our carefree days of going out on Saturday nights were over for a while. All of our friends were starting their families so our social lives revolved around our kids, none of us were carefree anymore. We found ourselves going to each other's homes while the kids slept or played together.

Luke was a good baby except for one short episode with colic. Our air conditioner wasn't working correctly for a few weeks during that first hot summer, so Luke and I sat stuck together by sweat in our living room in a rocking chair with a fan blowing hot air around us. He was crying pitifully and could not be consoled. I was crying too, for many reasons. *Why the hell do we have to wait so long for the new air conditioner? Why won't Luke go to sleep?*

I was so frustrated. Before having a child, this wouldn't have been such a big deal but now I had a baby to consider. Motherhood was hard. Although this was only about six weeks into being a mother, every day I was becoming more aware of my new responsibilities.

Luke was an adorable baby. His red hair had turned more of a strawberry blonde and he had inherited Dan's blue eyes. Whenever we went out in public, he was always noticed. I was the proud mother of this precious little guy. He had a great temperament and seemed content most of the time. He started sucking his thumb so any crying could be quickly taken care of without having to go look for a pacifier. He had a favorite blanket that he eventually called his "BT." My mother had made it and Luke loved holding onto its soft pink edging.

As time passed, we were thrilled by all the milestones he met – turning over, smiling, sitting, crawling, pulling up, and finally walking. We loved watching him as he proudly moved into being a toddler. Dan and I were handling being parents with ease. We didn't find many reasons to argue. Dan was always good to help with the household chores and didn't mind changing the baby or staying with him when there were errands to run. He also didn't seem to mind all the attention I gave to Luke, looking on lovingly when I was breastfeeding. We supported each other, knowing whatever we were sacrificing by being parents could never diminish our joy.

I faithfully wrote about Luke meeting all the developmental milestones in his baby book, not wanting to forget anything. As a gift to Luke, I kept a diary while I was pregnant, writing in it every week after he was born. I continued writing every month and eventually every year as he got older. Having lost Robert so young, I had some fear of dying young myself. I knew it *could* happen.

The thought of my children not knowing who I was or my thoughts and feelings about them prompted me to keep the diaries through the years. I wanted to savor this experience. I couldn't imagine motherhood being anything but rewarding and fulfilling. I was a naïve new mother.

Although adjusting to all the responsibilities of parenthood was difficult, Dan and I still continued to make going out together a priority. We always planned a special wedding anniversary trip. Since it was in October, we looked forward to pulling out our sweaters and enjoying the beautiful array of trees turning all shades of red, yellow, and orange in the fall. We went camping the first few years but eventually started staying in a hotel with creature comforts, such as a bed and a bathroom! We didn't have to spend a lot of money to enjoy ourselves, just getting away by ourselves and reconnecting was enough.

We were celebrating our fifth wedding anniversary and our first with a child. The stresses of new parenthood had taken its toll. We didn't spend enough time together. Dan was in the business world all day and I was in the *mothering* business. There were many days when I felt unproductive, slightly bored, and a little crazy.

We planned a weekend trip to the mountains of North Carolina to attend a football game. I was looking forward to our first trip as a family. I went to purchase an anniversary card for Dan but all the super romantic ones didn't quite seem to fit anymore. There was a feeling of distance between us. I chose a light-hearted card and hoped Dan would remember a card for me.

We joined several friends and Luke slept through most of the game. Dan was partying as if he was still in college. I was feeling the weight from the responsibility of taking care of our son. The game ended and we made our way to our motel. This anniversary was not measuring up to past years which always revolved around romance.

To make things worse, we just happened to be on the same floor where most of the college kids were staying after the game. They partied well into the night, running up and down the hall and slamming doors. This was Luke's first outing besides being at his grandparents' house so all the noise was disruptive to his sleep. At home, where he could sleep through anything, was not true in this motel room. I had never felt so old. Dan's snoring was incredibly annoying as I was left alone to try to console our crying baby.

We had survived our first year of parenthood. I still felt we had a good marriage but all of life's responsibilities had been hard for us both to accept. We had been married for six years. Our carefree days of having fun and partying whenever we wanted to were long past. We continued to try to have date night on Saturday nights. We would ask other couples to join us for dinner or go to a concert. We still enjoyed each other's company so it was always nice to be reminded of this. Away from home we could laugh and enjoy ourselves more easily.

I saw an announcement in our church bulletin about a weekend retreat called *Marriage Encounter*, referring to it as a weekend for couples who had good marriages but wanted to make them better. This sounded like an experience we could benefit from. I knew Dan and I needed to keep our marriage a priority. I wanted to feel closer to Dan on an emotional level. We asked my parents to stay with Luke and we headed off for our marriage enrichment weekend.

They asked us to take off our watches and not to turn on the TV in our hotel room so we could completely focus on each other. It was intense. Several older couples gave presentations on various issues of marriage – spirituality, sexuality, finances, communication, and family dynamics. It was intimate and moving to hear their personal stories. It let us know that all couples struggle to find a balance in their relationship.

We were required to do a lot of writing and use as many analogies as possible to express our feelings. I took to this quite easily but Dan struggled since exploring his feelings was not something he did easily. I wrote this to Dan, not knowing how prophetic it would become.

I felt a real eagerness toward life when we first married – looking forward to the future – wondering like a child looking at Christmas presents as to what will be inside. I still feel that same way. Life is sort of like a Christmas tree – bright and shiny and fills you with wonderment. All the packages are the different experiences in life, each wrapped in different colors and kinds of paper and bows. Slowly, you open up the packages and find something new. We have only opened a few of our packages. I like what we've gotten so far. Life has been good to us. But I'm sure along the way we will be disappointed at what we get. We'll be hurt – maybe at each other or maybe life in general. We may want to exchange that gift. But we can't – that's just part of life. We may feel cheated and feel that we wish we had a gift that someone else got. But we must look at all the other packages under the tree and know that we have many more gifts coming our way.

Love as always,
Karen

We left the weekend feeling enthused about our relationship with a new awareness of our feelings and our marriage. We needed to work on our communication but our love was as strong as ever. Several couples from the weekend were asked if they would like to become more involved in the program. We were chosen and considered it an honor. But they mentioned another program called *Evenings for the Engaged* that also needed young married couples to implement the program. We decided this is where we would direct our time and energy.

It felt good to have a renewed sense of commitment to each other and our marriage. We started the program in our home for six weeks, one night a week. Dan and I wrote and presented each of the topics: Finance, Communication, Sexuality, and Spirituality. The program was designed so the couples would see a working marriage in the setting of your home as you did the presentations. We were proud of our work, finding it rewarding. It gave us mutual involvement in a valuable program. The program eventually evolved into *Weekends for the Engaged*. Many of the couples did not live in the same town, and a six-week commitment was keeping them away. So the format was changed to meet their needs.

Dan and I continued our commitment to the program, moving from coordinating all aspects of the weekend to eventually just being one of the presenting couples. The primary theme throughout the weekend was "Love is a Decision." Felt banners with these words were given to each couple to display in their home.

The program's emphasis was based on the fact most people believe love is a feeling and feelings come and go. If you truly love someone, this feeling is replaced with the *decision to love* in difficult and stressful times common in all marriages.

We were given a plaque when we retired from the program inscribed with the words, "To Dan and Karen LaGraff for Fifteen Years of Continuous Work for *Weekends for the Engaged*." We were involved in this program all through the years of raising our children, the ups and downs of jobs, financial problems, and you name it. Although we were committed to the ideals of the program, we struggled with always implementing those in our own marriage. I didn't know then how much the words "love is a decision" would come into play later in our lives.

Although there were frustrations and hardships associated with parenting, we never considered having only one child. We discussed possibly four, but I had my doubts, knowing the work required with one child and couldn't imagine that times four. But within two years, we decided we were ready for another baby. Luke was two and we loved being a family. He had started talking and we were amused by the way he put words together, keeping a running list of his funny phrases. Our social life revolved around couples with kids. We rarely went out without Luke and included him in every part of our lives.

The summer after he turned two, I was pregnant again. We were thrilled and shared the news as soon as the test was positive. The kids would be three years apart, just like we planned. Luke was keeping me plenty busy since he was out of his mother's day out program for the summer. I was hoping our next child would be as easy as Luke.

We made plans for a small family reunion in North Carolina when I was two and a half months pregnant. We packed our car with food, toddler equipment, swimming necessities, and headed off to the mountains for a much-needed vacation. In only a few days, I started spotting after several trips to the bathroom. I just thought it was because of too much activity. I didn't panic since I was assuming it would stop after I slowed down.

But when we got home, the bleeding continued and got worse as the week progressed. The doctor ordered bed rest, hoping the bleeding would stop and the pregnancy continue, but it didn't happen that way.

During the middle of the night, the cramping increased and was now like early labor. Only this time there wasn't going to be a happy ending. We were advised by my doctor to go to the hospital. We called Skip and Lee Ann, who had moved from next door to the end of our street, and asked them to stay with Luke. We headed off to face the inevitable.

The miscarriage occurred and we were sent home. Just like that, it was over. In a matter of a few hours, this life had come to an end. The sudden drop in hormones left me feeling the loss, a different sadness, unlike any other I had experienced.

I tried to stay busy and having a two-year-old was helpful. I was thankful Luke was too young to know what had happened. When we called family and friends to tell them, I regretted sharing the news so early in my pregnancy. The doctor said to wait at least two months before trying again. I continued to have a feeling of loss but since I had a healthy baby already, and knowing we could try again, kept me from sinking into a depression. I continued to feel an emptiness but seemed to be able to move forward without too much trouble.

We were both feeling a sense of loss but it helped that we were still completely involved in parenting Luke. He was such a fun-loving little boy, almost always in a good mood. And he was an easy child to discipline. I couldn't picture what it would be like to have a difficult child. There was some feeling of pride, thinking that because we were making good parenting decisions this was why parenting was easy.

But the reality was, Luke was unusually compliant. If he was doing anything we objected to, we could suggest another activity and he was just as happy doing that. He was not a strong-willed child in any way. With his temperament, we could take him anywhere and he could easily entertain himself.

We had made a decision not to spank our children. We never thought it made sense to hit your child as punishment. Luke made this decision easy. When he turned two, we waited for the terrible twos but they never happened. He was what we considered the perfect little boy. *Could we be this lucky again?*

During this time, I wasn't working outside the home but started working on my Master's degree in Education. Although I was enjoying staying home with Luke, I needed to feel I was accomplishing more than just making it through another day. I knew I would eventually go back to work, and having a master's would help me get my foot back in the door as a teacher.

I started taking one evening class each semester. This was the first time I ever totally applied myself in school. I put off taking an educational statistics class until my last semester because of my dismal performance in previous math classes. There were formulas and long involved problems that made me anxious just thinking about them. Getting my masters required that I get at least a B in statistics which I wasn't sure I could do. It was my last semester and I had never been so nervous over a final test. I said a prayer before going in, even though I knew God had more important things to do than help me pass this course.

When I returned the following week, the instructor had our tests in hand.

"I decided to base the grades on a curve. The test was tough and the person with the highest grade should be proud." Then he walked over to me and said, "Congratulations." *Oh my God, is it me?* I was stunned. I looked down at my test and the 89 had been crossed out with a large 100 replacing it. *Oh my… how did I ever do this?*

If they had given superlatives in graduate school, I could have gotten *Most Improved Student.* I was incredibly proud of my 4.0 at the end of the six years it took me to finish. Dan was completely supportive of my decision to go back to school. He would come home early on the day I had class and take over all the responsibilities. I could go and be part of the adult world for a short while.

Dan was continuing to work in the insurance business, at the same place he started right out of college. He had a great work ethic and personality so he was successful, just as I knew he would be. But he had to work in a small cubicle, wear business clothes, make phone calls, and complete lots of paperwork. This was not exactly what Dan was best suited to, but he never complained. He knew he was supporting the family. He eventually branched out, specializing in retirement plans, working as a partner with other men in the business. Each pay increase allowed me to continue to stay home. For this, I was thankful, since I loved being home with Luke. I knew the time you have when your children are little is short and I didn't want to miss a thing.

Dan's father also enjoyed time with his grandson. He flew down for visits by himself and loved dressing up to take us to his favorite restaurant. By this time, Dan's other aunt, Mary, had died in a nursing home. This was the end of the line for Jack. He was now alone in the house where five children and four adults had lived.

But he surprised us all and had never done better, seeming content for the first time since I had met him. He stopped drinking and was finally at peace with himself. He had several health issues but seemed to like having time and space to himself. He was a wonderful Grandpa. He continued to have a great sense of humor even without the alcohol.

Dan and I planned a trip to Lockport to visit him and attend Dan's class reunion. I had a child now and this was a big deal for me to be away from him. It always made me nervous but not to the point of not being able to go and enjoy myself. Jack put flowers in a vase in the bedroom Dan and I were sharing and was going out of his way to treat us as special guests.

"What are you going to wear?" he asked me.

" I brought a dress but I don't know if it's dressy enough."

"Well, we'll just have to take you out tomorrow to see what we can find for you."

The two of us ventured out the next day to the local ladies' dress shops. I felt like I was his mistress and I think a few of the salesladies thought so, too. He would sit and comment when I came out in each outfit.

"No, don't think Dan would like that. Too dull."

"Oh, yes, this one is lovely."

Finally, a red and black sleek dress was chosen. "Oh, my, you look like a million dollars."

He then decided I needed jewelry, shoes, and a purse to go with it. What's a girl to do? I was loving this even if it was my father-in-law. The earrings made the outfit. They were black onyx with a row of diamonds (fake!) along the top and sides, larger than I normally would wear but fit the outfit and occasion perfectly. I wore the dress and earrings to Jack's funeral several years later. It was the hottest day of July but it gave me comfort. I loved my father-in-law.

Five months passed before we conceived again. I was enjoying being pregnant once again, even with the morning sickness. Possibly because I had lost a baby, all the annoying effects of being pregnant didn't seem to bother me. I was all about eating healthy, exercising, and wondering what it would be like to have two children.

As we prepared for the arrival of our next child, we answered the typical questions, "What do you want, a boy or a girl?" with "We don't care as long as it's a healthy baby." Pretty much what most couples say, with little thought to the possibility of anything seriously going wrong. After having the miscarriage, I felt this baby was meant to be. We had chosen the name Jordan Daniel, for a boy, and I continued to like Lauren Elizabeth, for a girl.

We tried to prepare Luke for the arrival of a sibling. He took most everything in stride so we anticipated he would adjust easily. We moved Luke into our front bedroom and I decorated it to suit a preschooler. The baby was due in August, the hottest month of the year, and I had gained as much as I had with Luke. The pregnancy had been uneventful, with no spotting or cramping. All my appointments revealed no problems. We had one scan and measurements were made showing the baby progressing normally.

Once again, I was past the due date but waiting patiently. I knew what I had in store for me. I was not looking forward to going through labor. I wanted to try again to go without an epidural but wasn't sure I could. Everyone said you forget the pain but I remembered it well. The labor began in the middle of the night as it had with Luke. We called Skip and Lee Ann to stay with Luke and then we headed off to the hospital.

The labor progressed quickly. In fact, so quickly I didn't get any pain medication, not even a shot. It was a completely natural childbirth. Anne, our nurse-midwife, coached me through all the stages. It wasn't like my first birth experience where we were left alone and checked on from time to time to see how much progress I was making.

I remember Anne's words as she worked to pull the baby out and suction his mouth. She was going to allow Dan to cut the umbilical cord and said "He has a complete knot in his cord. He must have done a flip at some point to do this." She didn't seem to be particularly alarmed since Jordan was crying heartily and had good color. It seemed she just looked at it as a strange occurrence.

"It's a boy." We were thrilled. I had made it through labor and we had our second child. While he was whisked away to be weighed and cleaned, we made our way to my room and waited anxiously for Jordan to return to us. It seemed to be taking longer than it should have. Soon a nurse entered the room, "We're going to be keeping Jordan for a while longer. He seems to be having trouble coordinating his swallowing and breathing." We weren't concerned since she made it sound rather common.

Throughout our hospital stay, Jordan continued to have episodes where he struggled to breathe normally. His arms would flail as if he was strangling. It would occur suddenly, not when he was breastfeeding, but seemingly for no reason. He was smaller than Luke had been, 7 pounds, 8 ounces, still considered a healthy weight. His Apgar scores were 8/9 so this gave us confidence there weren't any major problems.

But since he was having these issues, the nurses wouldn't allow us to keep him in our room. At one point, when the nurse brought Jordan to my room for nursing, she said to me, "Your baby scared us to death. He didn't turn blue, he turned indigo." Just what a new mother needed to hear.

We were greeted at home by my parents and the new big brother. Luke seemed a little shy and unsure of what to say or do. He had turned three in May and this was the end of August. We thought this was perfect timing since Luke was potty trained and getting ready for pre-school in September. I would have time to spend with Jordan since Luke would be in class from 9 till 12 three days a week. Things seemed to be falling into place.

I was excited about our new larger family. It was time for our first family outing. It was my thirty-first birthday so we decided to take a picnic to a nearby lake. We loaded all the necessary baby equipment and a few balls for Luke to play with. We headed off to celebrate both my birthday and the new addition to our family. There was a brisk fall breeze, enough for me to wear a jacket to shield myself from the wind coming off the water.

It was the beginning of the change of seasons, filling me with nostalgia. The leaves were swirling around us as we enjoyed our food on a blanket by the water's edge. Bundled up in his travel bed, Jordan, not yet a month old, was sleeping peacefully. Dan and Luke were kicking around a soccer ball, and I sat in gratitude for what my life had become – a sweet family of four. I was completely content. Everything about my life seemed, at least for that afternoon, *perfect.*

Chapter 8

September 1981

Perfect didn't last long. During the first few weeks, Jordan slept for unusually long periods. I was busy with laundry, cooking, and getting Luke off to preschool or keeping him entertained, so I was thankful for the time to tend to my responsibilities. It soon became a problem. When we went for his first checkup, Jordan hadn't gained any weight. He was sleeping through his feedings. I felt guilty for not being more aware of what was happening. The doctor recommended nursing every two hours, and if he wasn't crying to be fed then I was instructed to wake him.

Breastfeeding every two hours seemed to be taking up most of my day as we adjusted to this new schedule. I was thankful Luke was so easy and he was often saying funny things that kept me laughing. One day when I was nursing Jordan, Luke was asking lots of questions and I tried to describe to him how it all worked. Trying to explain to a three-year-old that mothers have milk inside their breasts to feed their babies even made me in awe of my body. He stared and looked puzzled. Then he asked, "Is there appie juice in there too?"

He was loving and gentle with Jordan and showed no signs of being jealous. He loved playing with his toys and being outside. Dan built a picket fence around our front yard so Luke could spend as much time as possible riding his push toys or kicking, bouncing, or throwing any type of ball. With all the attention I was giving to Jordan, it was a relief that Luke liked to be outside and could entertain himself. He got along well with other children so we often planned play dates.

Soon after Luke started preschool, I got a phone call from his teacher.

"I hope you don't mind me calling about some incidents I've observed with Luke. He has been picked on lately by the older kids and he won't stand up for himself. I don't want him to start hitting any of the children but I hate to see him so passive. I talked with him about defending himself."

I wasn't surprised to hear this. Luke was so easy going and I was sure kids were taking toys away and he was letting them. But how do you tell your child they need to be meaner? I was pulled in two different directions with two different children with different needs. Motherhood was becoming complicated.

Even with the increase in nursing, Jordan was still not gaining weight as he should. The next approach was to supplement nursing with formula. He had become frail and not filling out as a newborn normally does. He continued to have episodes struggling to breathe and swallow. When we asked the doctor about it, he said, "He'll most likely just outgrow it."

Jordan always had a runny nose and would often cough until he gagged. Because of this chronic congestion, the doctor suggested we test for cystic fibrosis. He felt there were enough symptoms. He failed to give me any information, telling me it was a simple skin test and was treated with a special diet. *Well, this doesn't sound too bad. I think I can handle this.*

After I returned home and read the information explaining the disease in detail, I was distraught. The doctor hadn't told me it was a terminal disease. I braced myself for the bad news. Then the test came back negative.

I was relieved but the symptoms persisted with no answers to all our questions. As Jordan got older, different doctors had different opinions. We were left to meet Jordan's special needs on our own. Not knowing was the worst part, and it would be years before we got a diagnosis.

I was always calling the pediatrician for advice or we were sitting in his office. Jordan had so many different problems and I just wanted someone to put all the symptoms together and say, "Well, now we know what's wrong. He has _____." But as we found out later, doctors don't always have answers. Through the years, many doctors gave us incorrect or misleading information.

Jordan was having other medical issues. He was plagued with chronic ear infections, taking repeated rounds of antibiotics. We were referred to ear specialists who suggested ear tubes to alleviate the pressure in his ears. This ended up being a surgery we had to repeat every several years. The infection would temporarily clear up, but within six months the doctor would recommend doing it again. When he got older, the doctor finally told us he needed a mastoidectomy.

This involved making an incision behind both of his ears and graphing new tissue into the ear canal. This was followed by a six-week regimen of intravenous antibiotics delivered into a port in his chest. This was a major ordeal, not only for Jordan but for me. By that time, Jordan was ten and this procedure was repeated every four hours. The port was into a major blood vessel and if pulled out would result in him bleeding to death. *How am I going to live with this kind of pressure?* We secured the port with a heavy bandage and wrapped his chest with a tight cloth followed with a type of vest he couldn't take off. It was a long, long six weeks.

After supplementing breastfeeding with formula, Jordan started gaining weight. But as soon as one worry subsided, another one took its place. He was having problems having bowel movements which were first attributed to not getting enough to eat. Soon we were having to give him suppositories for him to go regularly. Then we noticed he was rather floppy. He was hard to hold upright in your arms because of his low muscle tone. Doctors suggested that this was the reason for his inability to have bowel movements. We were becoming more and more concerned and more and more worried.

On the bright side, Jordan was mentally aware of what was going on around him. His gorgeous green eyes and feathery light brown hair made him appear perfectly normal. He smiled appropriately when engaged with another person, would follow objects with his eyes, and reached for favorite toys. He was content to lay on a blanket on the floor and watch Luke play around him. He was what you would describe as an unusually good baby. He rarely cried or was fussy. Initially, we looked at this as a positive but as time went on, it became evident he was too good to be true. This was not normal.

At his six month checkup, his pediatrician noted he still had *head lag* which meant that when the doctor took both of his hands to pull him up from a supine position, his head would lag behind. Not a good sign. He felt an evaluation by a physical therapist might be helpful.

We started physical therapy hoping they could work with him and in time, this would be another problem he would outgrow. But physical therapy didn't help much. This was the beginning of seemingly endless appointments by doctors and specialists across the United States as more and more problems began to present themselves.

Jordan was not progressing. He wasn't meeting the milestones for a typically developing child. He didn't turn over, crawl, or sit within a normal time frame. When he was nine months our pediatrician was concerned enough to suggest an appointment with a pediatric neurologist. This meant traveling to Emory University in Atlanta for the appointment, which was scheduled for three months ahead, giving me more than enough time to imagine all possible illnesses and diseases which might be causing his delays. All of our friends and family were anxiously awaiting whatever news we might bring home.

I dressed Jordan in his cutest outfit for our trip to Atlanta. He might have problems but there was nothing wrong with his physical appearance. His smile was warm and he had a tenderness about him that made me want to hold him close. Everyone always mentioned his expressive eyes. He was aware of everything going on around him. He seemed normal in almost every way.

Since we were seeing a pediatric neurologist at Emory University, we expected extensive tests but were soon baffled by the doctor's examination. He asked a few questions, looked at the report sent from our doctor in Chattanooga, and then pulled out a set of car keys from his pocket. He held them in front of Jordan and moved them from side to side. Jordan followed them with his eyes. He set Jordan on the floor and put a small rubber ball out of his reach. Jordan scooted over to the ball and reached for it.

The doctor nodded and proceeded to tell us, "Jordan is behind what he should be for a nine-month-old. He is developmentally delayed." *Well, duh, we already know that.*

"We'll just have to watch his development."

This is what we waited for three months to find out? Although I was thankful he didn't give us devastating news, I wanted reasons for Jordan's delays. We didn't get any.

All the worry was wearing me out. Every time I turned around, I felt I was hitting a brick wall. We weren't getting any answers and the problems just kept mounting. Dan was a source of emotional stability for me. He took it all in stride and made me feel we could get through this. *We can do this.* Although I was doing most of the doing. Since Dan was our only breadwinner, I was left with most of the child care. With Luke this was easy but now I was faced with a new set of circumstances.

I was overwhelmed at times. Sometimes I didn't know how I could cope, but I knew I had to. I was Jordan's mother. I loved him. But loving him didn't make things any easier. I rarely cried but frustration left me anxious and depressed. Dan and I never talked about the emotional side of how heartbreaking it was to see our child falling further and further behind. We did what had to be done next and tried to think positive.

Jordan was now almost one. He was still not crawling or sitting without support. And all the other medical problems continued to plague him. We were still searching for answers. Dan's brother, Mike, and his wife Susan were living in Cleveland, Ohio, and we planned a family vacation to visit. His brother had suggested we might get answers if we took Jordan to the Cleveland Clinic. So before we left Chattanooga we made a series of phone calls to find a renowned pediatric developmental specialist. Our appointment was scheduled and we waited with the hope of finally knowing what was causing all of the problems.

I'll never forget the doctor's words, "It doesn't appear to be anything mental." Although this might mean he could be physically handicapped, it cleared the worry of any mental handicap. I was feeling better already. The doctor was leaning toward a diagnosis of a muscle disease which required a muscle biopsy. Since it is a teaching hospital there were medical students and interns constantly coming and going out of our room. It became impersonal as I answered their questions. I felt like we were a case number. My stomach was in knots the entire time, knowing we might finally find out what was wrong with our son.

Jordan's roommate was a little boy with a genetic muscle disease and was full of life. His parents encouraged us, and after seeing him it was easy to think this might not be so bad after all. This little boy seemed limited only by not being able to walk. Life for him still held possibilities. All this was rolling around in my head when the doctor suddenly changed the course of his diagnosis.

After taking measurements of the circumference of Jordan's head, he discovered it was not what it should be for his age. This led him to believe it wasn't a muscle disease after all, but an issue with brain development. This was not told to us in so many words. We were told, "You should get your son in an infant stimulation program as soon as possible." They had no answers to any of his other problems. They didn't offer any other suggestions. We were stunned. We were at one of the most prestigious hospitals in the country and this was the best they could do.

We returned home to celebrate Jordan's first birthday at the end of August before he began the infant stimulation program in September. We celebrated with a small party in our front yard and invited many of our friends with young babies or toddlers. I put him in his high chair as friends and family gathered around to sing "Happy Birthday." The high chair was the one I used to deliver the news to Dan that we were expecting Luke. That seemed like a long time ago. So much had happened since then.

Jordan looked completely normal as he ate his chocolate birthday cake wearing a colorful birthday hat and a bib designed to look like a tuxedo. I remembered how joyous Luke's first birthday party felt. I wasn't feeling any of that today. I was feeling anxious, not just on this day but every day. I was good at keeping it all to myself.

It was hard seeing my friend's children at the party who were younger than Jordan but much more advanced in their development.

I knew I should be grateful since I already had one healthy son but I wanted two.

During the party, my friend's daughter came up to me and said, "Jordan can't do much, but he sure can smile." I didn't know whether to be insulted or inspired by her comment. My friend immediately started apologizing for her daughter. It was a comment only a child would make.

After the party was over, I thought about what she said and decided it was just what I needed to hear. It took many years but eventually, I came to realize Jordan didn't judge himself with other kids and I shouldn't either. If we could just keep him smiling, this would be my goal.

We followed up on the advice to enroll Jordan in an infant stimulation program for children with disabilities. I was full of apprehension as Dan and I went for a tour of the school. We met the director and looked on as the teachers engaged the students in various activities. The teachers and the environment were positive and encouraging. *Does Jordan belong here? Maybe he'll just have to attend until he catches up.* I was thinking positive but was also trying to be realistic. We enrolled him in a halfday Monday, Wednesday, Friday program.

Luke was now attending a half-day preschool every morning. It was a combined effort in the morning to get both boys up, dressed, and fed. Dan took Luke to his program and I took Jordan to his. I picked Jordan up at noon and would quickly swing by to get Luke. This gave me a little time to myself but it seemed to be filled with chores and frequent doctor visits for Jordan.

But during all this stress and uncertainty, we were enjoying Luke since he was beginning to show a true personality. He loved to dress in Spiderman or Superman outfits. I bought a variety of hats for his playroom. He would come out in the strangest combination of clothes and top it off with one of the hats. He wore a pair of brown rain boots, about five sizes too big, which seemed to be a favorite prop for his imagination. He could easily entertain himself, which made it easier for me since much of my time was attending to Jordan's needs.

Luke was easy in every way but one, he was incredibly picky about his food. As a toddler, I tried to expose him to a variety of foods but he seemed sensitive to smells and textures. As he became older, this became more frustrating since he would refuse to eat what I cooked. He would eat meat and bread but few fruits and vegetables. I worried about it but there was nothing I could do to change his eating habits. It was my first lesson in learning I wasn't always the one in control. He had a mind of his own. If this was his only problem, I would just have to put it in perspective with Jordan's problems. *No big deal.*

As time went by, our lives revolved more and more around our sons. Luke became social and loved having his preschool friends over to play. Skip and Lee Ann now had a daughter, Leslie, who eventually became one of Luke's good friends. Another daughter, Lindsey, followed several years later. They were frequently at our house or Luke was at theirs. With Luke having friends and being involved in sports, it kept us grounded and in a more normal world. We were thankful he was developing as he should.

At this point in our marriage, I hadn't worked in almost eight years so money was tight. We watched our spending closely, especially with the medical expenses related to Jordan. His early intervention program was expensive, as was Luke's preschool. Dan was working under a lot of financial pressure which added to all the other stress we were dealing with.

Soon Dan and Skip brainstormed some ideas and thought they had come up with a way for all of us to become more financially secure. We frequently rode by a run-down restaurant located along the banks of the Tennessee River. It had a sweeping view of downtown and the bridges that provided access from one side of the city to the other. When we drove by this place Dan always said, "Somebody needs to get a hold of that place and do something with it." Not long after that, we were the ones doing something with it.

Skip had always wanted to own and run a restaurant and Lee Ann was ready to go back to work after having children. The only problem was none of us had any restaurant experience other than working as servers or cooks. But this didn't stand in the way of all of us borrowing money, leasing the property, and putting our lofty ideas in place.

The summer was spent remodeling. Dan, the handyman, could do most any job. He was planning to continue his career in the insurance business and would serve as the maintenance man for the restaurant. Skip and Lee Ann would run the actual business, and I would come out on the weekends to help. We had a business plan.

Opening night was September 1, 1984. Cooks were in place and waitresses hired and trained. We were slammed the first night. Our disorganization and inexperience were obvious to everyone. I overheard a diner say, "I came here for dinner but I've waited so long, it's going to be breakfast!" Our friends with any experience waiting tables were asked to help. It was chaos.

Over time we became more organized and functioned more efficiently. We hired an excellent cook so the food was good. Skip and Lee Ann trained more staff and soon it became a popular dining destination. Eventually, a large deck was built overlooking the river with the three bridges connecting parts of the city and the mountains in the background. Sitting on the deck, watching the sunset, became a favorite place for many locals and tourists.

We were in our mid-thirties and in positions of responsibility I never imagined we would be in. I thought often about what we used to do on Friday and Saturday nights when we were in our twenties. I worked as a hostess on weekends and often did food inventory one day a week. In our early days as restaurant owners, we didn't have a PA system. When people came for dinner, I wrote down what they were wearing, and would have to find them in the crowd when their table was ready – lady in royal blue top, white pants – man in green polo shirt, khaki pants. Not very impressive.

This was the early eighties and The Sandbar became a recommended restaurant and eventually, we added a nightclub. We were getting in over our heads. Bands were booked for both Friday and

Saturday nights. The place was crowded with young twenty-year-olds. Hootie and the Blowfish, the Dave Matthews Band were two of the early bookings. They hadn't reached their fame at this point. Several old-timers also came, Pete Segar and Arlo Guthrie. Skip was in his element since he was more of a music connoisseur than any of the rest of us.

Dan loved his new responsibilities as a maintenance man. He worked in the business world during the day, wearing a dress shirt, tie, and frequently a suit. So he enjoyed putting on his work jeans, tee-shirt, and boots and doing real physical work. He liked to stay busy and never complained about all the work necessary to keep this old, wooden building look and function as a respectable restaurant. There was always something needing to be repaired, replaced, or cleaned.

This meant that on Saturday morning, and often Sunday afternoons, he was away doing what needed to be done at the restaurant, and I was left to handle the responsibilities of the kids. Even though being a partner in the Sandbar wasn't an investment that had much return for us, it was a fun learning experience. We also had something else to concentrate on, something to distract us from Jordan and all his problems.

Luke was now seven years old and very undemanding, but Jordan who had turned four continued to overwhelm us. He finally started walking at three and a half years old. I carried him around on my hip for what seemed like forever so we were elated he had finally achieved this milestone. Although he continued to have low muscle tone, we were assured he wouldn't be physically handicapped.

But other problems continued and by age four he still hadn't started talking. He had babbled as a baby so we assumed this would lead to words. We were holding onto the hope that his speech would just be delayed. I knew that some children never walked and were confined to a wheelchair, but I honestly never knew or had seen anyone who couldn't talk.

The first years of Jordan's life were heartbreaking and an endless search for answers. He still suffered from chronic ear infections requiring round after round of antibiotics. The problems with his bowel movements continued with me having to give suppositories regularly. This problem took an entire afternoon with him crying and cramping and still not being able to go. The ongoing congestion continued and he was tested again for cystic fibrosis. He started having hives causing different parts of his body to turn blotchy red, swell, and itch. In addition to all of this, he started holding the back of his head, grinding his teeth, and rolling his eyes, as if he had a terrible headache.

This prompted a visit to a local pediatric neurologist. He ordered an EEG and a CT scan which revealed no abnormalities. After several visits, with still no answers, the doctor picked up on my frustration, remarking over the phone, "Mrs. LaGraff, you worry too much. You need to go on vacation." *Ok, I would love to do just that. Do you think you could come and stay with my kids?* I wanted to scream. All the specialists were only looking at what they were trained in, and no one was looking at the big picture. We were in a maze and every way we turned there was another obstacle.

Somewhere in my exhausted and anxious mental state, there was still a longing to have another child. I wanted the joy again that we had experienced with Luke, watching him move through each developmental stage so effortlessly. But of course, there were no guarantees. Afraid we might have another child with problems, we decided to have genetic testing to make sure we weren't dealing with an inherited condition. The results showed Jordan's problems weren't genetic, and our chances of having another child with problems were the same as the general population. So now we did have one answer.

I just wasn't sure I could handle another child with the responsibilities of having an active normal seven-year-old and a four-year-old with severe limitations. But our fears were not enough to keep us from pursuing another chance at having a child.

Soon I was pregnant. There would be a five-year difference between Jordan and the new baby, eight years between Luke and the new baby. *I can do this.* Once again I suffered through morning sickness that plagued me in every pregnancy. I was surprised I didn't worry more, but being incredibly busy didn't allow me much time to think about the *what ifs*. We were cautiously hopeful and excited about having another child.

However, friends and family were taken aback by our news. I knew they felt we had our hands full and thought we must be crazy to have another child but we were excited. We decided to announce the news to my parents at the Thanksgiving dinner table.

Before the meal, as we held hands to say what we were thankful for, Luke announced, "I'm thankful I'm going to have a new brother or sister." He was seven and in second grade, old enough to know what this meant. He was excited about the news, already saying he wanted another brother. Probably a brother without all the problems Jordan had and someone he could play with.

My parents didn't know what to say. After the shock of the moment, my father finally said "Well, that's great." I knew they didn't think it was great at all.

My parents had thoroughly enjoyed Luke but backed off being very involved with Jordan. They were getting older and struggled to deal with Jordan's medical and behavior issues. They were cautious about saying too much. My father told me after we once left both kids with them overnight, "Your mother just can't do this anymore." My heart sank. I suddenly felt even more alone in this journey with a handicapped child.

My parents were still active but I knew I couldn't depend on their help with three children. My father had retired from all his businesses when he was sixty-five. I often wondered what he would do with himself when he no longer worked. His work had defined his life. He turned toward his flying hobby. He ordered an experimental airplane kit, a Long EZ, and hired another man to help him build it.

It was a beautiful plane with an exceptionally long wingspan, a two-seater, with the engine and propeller in the rear of the plane. It got people's attention which my father enjoyed. He entered it in many competitions, winning awards for best experimental aircraft and usually for being the oldest pilot. He continued flying until he was eighty-six and could no longer pass the annual pilots physical required to keep his license.

After spending four years building this experimental airplane, he flew to Alaska by himself. He had dreamed of this his whole life and was gone for six weeks, calling my mother at night to let her know he was safely on the ground again. Mother was a worrier so she looked forward to these nightly updates. He named his plane *Sweet Stuff II*. Mother was *Sweet Stuff I*.

Just the word *experimental* airplane sounded scary to me. I'm glad Mother didn't know, only a month after getting home, he would be having triple bypass heart surgery. He had experienced symptoms on his trip but didn't share this information with her.

Fortunately, for my mother, my father also had another hobby. After his retirement, they bought a motor home and traveled extensively across the United States to almost all fifty states. My father's interest in flying had often excluded my mother since his flying was frequently business-related. They did take occasional leisure trips in the plane but the motor home gave them mutual travel adventures. I was happy to see them enjoying life, finally away from their work responsibilities. It was strange seeing my father in a pair of shorts sitting in a lounge chair. *Does he even know how to relax?*

So my parents still had their own lives to live. They loved their grandchildren but at their age, I didn't expect them to take on caring for Jordan. It was almost more than I could handle. I didn't have any family support to rely on as far as physically being there to help. I relied on my sister, Diane, for moral support but she was eight hundred miles away in Florida.

At Jordan's school, I started meeting other mothers with children with various types of disabilities. We referred to each other as *handicapped friends*. When Dan and I first visited the early intervention school, we were exposed to children with a variety of disabilities. Our eyes were opened to a world we knew existed but had no previous exposure.

The other mothers were tremendous emotional support. Sherry's son, Chad, was involved in a car accident when he was fifteen months old causing severe brain damage. Sharon's son, Robbie, suffered trauma at birth causing cerebral palsy. Nora's daughter, Sarah, had a genetic condition called Rhett's Syndrome. Bev's son, Ben, had complications from a premature birth causing cerebral palsy and autism. Crista's son, Zach, had profound mental disabilities due to unknown reasons. Even though our children's problems were different, the heartbreak we shared was the same. We began to have lunches together, go on out of town shopping trips, and celebrate birthdays.

From other friends who didn't understand, I was hearing the typical platitudes, "God only gives special children to special people." "Everything happens for a reason" or "God never gives you more than you can handle." Platitudes again! I didn't have the nerve to say what I felt; *I don't feel chosen. I don't feel special. I don't feel God did anything to make Jordan's life so limited.*

I struggled to accept the circumstances I was facing. I did know, after having dealt with adversity of a different kind, you don't understand any situation until you have lived it. I cringed when people often gave advice or said to me "I know what you mean." "I understand." *No, you don't know what I mean. No, you don't understand.* At least this was teaching me that if I had a friend facing a difficult situation I hadn't experienced, it was important to just listen and learn from them.

With me being pregnant, my days as a hostess at the Sandbar ended. I was now staying home more with Luke and Jordan. It was getting harder to get a babysitter who was comfortable with Jordan. Dan and I still tried to go out as frequently as we could. I needed a break from the constant mothering, the constant worry, the constant fear. It was all exhausting.

Dan often went out on his own to be a part of the excitement involved in running a restaurant. He didn't adjust as well as I did to staying home at night with kids, particularly on Saturday nights. He was much more social so this gave him the outlet he needed to be involved with friends. He also needed to meet his responsibilities as part-owner of the Sandbar. They depended on him to keep the place running.

Occasionally, after a long night working at the restaurant, Skip and Dan would finish the evening off with too many drinks. Dan still had problems knowing his limits when drinking and often drove home after having too much. This started to be a source of conflict. I didn't like that he was driving when he shouldn't. He was putting himself and our family in jeopardy. Nothing I said changed his behavior, so I was left feeling resentful and frustrated. It was an area we couldn't seem to talk about.

Luke had now finished his first year of school and proved to be a good student. His kindergarten teacher had given him a glowing end of the year report the previous year, He "played well with others," "showed interest in books," "loved exploring outside." This felt like assurance he would continue to be well adjusted.

The only area during first grade causing any problem was religion. *Religion?* He came home after the first six week grading period with an F. I was shocked but also thought it was a little funny. When I told my father, he couldn't stop laughing. He saw this as a sign that Luke had more Baptist in him from the Campbell side of the family than the Catholic LaGraffs.

Luke had failed to memorize several assignments about Catholic dogma, prayers, and rosaries. It was far too advanced for a six-year-old to memorize, much less learn and understand. I wasn't impressed with Luke's first experience learning about the Catholic faith.

Even at this young age, Luke was showing more and more interest in sports. He started playing soccer and was involved with baseball in the summers. We were just beginning the seemingly endless job of taking kids to practice, picking them up, and attending all the games. It felt like a full-time job. *How are we going to manage a new baby in this hectic lifestyle?*

PART FOUR

You never know how strong you are
Until being strong
Is the only choice you have.

- Bob Marley

Chapter 9

July 1986

The baby was due July 12th, and it was the 19th. Late again. It was one of the hottest summers ever. I stood in front of our air conditioner for twenty minutes, trying to stay cool. I had lost my appetite and had a peach milkshake for dinner. I rationalized that at least the baby got calcium and some fruit. Dan and both boys were asleep for the night. I was restless and couldn't sleep.

Several hours later, my labor started with mild cramping. This gave me time to make plans for Luke, who had a softball game later that evening, and finding a sitter for Jordan. It was going to be a scorching hot summer day, expected to be 100 degrees. I was surprisingly calm as I packed my bag, started laundry, and read the paper. I was trying to distract myself from the day ahead of me. I took pictures of Luke and Jordan asleep in their beds, knowing all of our lives were about to change.

After we arrived at the hospital, the day dragged on and on since the contractions were coming and going. We read magazines and watched TV to pass the time. Dan set up our video camera across the room. I wasn't sure I was all in for filming the birth but knew, in the end, I wouldn't care.

Anne, our nurse mid-wife, was with us all day in the birthing room. Later in the afternoon, she suggested I walk around to increase the frequency and intensity of my contractions. I just wanted to lie there and not move, with as little distraction as possible. The pain was enough at this point that I wasn't making any conversation. *Just let me do what I have to do.*

But Dan encouraged me and counted as I got up and walked, counting whenever I frequently stopped to hold onto the wall and breathe through the contractions ... *he, he, he, he, he* .... This helped move the labor along. When I returned to our birthing room, I noticed the sun setting behind the mountains outside the window. It felt symbolic of this important day since I knew this would be my last baby. Even as I was in the throes of intense labor, I was feeling sentimental.

Anne was providing much-needed labor coaching. She had delivered Jordan, so she knew we had fears. She was positive and encouraging. I put all thoughts out of my mind about another baby with problems. *I can't go there.* We had tied all our hopes on what the geneticist told us, "Your chances of having a normal child should be the same as any other couple."

Although I always wanted a Lauren Elizabeth, I was not disappointed when Anne announced, "It's a boy." Our only concern was if he was healthy. But I also knew we couldn't know this for sure. Only time would give us those answers. But I wasn't going to let this stop me from enjoying this moment to the fullest.

I did notice he had webbed toes on one foot. *Is this a genetic marker for a disease?* Then I remembered my mother had the same toes. He must have inherited this from her. He certainly was crying appropriately. He looked healthy at 9 pounds, 21 inches long, with tufts of light brown hair, ten fingers and ten toes, a slightly round face, and dark eyes. Love at first sight.

It was Saturday night, the busiest night of the week at the Sandbar, but Lee Ann offered to bring Luke to the hospital to meet his new brother. By the time he arrived, Michael Alexander was cleaned, checked out from head to toe, and bundled up comfortably in a warm blanket.

Luke had his concerns when he asked, "Why are his feet black?"

We laughed and assured him it was only the ink from getting his footprints.

"Can I hold him?"

Dan gave instructions about supporting the baby's head. He put Alex in Luke's lap. It was a poignant moment watching Luke smile and tenderly touch his new little brother.

Although I was thrilled to have the birth behind me, I knew the hardest parts were yet to come. I only had two days before I would be faced with how I was going to handle three children.

When we left the hospital, we were the picture of the all-American family – Alex in my arms, Luke pushing the wheelchair, Dan walking along beside carrying suitcase and flowers, and Jordan following along behind all of us. We were on our way home to find out how this was all going to work.

We got off to a rough start since Alex had full-blown colic for close to three weeks. We were both losing sleep. But I was thankful he was born in the summer, and I didn't have to get the other kids off to school. His crying started around 10 o'clock, like clockwork. I planned my evening around it, putting all the necessities in place on the table beside my rocking chair – pacifier, blanket, a glass of water, diapers, diaper wipes, remote control.

Ten would turn into eleven and then twelve, sometimes one a.m. I watched *The Tonight Show with Johnny Carson, Late Night with Dave Letterman*, and whatever I could find afterward. I would carefully work to get him to sleep, and as soon as I thought it was safe to move him, the crying would start again. I knew his colic wouldn't last forever, but how long?

At the end of the day, I was exhausted and then would have to face giving baths, and then the crying would follow. I longed to just snuggle on the couch with a book or maybe have a glass of wine and conversation with my husband. But I was always faced with *BATH-TIME*. It became the most dreaded part of my day.

Luke loved his bath and would languish in the tub, lost in the world of make-believe with his toys. It would take repeated threats to get him out. Jordan needed help undressing, bathing, washing his hair, drying, and getting on his pajamas. I would try to bathe Alex in the mornings, but it didn't always work out that way. Between the three sons, I gave baths for seventeen years.

But even with all the stress, we were thoroughly enjoying our new baby. He put so much joy back into our lives. He was full of smiles, with blonde hair and green eyes, and miraculously doing everything he should, when he should. It was amazing watching him accomplish all the milestones Jordan struggled to master. We appreciated all the developmental stages as they unfolded.

Dan and I continued to have a strong commitment to our family. We supported each other, and there was little arguing. Maybe not enough arguing since I became more willing to let things go rather than dealing with any kind of confrontation. I just wanted to keep the peace at almost any cost. Even though I took on many of the domestic responsibilities, he was always willing to help out when I asked.

He was carrying all the financial responsibility, which was beginning to be quite a burden. Any hope of making money in the restaurant business was soon replaced with the realization it wasn't going to happen. The Sandbar became a money pit. We were bringing in new partners every winter to make it through until summer rolled around again.

Luke was getting more involved with sports, and Dan was an eager Dad who enjoyed watching his son's athletic abilities. Luke was involved in both baseball and soccer, so there were always practices and games. He was a social kid and loved having his friends over. But he was starting to be more concerned over their reactions to his brother Jordan.

Jordan had been in his infant stimulation program for five years. He had made some progress, but overall it was looking bleak. His diagnosis was changed from developmentally delayed to mentally handicapped. I knew there were different levels of severity and was hoping he might be at the high end of the scale.

His teachers worked with him on completing small motor tasks, such as putting pegs in a pegboard. Jordan was unmotivated. He would make noises, and completing the task required hand-over-hand instruction. I was in favor of giving him a treat, maybe a Cheerio or M&M, to motivate him, but this was looked down on. I became involved in working with him at home, always looking for signs of progress. There was little.

Jordan became obsessed with paper, chewing on all our magazines and the books Alex and Luke left lying around. He would flip the pages, bite on the corners until the paper was soft, and chew it before eventually spitting it out. There were little spitballs all around the house. He was ruining many of my favorite children's books, just as I was beginning to share them with Alex.

We were thankful Jordan could feed himself. However, he couldn't do it without supervision. He ate amazingly fast, so there was always a fear of him choking. When he was older, we couldn't leave him unattended because he would pull food out of the refrigerator and eat with his hands, getting crackers, chips, and cookies, out of the cabinets and eating one after another. Usually, this might make a child heavy, but another of Jordan's quirky habits was that once he started walking, he never sat down. He was on his feet all day long, often rocking back and forth, using calories as he paced around the house.

I wrote in Jordan's diary just after he turned one, *You move around the room doing an army crawl but don't get up on all fours yet. The things that seem to get you moving the most are the telephone cord, the living room curtains, the shower curtain, the fan, and any plants on the floor.* Although I didn't know it at the time, all these were a good indication of what we were going to be facing next ... autism.

Jordan wasn't interested in toys the way children typically were at his age. He would reach for them, possibly shake them, and put them in his mouth. He was intrigued by movement and responded physically to any kind of music. At twenty-four months I wrote, *I just wish all your problems would go away, and you could get on with the process of growing. You've had a rough time, but you're so happy most of the time. You always have a wave and a smile.*

As Jordan's strange behaviors began to increase, we became more alarmed and worried. If we gave him a cup of milk, he would down the whole drink and repeatedly bang the cup on the table. If we took the cup away, he would find another object to bang. We learned later this was called a self-stimulating behavior.

During this time, the movie *Rain Man* was bringing a lot of attention to autism. It was just getting noticed, and kids were beginning to be better understood and getting the services they deserved. As we read and became more aware of the symptoms, we knew it was time for an evaluation.

Luke was now ten, Jordan, seven, and Alex, nearly two. The closest center doing evaluations was in Wilmington, North Carolina.

With it located along the coast, we decided to make this a family vacation, stay in a motel, and make the best of our situation. It was our first vacation as a family outside of the trips we had made to stay with family members.

We tried to squeeze in as much fun as possible, taking the boys to the beach, going out for seafood, and playing in the pool. Alex turned two while we were there, and we celebrated his birthday at Chucky Cheese. But we had to leave early because Jordan wasn't handling the loud music and animated characters well.

We took Jordan in for his evaluation and watched behind the two-way mirror. It was evident we were not going to get good news. It was no surprise when we heard the results.

"Jordan is profoundly mentally handicapped with mild to moderate autism. If he doesn't acquire expressive language by the time he is ten, he most likely will not develop any speech." Although we were in the psychologist's office for more than two hours, my mind was only able to focus on the word "autism." He had just made it official.

It wasn't that I was shocked or surprised, just overwhelmingly sad, a new and different kind of sadness. He might never talk. The analogy I wrote about life being like a Christmas tree and life experiences being the gifts was playing out in our lives. We had been given the gift that we might want to exchange but couldn't.

I continued to hold out hope that Jordan might develop expressive language. He did have ways to let us know what he wanted and didn't want. If we were driving and weren't going where he wanted to go, he would start to scream. His screaming certainly got your attention.

It took time for us to see the full-blown effects of autism. Jordan went in and out of stages of bizarre behavior. He had trouble falling asleep and wouldn't stay in bed, and if he did stay in bed, he made loud noises, turning the light on and off, on and off throughout the night. We tried taping down the light switch, but he would rip it off and start again. He took the sheets off the bed and flipped pages in his books endlessly.

As much as I felt sorry for him, I also felt sorry for us. We didn't know what to do most of the time. Dan would eventually go to Jordan's bedroom and lay down with him, trying to hold him still long enough for him to relax and go to sleep. Sometimes it worked and sometimes it didn't.

Jordan went through a stage of pulling his hair on the top of his head. He did this with such strength, at the end of one summer, there was a bald spot about three inches wide on top of his head shaped like the state of Georgia. His anxiety caused him to twist his arms around each other and bite on the side of his hand, creating a callus. He was easily overstimulated and didn't know what to do with his feelings.

Another quirky behavior caused him to dislike the kitchen cabinets open. Anytime he came through the kitchen, and a cabinet was open, he closed it. Luke and Alex would open all the cabinets and time Jordan to see how fast he could close them all. It was good to see them interacting with him. They would try to engage him in other activities, but he had little interest.

One of the hardest parts of Jordan's mental limitations was that he didn't participate in regular childhood activities. He didn't play with toys. Children navigate the world through play, so the world to Jordan was a bit confusing. He couldn't imitate, so you could try and try to engage him with no response. During a particularly hopeful time, we hired a tutor who came to the house to work with Jordan. They worked on putting pegs in peg-boards, putting objects in and out of boxes, working simple puzzles, and following simple commands. Progress was slow.

Another thing that broke my heart was there weren't play-times arranged with other children. He had no friends. He was always with us – no sports activities, no birthday parties, and no sleepovers. There were a few babysitters who would sit, giving us an occasional break from our parental responsibilities. Typically, our only night out was Friday to the Pizza Hut, but we had to be home by 8:30 when the sitter was scheduled to leave.

I always tried to include Jordan in our holiday traditions. I made him an Easter basket with candy, and he was more interested in the Easter grass, putting it in his mouth or eating the candy without bothering to take off the wrapper. He wasn't interested in hunting eggs.

He always had a Christmas stocking but only filled with food. He loved his food. He was never excited on Christmas morning like his brothers. He cared nothing about the presents. After Luke and Alex finished opening their gifts, they would urge Jordan to open his, but he was always distracted by the wrapping paper. They thought it was funny to watch him rip it off and put it directly in his mouth.

He did, however, love Santa. There was something about a big, jolly man in a red suit with a white beard that fascinated him, enough that he occasionally tried to pull the beard off. Even though it was stressful to take Jordan to see Santa, I always took him, even when it wasn't *age appropriate*. I loved seeing him smiling and happy.

For Christmas one year, Dan got all three boys a small trophy for their accomplishments. Luke received one for *Most Improved Forward in Soccer*, Alex's was for *Most Points Scored in a Soccer Game*, and Jordan's was engraved with *Jordan LaGraff, #1 Cup Banger*. The only way to get through all this was to have a sense of humor.

It was especially hard taking Jordan to doctor appointments, which we spent much of our time doing. He was at one kind of doctor or another all the time. On the day of any appointment, I was full of anxiety. I would try to prepare myself for what I knew was coming.

In the doctor's office, Jordan would never sit down, so I followed him around the waiting room. The people waiting would try not to stare as Jordan made noises, chewed on his arm, chewed the magazines, and was in constant motion. The parents would not stare openly, but sneak looks over the top of their magazines. I saw the looks of sympathy they gave me. Glad it was me and not them.

The children, however, did not know what to think about Jordan. They stared. Jordan was different. He was loud. He did not understand personal space and would often get in someone's face or possibly even grab their drink off the table and take a gulp. I always thought this behavior should have gotten us in to see the doctor quicker, but it never seemed to make a difference. The wait time was excruciating.

I was always searching for books offering suggestions on ways to cope, for inspiration, or simply to help me feel I wasn't alone. I felt apprehension about having hope since I didn't want to be disappointed when there was little to be hopeful about. I wanted to be realistic about the severity of Jordan's problems. I didn't dwell on expectations for his future. I wasn't praying for a cure because I knew there wasn't going to be one. Once again, I was asking God to help me through this parental challenge, although truthfully, I was often overwhelmed.

Luke and Alex kept me from sinking too deep into looking for answers and being preoccupied with Jordan's problems. Both of them were loving and kind to Jordan. They often helped get him dressed and get him in and out of his car seat. There were never any signs of jealousy. They both accepted Jordan just as he was.

We settled into a hectic lifestyle dealing with our three sons. Luke was in elementary school and involved in sports activities after school and on the weekends. He had lots of friends and was always going to a sleep-over or birthday party. Jordan was in his infant stimulation program three mornings a week and still going regularly to doctor appointments and therapies. Alex was attending a Mother's Day Out program two days a week.

Dan and I continued to work as a team. He was patient with the boys and could take over when necessary. I was no longer working outside the home, so he carried full financial responsibility. We did the best we could, trying to give each child what they needed but often overlooking our own needs. There was no time to be selfish.

As time went on, we found ourselves living paycheck to paycheck. I felt it was time for me to find work outside the home, both for money and for the chance to interact with other adults. I was going slightly crazy attending to children day in and day out. I got a job working as a tutor two nights a week at Sylvan Learning Center, so Dan had to be home to watch the kids. This gave me a break from the nightly baths and some spending money.

Eventually, another job opportunity opened up, and the University of Tennessee at Chattanooga hired me as a student-teacher supervisor. This was a more involved job requiring several visits to schools and doing observations. I felt like a professional again. It was a perfect part-time job. It was flexible since I could schedule the appointments myself.

But I knew I needed to think about looking for a full time teaching position if we were ever going to get in a more stable financial situation. I paid the bills each month, and we were scraping by paying minimums. There were costs for private school for Luke, infant stimulation program for Jordan, plus his increasing amounts of doctor bills, and Alex's pre-school program. Money was tight.

We were pulled in many different directions, having two typically developing kids and Jordan in the middle, demanding much of our time and energy. When Luke began junior high school, Dan finally permitted him to start playing football, which he had wanted to play since he was a little boy. Even at this age, when anyone asked him what he wanted to be when he grew up, he always replied, "A Dallas Cowboy." Luke was athletic but not built like a football player and didn't have the aggressiveness necessary to be successful in football. Both boys leaned toward soccer and excelled as they grew older.

Saturdays often found me taking Alex to a friend's birthday party, going to Luke's soccer game, doing laundry, buying groceries, and cleaning the house. Due to Jordan's limitations, we qualified for help through a state agency providing care after school and on Saturday. The caregiver would come to the house from 3:30 until 8:30, entertaining him and bathing him. On Saturday, the hours were from 10 until 2. It was a tremendous help that made our lives more manageable.

We became close to several of his caregivers, but it seemed there were always strangers in our home. It did give me more freedom if I had to grocery shop, run errands, get my hair cut, or meet a friend. But whatever I did had to be squeezed into that time frame. There was always a never-ending *To-Do list*.

We all looked forward to the summers when we were on a more relaxed schedule. We joined a community pool, which gave the boys a great source of entertainment. The boys would meet their friends there, coming home tired and sunburned. Jordan's school program continued through the summers so this freed me to concentrate my attention on Luke and Alex. Summers involved endless sleepovers, movies, play dates, trips to the mall, and sporting events. But this still felt more relaxing than the pressure during the school year.

Luke and Alex spent several summers through the years going to a YMCA camp, a rustic facility on a beautiful lake that combined outdoor activities with crafts. Soccer camp was always on their summer schedule, joining many of their teammates to improve their playing skills.

They always spent a week with my parents in Ducktown, which gave them opportunities to bond with their grandparents. My father often took them flying, hoping to instill an interest in becoming a pilot in at least one of his eight grandchildren. I wished Daddy had pushed me a little harder to learn the basics of flying. My fear was too strong, and learning to fly a plane was something I never considered myself capable of accomplishing.

Luke's social life began to become more important to him. He always wanted friends to spend the night. One friend would be leaving, and he would want to call another to come over. With more people coming and going, our house was feeling smaller and smaller. If we were going to stay in this house, we needed more room. When Luke was in the sixth grade, we renovated the downstairs, added a bedroom, a bathroom, utility room, and extended the playroom.

The playroom was perfect for a bunch of rowdy boys. It was far enough away from our bedroom that we couldn't hear the noise and it gave them plenty of space to entertain themselves, which was usually with video games and rented movies. But they also made home movies of themselves creating *Saturday Night Live* skits.

Just after we finished the renovations, it was time for Luke's twelfth birthday. He wanted a sleepover with four boys, asking for Oreos, popcorn, and Cokes for snacks. They settled in for the night with video games and movies. I checked on them before going to bed.

The next morning, I went downstairs, and Luke was sound asleep. All his friends were still awake playing video games. Their faces gave away their guilt. I looked around at my newly painted, newly wall-papered, newly carpeted room. Ground up Oreos covered the new blue carpet, mixed with popcorn. There were smashed Coke cans, candy, and gum wrappers everywhere. The room was a mess.

Even though there was a new bathroom downstairs, they chose to pee in the unfinished part of our basement. *Why?* I was livid. A friend told me later that this was what I should have expected from a bunch of boys. *Boys will be boys* excused a lot of bad behavior. And I had three. At least Jordan wouldn't be having any sleepovers.

"What happened down here? We just remodeled this place. This carpet is brand new," I shouted. We had spent most of the money we inherited from Dan's father's estate to make the much-needed renovations. Now we felt we could stay in this house we loved and were proud to have done much of the work ourselves. I should have known better than to let these boys take over the room. A bunch of twelve-year-old boys could have cared less. I jerked Luke out of bed.

"Why did you do this? You know how hard we worked down here. Get up. You're going to vacuum these rooms right now. And pick up all these wrappers and cans and put them in the trash. I can't believe this mess."

He was still half asleep but didn't argue with me. They were all unusually quiet. I called their parents and told them to come pick them up. The party was over. Luke was grounded for the first time. At the time, this all seemed like a huge deal since it was my first experience feeling betrayed by my child. Years later, it seemed unbelievably innocent.

While Luke was at an age wanting more independence, Alex was at an age where it was still okay to spend time with your parents. He was a fun-loving kid, and we bonded closer to him. After everything we had experienced with Jordan, he put much life back in our family.

Since there was an eight-year difference between Luke and Alex, there wasn't much sibling rivalry. Because of this, we avoided having kids fighting continually with each other. Both boys developed a special relationship with Jordan, developing sensitivity to others, and being exposed to the world of the disabled.

We attempted to involve Jordan in Special Olympics, but he had little interest. Someone would have to run with him, pushing him to participate, or he would stop and not want to finish. Any sport involving a ball would have to be hand-over-hand. It was hard to accept he was too profoundly handicapped to take part in one of the only outlets for people with disabilities. This was another closed door for Jordan.

When Jordan got older, one event he did enjoy was a prom given for the developmentally disabled by a local Christian high school. The high school students decorated, prepared food, and planned the music. But the best part was watching their genuine interaction with the disabled participants. They weren't hesitant in any way, getting them food and encouraging them to get out on the dance floor. The young, beautiful, teenage girls were all in prom dresses, and Jordan wore a tuxedo, just like all the other teenage boys. He looked incredibly handsome.

He had always shown interest in music and pretty girls, so he was enjoying this much more than any sports activity. He danced with the crowd of other teenagers and smiled the entire evening. He seemed to be having the time of his life. But it was hard not to wish more for him. *If only he could talk.* I was trying not to impose my selfish longings on him. *He's having fun, isn't that enough?* For several years, Luke and Alex and Dan and I would accompany him to this much-anticipated event. One year the three boys rode together to the event in a limousine.

Soon it was time for Luke to go to middle school. I had not been particularly impressed with Luke's Catholic education, so I wanted a change for him. There was a new public magnet school, the Chattanooga School for the Arts and Sciences, getting lots of publicity as being the best school in the city. It was a Paideia school with new innovative teaching methods. I felt this could be a great opportunity, but Luke didn't see it that way. He didn't want to move away from his friends. He tried to manipulate us by saying, "You only want me to go there because it doesn't cost any money." I tried to explain the new experiences he was going to have.

"You can learn to play an instrument. They have a band director. And you will have a choice which foreign language to take. Plus, there's a drama program. You might want to be in a play."

"But none of my friends will be there."

He never showed much enthusiasm. Thinking this was in Luke's best interest, at least educationally, we decided to move him. So his sixth-grade year was spent in a public school.

But after spending a year there, it was not a good fit. Most of the kids began there in kindergarten and already had their cliques. Luke continued to hang with his old friends from St. Jude, the Catholic elementary school. When we started talking to him about the next school year, he was asking to go to Baylor, an exclusive private school, not affiliated with any church. We allowed him to be tested and interviewed, wondering how we would afford it if he were accepted.

He received an acceptance letter. We made another decision on Luke's behalf, thinking he would thrive in Baylor with such a strong reputation both academically and athletically. Luke went on to attend seventh, eighth, and ninth grade at this school. We were lucky and got financial help, which made it somewhat affordable since our finances were always a concern.

Luke got involved in soccer, but little else. The school offered a variety of opportunities, and I pushed him to get more involved. His school reports began to come in, saying, "Luke is not working up to his potential." He was passing but not doing enough to justify all the money we were paying for this private education.

We had to make a decision. *Are we doing the right thing?* With more expenses required for Alex, and Jordan's continuing needs, we faced the fact that we couldn't keep Luke in this private school. For his sophomore year, we moved him again to the private Catholic high school, where all his friends from his elementary school were going.

Now it was time for me to make some changes. I needed to go back to work full time. We needed it for financial reasons, and I needed the interaction with other adults and to feel productive again. I wasn't sure how I was going to manage, but if other women did this, so could I.

After completing all the paperwork and going on interviews, I was offered a full-time position teaching first grade in 1992. Luke was fourteen, Jordan eleven, and Alex six. Having not worked full time in fifteen years, I was excited but apprehensive. First grade was not my grade of choice, but I was trying to feel grateful to be employed again.

The school was old. It was built in the 1940s, and the classrooms had high ceilings with lots of windows and in need of being updated aesthetically. I couldn't spend my days in a dull and dreary room, and the kids deserved a more stimulating environment. So my interior decorating instincts kicked in, and I spent weeks making my classroom bright and cheery.

I covered all the bulletin boards with colorful patterned material and attractive trim. I spent my own money at a school supply store buying interesting posters and motivational quotes, forgetting the kids couldn't read yet. I paid a friend to paint scenes from several favorite children's books on the large pull-down window shades. The room needed painting, which I attempted to do by myself, This was a massive undertaking, and the first indication I was in over my head. I should have been reading up on behavior management techniques.

I thought I was ready for this new challenge. But on my second day of class, the principal walked into my classroom, which immediately made me nervous.

"You have a phone call in the office, Mrs. LaGraff. I'll watch your class while you take the call."

This only increased my anxiety. *What could have happened?* As I walked to the office, a million thoughts were going through my mind. *Is this about Dan, Luke, Jordan, or Alex? Or maybe my parents?* Something significant had happened, or the principal wouldn't have interrupted my class.

"Mrs. LaGraff, this is Paige at Orange Grove. There's been a medical issue with Jordan today. He had a seizure, and they've taken him in an ambulance to the hospital," she said. I couldn't talk. My mind was reeling.

"Are you okay?" she finally asked. "He was aware when they left with him, but you may want to meet them at the hospital."

"Okay, thank you," was all I could say.

"Do you have someone to drive you there?" she asked.

"I'll have to call Dan." I tried to call, but he was not in his office. I decided I needed to get there as soon as possible. *You have to pull yourself together. Just focus on getting to the hospital.*

I drove myself to the hospital and arrived before the ambulance. *How did you ever think you could do this? Go back to work when Jordan always needs medical attention.* I felt overwhelmed and discouraged. I was second guessing my decision to go back to work.

After an evaluation, it was determined he had a grand mal seizure, and appropriate medication was prescribed. We were told seizures often occur when developmentally disabled boys reach puberty. We left with an appointment to see a pediatric neurologist. This was another step back for us with Jordan. When questioned about Jordan's problems through the years, I had always said, "but at least he doesn't have seizures." Now there was another issue that complicated his medical status.

I had signed a teaching contract, so there was no turning back now. I was going to have to make this work. We needed the income since Luke would be going to college in a few years. I would get through the year one way or another. I had to.

Since having children, our lives had gone by in a blur. When you only have one child who is disabled, all your attention and worry naturally centers on that child. I had two other children, so I couldn't dwell just on Jordan's problems. I felt thankful for my other two boys despite being pulled in different directions with their age differences and interests. They helped keep me in the world of the normal activities of children and provided a source of pride and fun.

Although I was excited to be back in the workforce and interacting with other teachers, I was unprepared for the stress involved in working in a city school. This was more stressful than the stress I was feeling at home. Having been away from teaching for many years and previously working in rural or private schools, I hadn't encountered the kind of behavior I was experiencing at this school.

Every morning I left with a knot in my stomach and came home completely drained. The students were demanding in every way. I envisioned them as a herd of wild horses, and all day I was holding the reins, trying to rein them in. I would get them settled down, and in no time they would be off to the races again.

First graders need you to be both a mother and a teacher, and I was only prepared to be a teacher. My own three children weren't getting the attention they needed, so giving twenty-three other children what they needed was a career challenge I wasn't sure I could meet. My responsibilities at school and my responsibilities at home kept me in constant motion. It was a long year.

Joy, another first grade teacher, helped me survive my first year teaching full time again. She encouraged me to find the humor in the many not so humorous challenges. At the end of each day, I went to her room to unwind and get suggestions to try to make my class more manageable. I had been out of the classroom for a long time. I was feeling inadequate in many ways.

When a second-grade position opened the next year, I let my principal know I was ready for a change. She gave her approval for me to change grade levels, and I wasn't going to have to change rooms. I could keep my newly decorated classroom. I spent much of the summer planning and making activities for the second graders. I familiarized myself with the curriculum, and spent hours preparing bulletin boards, feeling excited about a new school year.

When the year began, I felt much better about my abilities as a second-grade teacher. The students seemed to be better behaved. After the tenth day of school, the enrollment numbers for every school go to the central office, and they let the schools know if the number warrants the number of teachers they hired. So several teachers were required to leave who were hired after me. I was relieved temporarily but soon found out that because of these changes, I would be placed back in first grade.

"But this isn't fair," I wanted to tell my principal. How many times had I heard that from my own kids? I was an adult but felt like stomping my feet and maybe throwing something. *I'm not a good first-grade teacher. I want to teach second grade. Please, please, please don't make me change.*

I had convinced myself teaching second grade would be much better. I would enjoy the curriculum more, and the students would be better acclimated to school. I was more than depressed about the situation, but there wasn't anything I could do. I felt a little like a child might feel being retained, not being quite ready for the next grade. I was going back to first grade.

There was tremendous pressure, both at home and at school. I was always thankful when I made it through another day, but once I stopped, the stress caught up with me. As soon as I lay down at night, my heart would start to jump around. I started having heart palpitations. I made an appointment to see a cardiologist. After testing, the doctor said my heart looked fine but suggested I start drinking decaf coffee and try to avoid stressful situations. *Well, I guess this means I can quit my job and not go home anymore.*

The heart palpitations continued along with the stress. My students were challenging on so many levels, and I brought their problems home. Every year when summer finally arrived, I felt a huge burden lifted. I had done all I could do. Teaching was harder than I remembered.

Dan and I continued to try to steal time away from all our responsibilities when we could. We planned a trip for the two of us to spend three nights in Hilton Head, South Carolina. I was excited about getting away from home and school. All the arrangements were made, and all three kids were going to be taken care of by Jordan's after school sitter. I allowed Luke to ask a friend to spend the night. I was doing plenty of worrying about going out of town, getting my usual trip anxiety. But after I was out the door, I managed quite well on not dwelling on negative thoughts.

Dinners out, drinks by the pool, and some much-needed intimacy were just what we needed. We called home several times to make sure all our arrangements were going smoothly. When we got home on Sunday afternoon, Luke was casually sitting in his usual chair in front of the TV, zoned out. I stopped to say hello and ask a few questions, which he answered with little emotion.

After unpacking our bags, I headed downstairs to the laundry room, which required me to pass through the playroom. I noticed the door open to the garage and walked over to close it. To my surprise, there was no door. It was off its hinges and lying in the garage. I noticed a hole in the sheetrock. *What the hell?*

I walked back upstairs.

"Would you like to tell me what happened downstairs?

"Oh, Brad just fell against the door," he said matter-of-factly.

"And what about the hole in the wall?" I asked, trying to control my anger.

"Well, that happened when Brad got mad at me, and we started wrestling." He was trying to make it sound so reasonable.

"And where was the sitter when all this was going on?"

"Asleep," he answered.

So I called Brad's mother, and she told me that while they were wrestling, her son's glasses were broken. So we called it even as far as expenses were concerned. My much-needed sense of calm from the much-needed vacation went out the window, or the door, I guess you could say. Luke was grounded for the second time.

We eventually settled into a routine with Dan and I both working full time. Luke was a junior at the private Catholic high school; Jordan was at Orange Grove, a private school for the disabled, and Alex was still at CSAS, the free public magnet school Luke attended in sixth grade. Now it felt as if our family was being pulled in five different directions, Dan's job, my job, and the kids in three different schools. It was a flurry of homework, projects, meetings, sporting events, doctor's appointments, sports practice, cooking dinner, going to bed, and doing it all over the next day.

My job was still challenging. I longed for more support from the parents. Many of my students were from low-income single-family homes. They loved and cared about their children's education, but out of necessity, their priorities were often more about a roof over their heads and food on the table. I worried about many of my students. I also worried about my ability to handle all the responsibilities of teaching and parenting. I didn't feel like I was doing a great job at either. I decided to transfer to another school to try to improve my work environment. I couldn't transfer to another family. I knew something had to improve.

Luke continued to be hesitant to get involved in extra-curriculum activities. He became increasingly quiet, but I just attributed it to being a turbulent, moody teenager. He had always been laid back, but it now seemed more like a problem. He didn't seem to have any fire under him to motivate him to accomplish what was expected at school and home. I hoped this was just another phase. He found a few lawn mowing jobs in our neighborhood, but I had to remind him of his responsibilities constantly. It felt as though I was always nagging him about something.

As Jordan's problems presented themselves through the years, we became more concerned about his future and ours. It was clear he was going to be non-verbal. He had never said one word. I couldn't even imagine how frustrating this was for him. He would always need caregivers for the rest of his life. I wanted to have a plan in place in case something should happen to Dan and me. We wanted him to have a life outside of just us.

We decided to put his name on a waiting list to be placed eventually in an Orange Grove residence in town. The school he attended provided housing in sixty-four group homes across our city designed for four clients. All the homes provided twenty-four-hour care, and some included nursing care. We thought we might consider this when Jordan turned eighteen, the age when a typical child leaves the nest. We received a call when Jordan was fourteen, with a potential placement available. We were told if we didn't take it, his name would be placed at the end of a years' long waiting list.

There was a lot to consider, but we decided to accept the placement that would soon be available. We knew, as responsible parents, this is what we needed to do. We would never expect Luke or Alex to take on the care of Jordan at any point in his life. Knowing this still didn't make it easy.

After going over to look at his house, as it was being built, I cried all the way home. It was only ten minutes from our home, but moving him there seemed so final as if we were giving up on him. I had hoped for a more positive future for him, but time ran out thinking he might improve. We were now faced with the stark reality that he would never improve. There was nothing to hope for anymore.

As the time neared for Jordan to move, I became increasingly anxious. I had trouble sleeping at night and couldn't concentrate during the day. Every time I looked at him, it brought tears to my eyes. I knew it was the right decision, but this was going to change our family dynamics. Alex was nine, and Luke seventeen.

I talked to Jordan about what was going to happen, but I never knew what, if any, he understood. He rarely showed emotions on his face or in his demeanor. We sat down with Luke and Alex and discussed the situation.

I started the conversation … "You both know that Jordan is going to be moving into the group home. He will continue to go to Orange Grove. There will be a couple there to take care of him and his three roommates. There will always be a nurse in case any of them get sick. He'll be able to go places around town and still come home some week-ends. Do you have any questions you want to ask?"

Both boys were quiet. I continued to explain, "We love Jordan just like we love both of you. But he won't be able to grow up and live on his own. With him being in a group home, he will always have his family there and his family here."

Dan added, "It's going to be different around here. We'll miss him, but we can visit him and he can visit us. We feel like this is a good arrangement for all of us." We were all quiet, lost in our own thoughts, wondering what our family life would be like now.

We met the young family who were going to be Jordan's house parents. They would receive free housing and be responsible for four young men, all with varying degrees of mental and physical disabilities. All of them attended a day program, but it was a large undertaking for a young couple. They were expecting their first child. We knew how much work was involved in caring for one disabled child, and they were going to be responsible for four. But they would have plenty of support staff, and the boys would be at school during the day. Once again, I was asking God for some sense of peace over the decision we had made.

PART FIVE

Trust me, you will lose everything
- Alcohol

Chapter 10

August 1995

The day arrived to pack Jordan's clothes, music videos, family pictures, and move to the group home. On a practical level, I knew it was the right thing, but emotionally I was struggling. Since the day we brought him home from the hospital fourteen years earlier, he had spent only a few nights away from us – no sleepovers, no summer camps, no visits with his grandparents.

I didn't know what to expect. I was afraid of turning over my role as his mother to someone else. *Is he going to cry when we leave? Will he miss us? They don't even know Jordan. How are they going to know how to handle all his quirky behaviors, his sleepless nights, his restlessness?*

Several weeks before move-in day, I decorated his room, hoping to make it feel a little like home. A new plaid bedspread with matching curtains, family pictures on the wall, and a large poster of Britney Spears made it colorful and personal. Jordan spent his childhood watching Barney videos but recently liked listening to Britney Spears. Finally, he had an age-appropriate interest. The house was new, with four bedrooms, a living room, a den, sunroom, two bathrooms, and a large kitchen. The house parents were warm and loving. We couldn't have asked for more.

I gave him a hug and kiss and tried not to become overwhelmed with sadness. He showed no emotion at all. Arriving back home, it felt strangely quiet. But the silence was loud, making me think of Jordan constantly. I knew this was a new chapter in all of our lives.

Dan and I tried to focus on the positive aspects that we had discussed with Luke and Alex. Knowing there were trained personnel twenty-four hours a day and a nurse on staff to handle any medical needs was reassuring. Jordan loved going anywhere in the car, so we knew he would enjoy going to appropriate places with his roommates. If anything happened to us, Jordan would have a life already established on his own.

Most importantly, he would be assured a day program after he turned twenty-two because he lived in a group home rather than at home. Many parents, with disabled children still living at home, were left with no programing available after their child reached an age when services weren't mandated by law.

We felt lucky in this regard, but there were still feelings of guilt and sadness. The years had been long and difficult due to Jordan's various medical issues and, eventually, the frustrating behaviors from autism. I learned a lot about myself and about life. Jordan opened a whole new world to us, much of it positive rather than negative. Our family was stretched, molded, and changed.

As time went on, I began to feel some relief from all the responsibilities. I called Jordan's house often but could only talk with the caregivers. *If only he could talk, I might feel better.* We brought Jordan home for visits every other weekend, which helped the transition for him and us. It helped that he never showed any signs of anxiousness when it was time for him to return. He often came home on Saturday and Dan would take him to school on Monday.

Jordan adjusted well to his new environment. This gave me the assurance I needed to adjust to his absence at home. It took time to get used to this new peace and quiet. It gave us freedom as a family that we hadn't experienced since Jordan was born.

Dan's brother, Mike, and his wife, Susan, were living in London and extended an invitation to our family for a Thanksgiving visit. *Perfect timing.* We spent ten days touring and exploring this fabulous European city. Dan and I hadn't been out of the United States, other than Jamaica, so this was educational and exciting.

Luke was a junior in high school and had his own opinion about the trip.

"Is this all we're going to do? Look at a bunch of old things."

He sounded just like a bored teenager, maybe a little ungrateful for this travel opportunity. He had gotten tired of touring all the historic buildings and cathedrals. He brought his rollerblades, and we allowed him to join some kids skating one evening.

Alex was in the third grade, so he was enthusiastic about everything. We were on the go and continually getting on and off the subway as we walked to various tourist sites. He kept busy by collecting the discarded tickets lying on the ground from the Tube. By the time we left, he had a huge stack.

The night before we left, Alex was running a 103 fever and was lethargic. He had most likely picked up germs from all the tickets he had handled. The mother guilt kicked in. *Why did I let him do this? I should have known better. What was I thinking?* As soon as we landed at the Atlanta airport, I had to call a sitter to stay with him the next day. He was too sick to attend school, and Dan and I had to get back to work. He was diagnosed with walking pneumonia.

Back at home, we were all adjusting to our new family dynamic. Jordan's absence affected each of us differently. But since he came home so often, it helped us all to accept the situation. Luke continued to become more aloof. He was making passing grades but still wasn't working up to his potential. I was beginning to worry about how he would manage college.

He got a job working at a golf course and later bagging groceries to pay for his gas money. He usually made plans on weekends to hang with friends, often calling to say he wasn't coming home but staying over for the night. Sometimes the guys went camping to some of the local forest areas. Since none of them were dating, I felt this was acceptable and almost always agreed to let Luke go.

Roller hockey was his new athletic interest. He and his friends skated on their own for several years, but as they got older, they joined a league at a local roller skating rink. Luke was one of the top scorers and loved the game. Although he was still laid back, he showed a surprising amount of aggressiveness when he played. It was fun to watch him play and entertaining to see him move so fast.

But he became more reticent at home, always quiet and private. I was worried about his lack of conversation and aloofness. I resorted to writing a series of questions so we could discuss his feelings about specific issues. I was doing whatever I could to get him to talk. This felt awkward for both of us. *Is he depressed, or is this normal behavior?* He was turning inward, not the fun, open boy from the past.

There were also signs Luke was struggling with being responsible. He had trouble getting to his job on time and procrastinated about everything. He rarely finished his chores on time. Being laid back was an asset when he was younger, but now it was presenting issues for him. He was still playing soccer and excelling, playing first-string on his high school team. They won the state championship in their division his senior year. But this was his primary extra-curriculum activity.

Since his bedroom was downstairs, he spent more and more time there away from the family. Any free time he spent with friends. Getting his driver's license opened up a whole new world of worries. I had a certain amount of confidence in Luke's driving skills since he had taken driver's education, but now he was asking to go places with his friends driving.

Although I was suspicious that he had started to drink, I never saw any evidence. When he socialized with friends, I made him come in through the front door rather than through the basement to his bedroom. I was usually asleep, waking when I heard the door open and close, but rarely got up to check on him. He hid it well.

I was becoming more aware of what little time was left for us as a family before Luke left for college. My melancholy was kicking in. I planned a ski trip for the four of us to Snowshoe, West Virginia, during Luke's senior year. The kids were excited to be traveling out of town and looking forward to the snow. We settled into a cozy condo with a fireplace. I could water ski but had never tried snow skiing. I managed to conquer the bunny slope, the easiest beginners slope, but never felt confident enough to move to a more advanced slope.

Luke already knew how to snow ski, so he helped Alex. Being a natural athlete like his brother, they were soon skiing the black diamond slopes together. Although they were eight years apart, they were playful around each other and enjoyed this winter vacation.

While looking in Luke's suitcase for some dry clothes for him, I found a 16 oz. can of beer. This answered my question about him starting to drink. I never knew how many he brought or saw signs of him being drunk. I didn't make a big deal of it and didn't even mention it. *Just being a teenager.*

Soon it was time to prepare for Luke leaving for college. We were okay with him checking into out-of-state colleges, maybe a small college where he could play soccer. But he showed little interest in this idea and little interest in college at all.

Graduation was dependent on his final grade in Algebra II. He had already taken it his junior year and failed, inheriting my dismal performance in math. There was a lot of pressure for him to pass this final exam, which he managed to do. He applied to our state college, the University of Tennessee, and was accepted. I was becoming more apprehensive as it became time for him to pack and head to Knoxville.

The summer before college, Luke painted houses for a neighbor. Our neighbor questioned me about hiring him, and this was the only advice I gave, "All I can say is, it takes Luke ten minutes to put mayonnaise on a sandwich, so I'm not sure how he would ever paint a house." He hired him anyway.

The neighbor frequently called to ask where Luke was because he hadn't shown up for work. He was always spending the night out, and I had no way of getting in touch with him. I was angry and frustrated because he wasn't even trying to be responsible for the commitment he made to this job. Being mature enough to handle the responsibilities of college was not looking good. He had only turned eighteen in May.

The morning we were leaving for Knoxville, I was emotional about my firstborn leaving for college. I cried a little before I even went downstairs to his room. *How can this be?* I had gone through this in my head a thousand times. I was feeling sentimental about this next stage of parenting, knowing it would just be Dan, Alex, and me at home.

"Do you have everything ready to go?"

He was still in bed. "Yeah, I think so." The smell of marijuana filled his room. *Oh, man, how do I handle this? Slow and easy ... don't yell ... be calm.*

I casually sat down on his bed. "It smells like you might be taking some marijuana with you."

"What do you mean?" he asked, suddenly wide awake.

"Well, the smell is hard to ignore. Where is it? You should know you can't take it with you to the dorm."

He had gone out with his oldest childhood friend, Brad, the night before.

"So, is this what Brad gave you as a going away gift?"

He had an easy out now, and he used it. "Yeah, he thought it would be funny."

"Well, where is it? I want to see it. You're not taking it to Knoxville with you."

"In my backpack."

I searched the backpack and found the pot along with a large bong. Necessities for a college freshman.

It was easier for Luke to blame his friend rather than take responsibility for it. It was his pot and his decision to take it with him.

"You do know it's illegal," I said sarcastically. "You could get thrown out of school if they find marijuana in your dorm room. I can't believe you would think this was alright."

I took the pot and the bong and left the room with a completely different feeling than when I entered. All the previous sentimental feelings were replaced with a sense of doom. I was afraid college was not going to go well for Luke.

Dan, Alex, and I drove to Knoxville to move Luke into the dorm. I continued to feel on edge. We helped him unpack and hang his Pink Floyd poster. This was a high priority. He followed us to the lobby to say goodbye, and we left him standing along a wall looking forlorn. He was tall and thin, and his long, red hair hung slightly over his eyes. I wanted to hug him and tell him, "You can do this."

This was all getting to me. *I need to get out of here.* Nothing more embarrassing than your mother crying as she leaves you at college. He waved at us as we left to drive home. I tried to talk myself out of jumping to conclusions. *Maybe all mothers are feeling like this. This is all normal. He'll surprise us and take this more seriously after classes start.*

Dan and I were now parenting just one child. This felt easy. Alex was continuing to be a joy in every way – a good student, athletic, and well-liked by others. Jordan continued to come home regularly and thrive in his new home environment. He was happy coming home and happy going back to his new home. His house parents assured us he was adjusting well. We had stopped worrying about where Luke was and what he was doing. He was at college studying.

But as I feared, his freshman year got off to a bumpy start. He started finding rides home every weekend and continued to hang out with his old friends. I was getting more and more worried. He wasn't. He was more and more nonchalant. He didn't seem to care about anything.

I found his pack of cigarettes and cried. Since Dan's mother died from emphysema at sixty-one and never got to meet any of our children, I was heartbroken he had started smoking. I went through his book bag, the one he always brought home but never opened and found a citation for having alcohol in the dorm. I saw notebooks with little or no notes in them.

What can I do to turn this around? I wrote a contract that he signed, agreeing to pass courses to get a car. I thought this might give him the motivation to try harder. But nothing worked. It was a long fall semester. After he came home for Christmas break, we found out how bad things really were. His grades came in the mail, F, F, F, F, F. Dan posted them on the refrigerator. We were sick.

Even though it was the holiday season, there was no celebrating at our house. I didn't bother to decorate the house since no one seemed to have any interest or enthusiasm. This was always a major job, with as many as thirty plastic containers stored away full of Christmas decorations. The boys always helped bring them down from the attic. This was the first year since I had been married that I had no Christmas spirit.

I did buy one new item, a Christmas doormat imprinted with the perfect slogan, "One big happy family lives down the street." We decided to spend Christmas in Florida with my sister and her family, thinking maybe we could be part of her happy family.

I was trying to convince myself Luke would stay home a semester, get a job, realize his big mistake, save his money to buy an old car, and return to college the next year. This was my plan for him, but as I found out, it wasn't his plan. He was lost and directionless. After a few weeks, he found a job working at a restaurant busing tables. He was fired since he could never get there on time and wouldn't show up whenever there was anything fun he wanted to do.

So now I knew he was drinking and smoking weed. I had noticed during the summer that his eyes were often bloodshot, and when I questioned him, he had an answer, "Oh, I just fell asleep with my contacts in, and it makes my eyes red." I had no reason not to believe him, but I was always suspicious.

He naturally lacked motivation, so smoking pot, that people use to chill out, wasn't working for him. It took away ALL of his motivation. I expected that he would experiment with marijuana but didn't think it would be this harmful to him.

Even though he was living with us, I tried to stay out of his business as much as possible. It was hard when I knew he was supposed to be at work at a specific time, and he would still be asleep downstairs or not at home at all. I would get calls from his bosses, wondering what was going on. "I don't know where he is," I often had to say.

This became his pattern of behavior, and it was out of my control. With Jordan, I had finally realized that there wasn't much I could do to help him. But with Luke, I felt I could influence, persuade, bribe, or shame him into changing his behavior. I was wrong.

After Luke had been out of school for almost a year, I came home and discovered the couch I bought for the playroom on his 16th birthday was gone. His clothes were gone from his closet. He had moved out to live with two friends. There was a brief feeling of relief, followed by worry since I knew he was in no position to support himself. I could never blame Jordan for not succeeding, but I did Luke. I tried not to but couldn't help myself. It was heartbreaking to watch this happening.

While Luke was floundering with his life, Alex was flourishing. He was a social kid with many friends. He played on a select club soccer team requiring weekly practices, out of town games, and tournaments. This was a family commitment since it meant we frequently were gone from Friday through Sunday, attending games. We couldn't do this with Luke since Jordan was still living at home. So we felt we should provide this opportunity for Alex even though I was still teaching full time and Dan working full time selling retirement plans. We looked forward to these weekends full of excitement and enthusiasm from the young, pre-teen boys.

Having an open weekend with no games scheduled, Alex asked to have several friends come for a sleepover. He planned a night to camp in our side yard with sleeping bags and tents. Dan let them build a small fire, and they were loud like typical middle school boys. They cooked hot dogs over the fire and had plans for s'mores later. Luke came in through the front door without noticing them.

"Hey, Luke, what's up?" Dan asked.

"Not much."

I figured it must be one of those nights when he didn't have anywhere to stay. We sat with him for a while, making small talk. It was obvious he had been drinking.

"Where's Alex?" Luke asked.

"He's with his friends in the side yard. They're camping out, so don't go out there and bother them."

"Why would I be bothering them?"

"Just don't go out there."

Soon Luke was telling us goodbye.

"See ya'll later. I gotta run."

I knew he had nowhere to go because he came over so late. He was most likely hoping he could sneak back into his bedroom window that he used to sneak out of. I was trying not to ask many questions. I was afraid of what I might find out.

"Well, stay in touch," I said, with a sinking feeling.

Dan and I decided it was time for bed. He went out one last time to check on the boys. Then we settled into bed. But in a short time, I heard Luke's voice.

"Hey, can I have one of those hot dogs? You guys having fun out here?"

Oh man, this is not good. Maybe Dan is already asleep, and I can handle this myself. Then came a loud laugh from Luke.

"Is that Luke out there?" Dan asked.

"I think so."

Dan jumped out of bed in only his underwear and was out the door to the side yard.

"What the hell are you doing back? I thought you left. I told you not to come out here."

Most of their conversation was hard to hear inside our bedroom. I couldn't understand all the words but their voices were loud. I got a knot in my stomach. Luke knew he was in trouble. Watching from the window, I saw Luke running and Dan running after him. *What's he going to do if he catches him?*

They ran across our yard and into the neighbor's yard before Dan grabbed him and tossed him to the ground. Luke squirmed away and ran. Dan slowly got up, brushing himself off and appeared just to be noticing he was in his underwear. I could see his look of disgust and anger as he shook his head and came back inside.

"I told him not to bother them. He never listens to me."

"Where'd he go?"

"I don't know and don't care. I'm tired of all his shit."

We were both quiet after that, lost in our thoughts, trying to go back to sleep. Alex and his friends thought it was all so funny. We did not.

Luke continued to move from place to place, staying with friends who would have him. He didn't pull his weight as a roommate, so he was often asked to leave. I always reasoned if only he had a place to live, he could get himself together. If only he had a car, he could get himself together. If only he had a job, he could get himself together. I helped look for cheap apartments, look for used cars, look for jobs, thinking it was the right thing to do.

Dan and I were at odds over all that was happening. He thought we should just let this unfold and stay out of it. I would try this approach, but my heart just wouldn't cooperate. I constantly worried, thinking about Luke driving under the influence. *What are the alcohol and drugs doing to him? What if he has an accident? What if he were to hurt other innocent people?*

He found a way to rent a house with two other friends. They didn't have a phone, so if there was anything important I needed to discuss, I had to go to his house. I planned a family dinner with my parents, my brother, and his kids, and I wanted to ask Luke to join us. But I knew the only way to communicate was to do it in person.

I drove to the rental house. I reluctantly climbed the steps, noticing litter scattered on the lawn and knocked on the front door. No one answered. I walked to the back of the house where his bedroom was located. The window was half broken out, and glass was lying on the ground outside. I looked in and felt nauseous, letting out an audible gasp.

His mattress was on the floor with no sheets. Clothes were strewn all around the room, piled everywhere. Liquor and beer bottles were littered around the room, and ashtrays were overflowing with cigarette butts, *Oh, my God,* My heart was pounding. It looked like a crack house.

He wasn't home, nor were any of his roommates, so I stood there staring and taking this all in. *How can he live like this?* I thought back to the days when I so carefully painted his nursery with primary colors. The beautiful tributes to motherhood I cross-stitched and hung on his walls. The pictures of sweet scenes depicting baby animals being lovingly cared for by their mothers. *So this is what life has done to my son. He is lost. What have I done wrong?*

After this happened, I convinced myself we needed an intervention. I talked with my parents and thought maybe with them involved Luke would straighten up. They weren't fully aware of the extent of his alcohol and drug use, but I had shared enough that they were concerned. After coming to our house, my father began the conversation by carefully asking Luke a few questions.

"Do you think you need to stop drinking?

"Yeah, I probably do."

"Do you think you should go back to school?"

"Yeah, I probably should."

"Don't you think you could be working?

"Yeah, I probably could."

Everything we said to him, he agreed was true. He was his usual compliant, passive self, never arguing or raising his voice. He respected my father and mother too much to do that. They encouraged him to try to get his act together. He was too smart to be wasting his life away. At least this might be a new start in the right direction. I was cautiously hopeful.

Luke continued to hang out with his childhood friend, Brad, who was a senior in high school. Brad, and many of Luke's old friends, were headed to Panama City, Florida, for spring break and asked him to join them. Luke was working at the Beverage Barn, selling beer and soft drinks, making minimum wage, so a week's vacation didn't seem feasible to me. But this was my way of thinking. He didn't have to ask my permission anymore since he wasn't living at home. He didn't seem to think not having any money was a reason not to go with his friends to the beach.

A few weeks earlier, Luke caught me in a weak moment when he stopped by my classroom, asking for gas money so he could get to work. *He has to get to work.* I didn't have cash, so I gave him my gas card, which he was supposed to return immediately. He took the card with him on vacation to Florida. I didn't know this until I got my bill and was in disbelief when I saw charges from his trip for food, gas, and beer. I felt betrayed once again. *How could he do this after all the help I have already given him? Why is it so hard to tell him "no"?*

I was becoming more and more convinced that Luke needed some professional psychiatric help. Maybe they could get through to him. *Was his behavior all due to alcohol and marijuana, or was something more going on?* I had always thought that maybe he had an attention deficit disorder without the hyperactivity component. He exhibited many of the symptoms, so I felt it was time to have testing done. Luke was always agreeable to whatever I suggested. So I took him to several different psychologists, all of whom gave different opinions.

After testing, the psychologist said he had a higher than average IQ. Another commented, "Do you have any idea how sensitive your son is?" My sweet, sensitive son was still in there somewhere. One suggested he was bipolar, but I doubted this because I had never noticed his behavior being very high or very low. One suggested he was having trouble being a responsible student and thought cutting down on his partying would increase his chances of being successful. *Oh, really .... that sounds familiar ....* I'd said it a thousand times.

At this time, he didn't have a car, so I would take him to the counseling appointment. Usually, the counselor would talk with only him but occasionally both of us. I continued to hold out hope he could make necessary changes with or without medication.

At one low point, Luke was completely broke but still trying to have a life on his own without working. At the time, Alex was twelve, and he and his friend, Devin, were always looking for ways to make money during their summer vacation. They decided to set up a lemonade stand at the top of our street. I took them to the store to buy their lemons, sugar, ice, and cups. They made signs, took my card table, chairs, and an umbrella to keep the summer heat from melting the ice, and set up shop.

They came back to the house to get lunch and were enthusiastic about how much money they made. "Mom, one car gave us ten dollars, and they didn't even want any lemonade." They were already talking about what they were going to do with all their money.

By late afternoon they were getting restless, and that's when Luke showed up.

"You guys look like you could use some help. How about letting me run the stand for a while? You guys can go back to the house where it's cool and play some video games. I'll just charge you ten dollars to stay here, and for each cup I sell, I'll take a quarter, and you can have the rest."

All of this sounded good to them.

They came back to the house, "Did you guys give it up for the day?" I asked, seeing their faces of relief.

"We hired Luke. He's going to stay at the stand, and we can play."

Picturing in my mind, my twenty-year-old selling lemonade and most likely smoking cigarettes, I didn't know whether to laugh or cry. He finished the afternoon at the lemonade stand. He brought back the table and chairs, the leftover cups and lemonade. He had made twelve dollars. Enough to buy some cigarettes and maybe a beer or two.

Holding down my responsibilities at home and at school often felt like two full-time jobs. It didn't help that every morning I woke up with a sense of dread, both by what was ahead of me at work and all that was going on with Luke. But as soon as I arrived at work, my mind was preoccupied with only what was in front of me, twenty-six third graders. But as soon as I got back home, I was obsessing over the latest crisis with Luke.

Dan kept himself busy at work, but also made time for working out several times a week. He was involved in several civic organizations that meant going to meetings and fundraising events. He was a leader and often found himself in charge. We seemed to pass each other coming and going through life. But we did try to get away alone when possible. Through Dan's work in investments, he qualified for a conference in LA. We both needed a vacation, so we made plans for me to go with him.

Since Luke wasn't living at home, we only had to make plans for Alex. Dan's sister, Susie, was now living in town, so we asked her to stay at the house. Arrangements were made around Alex's soccer schedule since he had practice and several games. Susie would stay with him on Thursday night. He was going to spend the night with a friend Friday night, and the parents would bring him back to the house early Saturday. Another family, also taking their son to practice, would pick him up that morning. I felt confident we had covered all the details.

I called home to assure myself all my scheduling for Alex was working. Susie told me that when she and Alex came home after school, Luke and his friends were on our screened porch smoking pot. *Oh, man, he's in trouble.* Susie told me she asked Luke and his friends to leave, and he did without any problems. She encouraged me to relax and enjoy myself while I could. This sounded like a good idea. I put it out of my mind.

Dan and I enjoyed a few drinks and a gourmet dinner at a fabulous restaurant, all taken care of by the sponsor of the conference. I bought some sexy lingerie and tried to forget I had kids. What was happening at home, for the time being, was not my problem. There was nothing I could do from California. What I didn't know I didn't have to worry about. Maybe I would just never go home again.

But back home, things were going very wrong. On Saturday morning, Alex was dropped off at the house, and he was waiting on his ride to soccer practice. He told me everything after we got home.

"I went in my room to get my soccer uniform, and there was a couple in my bed. I don't think they had any clothes on. I didn't know what to do."

"There were more people in your bed," he continued.

"The rest of the house was a mess, Mom. You should have seen it." There had been a party at our house. Susie went home since Alex was spending the night out, so she was not to blame. It was Luke's party.

When we arrived home, Alex was unusually quiet, and that's when he told me what had happened. He was tired of all the drama too. I was able to track down Luke and insisted he come home to change the sheets on the beds and clean the rest of the mess.

He didn't seem bothered by my reaction and said with little emotion, "This is what kids do when their parents are out of town."

When Alex went to bed that night, he came into my room holding a black bra. "I found this in my bed," he stated, not even surprised. *Oh my God, what is all this doing to him?* I knew what it was doing to me.

Luke's shenanigans seemed to be never-ending. I was always on edge, waiting for what was going to happen next. I got a call the morning after Halloween. It was the crazy lady who lived across the street. She never liked anything we did and looked for reasons to complain.

"Is this Karen?" she questioned as soon as I answered the phone. There was panic in her voice.

"Yes, and who's this?" I asked.

"This is Mrs. East, across the street. I just wanted you to know it looks like there's a dead body outside your basement door," she announced frantically.

"What? Why do you think that?"

"Well, I can see a body, and I've been watching for a while, and it hasn't moved."

"I doubt it's a dead body, but I'll certainly go check it out. Thanks for calling." I said sarcastically.

Dan must have left some yard equipment outside the door, and from her house, it looks like a body. I decided I better go check it out before she called the police, as she had done before for various ridiculous reasons.

As I walked down the driveway and got closer to the basement door, I could indeed see a body. I stopped briefly to decide what to do next. I realized it was Luke, only because I noticed his long red hair flowing out onto the pavement from the large orange and black pimp hat on his head. He was wearing a pair of green long johns and no shoes and was in a fetal position, apparently still wearing his Halloween costume. He was asleep right outside the door. Since the door was locked, that was the end of the road for this trick-or-treater.

Suddenly the words our neighbor used, "dead body," seemed like a possibility. Seeing Luke on the ground also brought out my maternal feelings. *Is he okay? Oh, my God.* So many mixed emotions. This was breaking my heart.

"Luke, Luke!" I repeated over and over. It took several hard shakes to get him to respond. As he opened his bloodshot eyes, my emotions quickly changed to anger.

"What the hell happened to you?" I could smell alcohol and cigarette smoke on him.

"I couldn't get in, so I just slept here," he replied slowly, slurring his words. His answers always made sense to him.

"God, Luke, you …. you … you can't keep doing this. Get up before the police show up."

"Why would the police come? I'm just sleeping in my own driveway."

"Well, the neighbor thought you were dead. So get up and come inside and go to bed."

I helped him into the house. He had no trouble finding his bed, and I was left to wonder once again how we got here and how do we get out of the continuing saga of Luke's addictions. I was confused about what my role was anymore.

Thoughts and questions rolled around my head…*What kind of mother am I? I am enabling his behavior. But how do I stop? I still want to protect Luke, but when does it turn into over-protecting him from the consequences of his actions?* I had already lost Luke on many levels, but the fear of his death kept me on a continuing search for ways to turn him around.

During this time, Dan and I did our best to be there for Alex. He was always hearing us discuss the most recent problem with Luke. We made a point to travel alone with him while he was growing up. During his summer vacations, we went to Chicago, Boston, and San Francisco, taking in the popular tourist sites. On a trip to New York City on the 4th of July, we were part of the audience on *Good Morning America*. Our souvenir pictures have the Twin Towers in the background during a ferry tour of the city.

Alex was always an eager traveler, easy to please when we made travel plans. He got all of our attention and deserved it since he was our only child who didn't have significant problems. I did my best to put whatever was happening at home with Luke out of my mind, and Jordan was being well taken care of. Alex deserved a mother who wasn't preoccupied.

I was always thinking of ways to provide Alex opportunities to steer him away from the path Luke had taken. To provide a more enriching summer vacation, other than hanging out with his friends, we involved Alex in an international organization called CISV – Children's International Summer Village. It was an exchange program involving children from across the world who gather to promote harmony and understanding of each other. It is a peace fostering summer program for children eleven through eighteen.

Alex traveled to England with other kids from Chattanooga, where each of them spent two weeks with a family. The following two weeks the student from England stayed with us. Alex also served as a junior counselor at a CISV village in Philadelphia for a month the following year. These experiences were growth opportunities for Alex in many ways.

We were intent on keeping him focused on the importance of his education. Summer seemed to be the time when many of his friends were drinking and experimenting with pot, which we were hoping to prevent him from doing, at least until he was older and could make a more informed and responsible decision.

I was trying to become less involved in all the drama associated with Luke, so I started focusing on other interests, like my husband, for example. Since Dan and I honeymooned in Jamaica, we decided to go back for our twenty-fifth wedding anniversary. This time we stayed at the Holiday Inn rather than the inexpensive bungalows across the street. We enjoyed all the usual beach activities, dining out, and watching the sunset. I had my hair braided by a local Jamaican woman, and we shopped in the various markets, trying to avoid buying too many souvenirs. We went back to Dunn River Falls since we went there on our honeymoon. It felt great to be reconnecting again and to realize we still enjoyed and loved each other.

I took all of our love letters from the years before we married, and we read them together. We had shared twenty-five years, so I bought a ring to commemorate the event, an aquamarine blue emerald cut surrounded by three small rows of diamonds on each side. Aquamarine reminded me of the water in the Caribbean and is said to be a symbol of youth, health, and hope. Our future together looked solid. Maybe if we were lucky, we would be here celebrating our fiftieth.

Our hotel offered several tours around Jamaica. I inquired about visiting a school. The Holiday Inn was accommodating and made the arrangements but questioned my interest. After I told them I was a teacher in the United States, they understood my curiosity. I was excited about seeing a side of Jamaica not usually seen by tourists.

I tried not to show my shock as the principal took us on a private tour, going to different classrooms, and seeing what they called the cafeteria and playground. There were close to fifty students crammed into small cinder block rooms without resources other than a blackboard. There were three students behind each wooden bench.

It was October, and the heat was sweltering. Dan and I were both wiping sweat from our faces as we smiled and interacted with the students. There wasn't a cafeteria but a room with snacks the children could purchase if their parents had money to give them. The majority of the kids had no money, so they didn't eat lunch. The playground was the large parking lot in front of the school, and there was no equipment. The kids were playing soccer with a large plastic soda bottle. It was an eye-opening experience and one that changed my perspective on teaching.

One teacher stood out among all the others since she was wearing a suit, with hose and heels. She was open and friendly and spoke in her beautiful Jamaican accent. I asked her if her students might be interested in becoming pen pals with my students. We were both teaching third grade. So this was the beginning of my relationship with Norine from Jamaica.

During the following summer, away from my responsibilities of teaching, I wrote a grant and received money to go to Jamaica. I asked six other educators to join me for a week at Chetwood Elementary School. Alex and his friend, Quinn, came along to help. We planned a week of activities around the theme, "It's a Small World After All."

We divided into groups, and each group read a non-fiction book about a different country followed by a fiction book about an animal native to that specific country. The teachers developed an art activity related to the books. The entire trip was a distraction for me and an enriching experience for Alex. We had never seen such poverty but also never witnessed kids with so much motivation to learn.

The children were eager to experience all we offered. We brought a variety of balls, their eyes lighting up in anticipation as we inflated them. Their recess involved all the kids in the school running wild in the parking lot entertaining themselves. But no kids were fighting, pushing, and shoving or being disrespectful to each other as I often experienced when my class was at recess with other classes.

We brought bubbles in a bottle, and the children chased the bubbles around, laughing with glee when they landed on heads, arms, and legs. Our funds were limited, but we gave all 500 students *Smarties*, a hard flavored candy. We told them these would make them even smarter than they already were. So throughout the week, they asked continually for another "sweet," as they called them.

The entire week was one we would never forget for many reasons. We felt more gratitude for the many resources in our schools that we didn't always appreciate. We even looked at our school library, the cafeteria, the air conditioning, playground equipment, and our music and PE teachers, with new eyes. We had nothing to complain about other than kids who often took it all for granted, just like we had. I was thankful for this shared experience with Alex, hopefully giving him more insight into who and what he might become as an adult. Maybe it was too late for Luke. He didn't seem grateful for anything. *Where has my son gone?*

Although I was teaching full time, keeping friendships with my *handicapped friends* was important to me. Although we weren't handicapped in a literal way, we had all come to realize everyone has handicaps of one type or another. Throughout the year, we planned dinners around each of our birthdays. One cold December, we flew to New York City, attended several plays, went through Central Park in a carriage, and ate at Tavern on the Green wearing Santa hats. Another year we drove to Abington, Virginia, riding a section of the Virginia Creeper Trail on bicycles and attending a play at the historic Barter Theatre. Trips to Williamsburg, Nashville, Atlanta, and Gatlinburg through the years each have their special memories.

Our common bond was our disabled children, and it was therapy sharing stories around their specific conditions. There were always funny stories, but we had just as many stories about our normal children. We spent most of our time laughing, realizing keeping a sense of humor was the only way to get through difficult life circumstances.

Whatever sense of relaxation I was able to achieve on various trips, it always seemed to end as soon as I got home. Luke's attempt at living on his own had not lasted long, since there was rent to pay. So he was back living with us. Dan and I got a phone call late one night. Phone calls late at night are never good news. It was the police.

"Do you have a son named Luke?" He and two friends had been pulled over for speeding. The policeman told me where they were and asked me to come. All three were wild-eyed but not stumbling around like they would have been if they had been drinking.

"Ma'am, if you could just take them home. I want to get them off the road. They can leave their car here. They are high on something, but I don't have a way to determine what it is."

I couldn't believe what he was saying. A flood of relief washed over me. He wasn't going to press any charges.

"Thank you so much, sir." I was talking for them since they couldn't even answer his questions.

The three of them got in my car. I was furious. But I couldn't even question them because no one could give me any answers. We rode in silence. I took the two friends to another friend's apartment nearby and then headed home with Luke. He went directly downstairs to his bedroom. There was so much I wanted to say, but it was useless that night. I was exhausted, in more ways than one. I was hoping this might scare Luke and be a turning point.

The next morning I went downstairs to give my lecture. I opened the door, thinking about what I wanted to say. His bed was empty. The bathroom was empty. The window was slightly ajar. He had snuck out of his bedroom window. *What the hell?* The same two friends had gotten a ride back to their car and picked up Luke during the night. As I sat in the den, wondering where he was, he walked casually in the front door.

"What are you doing? Where did you go? Don't you realize I was called in the middle of the night to come to get you and your friends, and I got everyone home safely, and what do you guys do but sneak out of the house? Are you crazy?"

"We were hungry, so we went to the Waffle House," Luke explained.

This seemed like a perfectly good reason. I was livid.

"You probably don't even remember last night. You guys got lucky. You got stopped by the police for speeding, and he knew ya'll were high on something. He let you go. He didn't arrest any of you."

"That was nice of him."

"I hope this teaches you a lesson. None of you should have been driving."

They didn't realize how lucky they were to have gotten off with only a reprimand.

I was trying to keep our family intact as much as possible, but with Jordan living in a group home and Luke practically living on the street, we didn't see much of each other. With Christmas soon approaching, I felt it was a chance for the family to reconnect. I always made a big deal out of the holidays, Christmas especially – decorating inside and out, preparing food and pulling out the best china, cloth napkins, and candlesticks.

I invited my parents to join us on Christmas Day for a late lunch. Years earlier, Dan, Luke, and Alex started a tradition playing a Christmas Day football game with another family with sons, so we always planned lunch around the game. I had the meal timed so we could eat soon afterward, and I used the time alone to finish the last minute touches, trying to make it all perfect.

My parents arrived first, complimenting the house with all its festive decorations and the smells coming from the kitchen. Dan and Alex came back first, and we waited for Luke. He walked in, and I could smell the pot. His demeanor was different. He was stoned. I took a deep breath.

As we bowed our heads to give thanks for the food and family, I was having trouble not showing my anger. I lost my appetite. I could barely get through the meal. I kept watching Luke and waiting for some inappropriate words or actions, but that didn't happen. I seemed to be the only one aware of what was going on.

I didn't want to ruin Christmas dinner with an emotional outburst. *Why doesn't he appreciate all the time that went into the preparation for this meal? Why doesn't he realize all the work that went into buying and wrapping all the gifts under the tree? Why doesn't he understand how much this hurts my feelings?*

It was unrealistic for me to expect Luke to consider such things. I was only looking at it from my perspective. He was dealing with addiction. He was dealing with denial. He was in his own world. The alcohol and drugs had changed Luke.

We finished lunch without any kind of drama, but when I got him alone, I questioned him.

"What were you thinking? Coming to Christmas dinner stoned with your grandparents here?"

"Well, Jimmy had some good pot, and we played a good game, and it was time to celebrate Christmas," he replied.

How could I argue with that?

By mid-2000, Luke was still struggling with having and keeping a job, a place to live, and a car. It seemed one of those was always missing. He was running out of options. It was time to look at rehab. I did extensive online research, trying to find the perfect place. I found one that seemed to be a possibility if our insurance would only pay. It was expensive, but we felt it would be a good fit for Luke and his personality. The Wilderness Treatment Center in Kalispell, Montana, was a 60-day inpatient facility for males 14-24, described as a ranch-based experience. Luke was 22.

212 So Much for the White Picket Fence

The information online sounded like heaven, "Treatment allows for the reconstruction of family wholeness and health." We were desperate for this. "Days are filled with individual and group therapy, informational videos, and lectures." One component made it stand out among other facilities, "We provide a 16 to 21-day wilderness therapy expedition into Yellowstone National Park." This might be enough for Luke to say "yes."

I asked him to come by the house, and I approached the subject with as much positivity as I could.

"Luke, it seems you've sort of run out of options. Do you have any plans for what you are going to do next?"

"Nah, I don't know," he said flatly.

"Well, Dad and I think it might be time to think about a rehab facility. I think you know this yourself. You know we love you, and it's been hard watching you struggling so much. Nothing seems to be working out for you here in Chattanooga. We've been looking at places online, and we think we've found a program that might work for you."

"I don't know about that."

"It might help you understand what's going on. I mean, you can't continue your life the way you have been since you finished high school. You have to start thinking about your future. You seem unhappy."

I tried not to be preachy or accusatory. I told him all I learned about the Wilderness Treatment Center. He sat for a long time without saying anything. You could never read any emotions on Luke's face.

Finally, without any questions at all, he responded, "Yeah, it all sounds good. I guess it might help."

I had several questions I wanted to ask but didn't. *Are you seriously ready to get help? Are you looking at this as a fun trip to Montana? Do you just want to go on an extended trip with free food and lodging?*

Many people cautioned me, "If he's not ready to change, it'll be a waste of time and money."

My thoughts were always ... T*hat's the job of the treatment facility, to give him enough information, so he realizes he's in trouble and needs help.* At this point, I felt it was the only option.

He was his usual compliant self. I didn't have to do any convincing. He seemed ready for help. He had been out of high school for four years and had made no progress toward taking responsibility for his future. It was a month before he would be leaving. I just hoped he wouldn't change his mind.

During the four years since he graduated, he had gone through twenty-seven places of employment. He was easily hired because he knew how to say the right things and was personable. He just couldn't follow through with the basics of holding a job, like showing up and showing up on time.

He worked in many different fast-food restaurants. McDonald's held the record for the shortest time of employment – two weeks. There was most likely a one-day work record somewhere. The variety of jobs was vast – Chattanooga Choo-Choo, Beverage Barn, Shamrock Carpet Cleaners, Kirby vacuum cleaners, Hot Dog Heaven, Baskin Robbins, Rock City, and the list went on and on.

One of Luke's jobs was at Video Park where I used to take him and his friends to choose videos when he was younger. When he got the job, he was without a place to live. After he closed the store one night, he decided it made sense to just sleep there on the floor so he would be ready to work the next day. You can imagine the surprise when his boss came in early to find him asleep on the floor of her store.

There were crazy stories to tell about all his work experiences, either about him or the other people who worked there. I knew he enjoyed creative writing, so I suggested he consider writing a book, with each chapter being about a different job, and name the book *Minimum Wage.*

Luke continued to be an irresponsible employee. He needed money to survive since we weren't giving him any. But it seemed he just worked long enough to pay for his alcohol, cigarettes, drugs, and food, and probably in that order. He rarely had enough for rent.

This was driving Dan especially crazy because of his own strong work ethic. We just didn't know how much of this behavior was due to his drinking, or was it a personality flaw. We wanted to take alcohol out of the picture to see what was what.

Since Luke had agreed to go to rehab, I was looking forward to a break from any further incidents. He would be gone for two months. I was full of both relief and apprehension as I drove him to the airport. I felt hopeful this was the turning point. I wouldn't be able to talk to him for two weeks, and only for short periods after that. After a two week evaluation, Carrie, the counselor assigned to Luke, called me to discuss his progress.

"He has adjusted well. He didn't have to go through any kind of detox. I'm a little concerned that he hasn't opened up very much. He's on the quiet side."

"Yeah, he's always been like that. Do you think he's depressed?"

"Since I've only known Luke such a short time, it's hard for me to say. He does seem to a person who is struggling with his feelings and dulling them with drugs. Do you know the extent of Luke's drug use?"

"Well, I just know he can't seem to manage life, probably from his alcohol and marijuana use."

"I'm afraid it's a little more extensive than you think. He has been involved with not only beer, wine, and liquor but mushrooms, LSD, cocaine, mollies, and was drinking so heavily he was having blackouts. But it seems his primary issue is alcohol." I felt sick hearing these words. He was slowly killing himself.

After four weeks, Dan and I flew to Montana to attend family week. Alex could have attended since it was open for brothers and sisters, but I decided he didn't need to be around all the drama. He needed a break from all of Luke's issues. Twenty other sets of parents were there, doing what they thought needed to be done to help their sons. We listened to their stories and shared ours, making us feel less alone.

Luke was twenty-two, one of the older boys at the rehab. But he was so out of it when he arrived he told them he was twenty-one. He didn't even remember the birthday he had in May. When we arrived, I didn't recognize him because his long hair was gone. He had a buzz cut, and it looked good on him, just different. He was eating regular meals, so he had gained weight making him appear to be healthy again. It felt good to put my arms around him. I didn't want to let go.

At the end of family week, all the parents and their sons gathered in a circle in the meeting room. The counselors explained that we would be doing an activity called "knees to knees." Each parent would sit in a chair facing their son, knees touching, and would share their fears, disappointments, and intentions. My heart lurched. This was going to be hard.

We listened as parents poured out their feelings of broken hearts and desperation, and their sons shared feelings of inadequacy, guilt, and fear. We sat and waited for our turn. Dan went first. You couldn't look away. You couldn't turn away. You couldn't walk away.

"It's been tough to watch what you've been going through. I know I haven't always done or said what I should have. Most of the time, I didn't know what to do or say. This has been hard for me, and I know it's been hard for you, too. I've been scared about what might happen to you. I want to help you get your life back in order. Just let me know what I can do."

Dan was more vulnerable than I had ever seen him. He didn't always show his concern or compassion, but he had been just as impacted by all of this as I had been.

It was my turn. My heart was pounding. As soon as I sat down, I started crying. *You have to pull yourself together.*

"I love you so much. It has been hard watching you make so many bad choices. You were always so loving, and the alcohol and drugs changed you. I've cried so many times worrying that you might overdose or get in an accident." I had to stop every few minutes to regain my composure.

"I hope you're learning about addiction, so maybe you'll have ways to cope with life. I know I have said and done things that hurt you and probably didn't help. But I've always wanted you to be happy and healthy. I'll support you however I can. I don't want to enable you anymore. I want to help you."

It was hard for Luke to share and open up in front of all these people. He didn't cry or show much outward emotion like many of the other boys did. But he did seem remorseful.

"I love you too, Mom. I don't know why I've made so many mistakes. Nothing seemed to work for me, not college or any of my jobs. I'm sorry for hurting you so much. I didn't mean to. I know I can do better. I want to do better."

This circle of mothers, fathers, and sons shared so many feelings – fear and anger, regret and remorse, guilt, and love. It was intense. I felt drained.

Before we left the circle, one counselor brought out a beautiful bird mobile as a visual.

"This represents a family where life balances out when all the members work together." Then he cut off one of the birds. As the mobile became out of balance, he continued, "This is what happens when one member is an addict. The entire mobile becomes dysfunctional." I could completely identify with this. I felt as dysfunctional as Luke.

At the end of the week, the counselors told us that more treatment would be needed to break Luke's pattern of addiction. This rehab would need to be followed with an aftercare program of two months if we wanted him to be successful. I hadn't even thought that far ahead.

Dan and I left with a better understanding of addiction and its many facets. There are both physical and mental reasons that contribute to a person's use. Although I knew this all along, it was good to hear it from the professionals. It was complicated. It wasn't as simple as *"Why can't you just stop?"*

Luke finished the program and headed to Minneapolis for a structured after-care program, a halfway house. Since he loved snow, maybe this was the right place for him to have a new start. He spent his first Thanksgiving away from family, and I was beginning to feel hopeful about his future. He was attending AA meetings and working in a coffee shop. This was a new beginning for him. He sounded good on the phone. He was more talkative and seemed to have a positive outlook.

He was scheduled to come home for a visit at Christmas, and I was making preparations for our family to reconnect for the holidays. I hadn't been this excited in a long time. Life had calmed down, and I was enjoying the peace. Alex hadn't seen his brother since September. We made flight arrangements, and I was marking days off the calendar. Then I got a phone call from the manager at the halfway house.

"Is this Mrs. LaGraff?" Thinking this was maybe a solicitation call, I almost hung up.

"Yes."

"This is Mr. Grayson, from the half-way house where your son Luke is living. I have some news I need to share with you." He had my attention now.

"Luke has broken our house rules. He was supposed to be at an AA meeting and instead went somewhere else on the bus. He also lied about it when I questioned him." My heart sank.

He continued, "Because of this, he won't be allowed to come home for Christmas." I wanted this to be a prank call. *This can't be happening.*

"But I've already paid for his ticket home," I said, thinking this might be enough to persuade him to change his mind.

"We have already made up our minds concerning this issue. We have rules, and Luke knew the rules. He made an unfortunate decision. He can continue to stay in the program, but he won't be allowed to come home."

My heart dropped. I had to sit down.

"Well, I don't even know what to say. We were so looking forward to him coming home. He's been doing so well. I know he needs to continue in a program, but … but this is awful."

This news left me shaking. I paced around the house as I tried to process what he had just said. My thoughts were jumbled, coming one after another. "*Why did he do this? How will I tell Alex that Luke isn't coming home? What can I do to change this?*

I called Luke.

"I just talked to Mr. Grayson. He's not going to let you come home. Why, why, didn't you go to the AA meeting? And then you lied to the director. This messes everything up. We were all so excited about you coming home. What happened, Luke? I thought you were going to start making better decisions."

"Well, I don't know. I've been going to all the meetings. I thought it wouldn't hurt to miss one. I'm sorry, Mom. I didn't think it would be a big deal. I guess it was. I should have just told the truth."

"Yeah, you should have. That just made everything worse. I'm so angry and disappointed. But maybe we can figure something out. I still want you to come home."

"Maybe there's another place I can go. I know I still need to be in a halfway house, but I'd like to be in a less structured place. I'd like to stay in Minneapolis."

Another decision had to be made. *They don't know what's best for our family. I don't want to disappoint Alex. I want Luke home for Christmas.*

So I rescued Luke from a bad decision and brought him home for Christmas. *What will we do with him now?* I had been feeling so much better being removed from the frequent turmoil of living in the same town as Luke. He was many miles away in a safe place, and I could finally sleep again. He was home again, but I knew he had to go back and finish a program somewhere.

I found another facility so he could continue his recovery. After talking with the director, she agreed to take Luke. Although I was happy to be with Luke during the holidays, there was tension in the air throughout his visit. I knew I had probably done the wrong thing. The guilt and happiness were a strange mix of feelings.

He flew back to Minneapolis after Christmas to live in a different sober living facility. He got a job in a call center. He was still required to attend AA meetings. Everything calmed down again for him and for us.

Dan, Alex, and I visited him the following summer. I hadn't seen him in six months and had missed him. We went sightseeing, out for dinners, and I felt I saw more of the old Luke again. Alex stayed with him at the halfway house, giving them time alone to play video games and watch movies. Luke appeared to be doing well. We talked to the director.

"Luke had a little rocky start, but he is doing much better now. He is well-liked and meeting his responsibilities."

I was full of hope. He stayed there until late August when we all decided it was time for him to get back to the real world. It had been almost a full year since he first left for rehab. He flew back to Chattanooga to begin again.

Chapter 11

August 2001

Luke was back in town. He didn't have a job; he didn't have a car, and he didn't have a place to live. To give him any chance of being successful, I knew he needed our help. I found a clean and affordable apartment, and Dan bought him a used car. Jordan's school was a few blocks away, so I suggested Luke check on possible jobs at Orange Grove. He was always patient and loving with Jordan, and grew up with opportunities to be around and interact with the disabled. He got a job as a classroom assistant. His life seemed to be moving in the right direction.

Meanwhile, I was still trying to stay on top of all my school responsibilities. At the end of the school year, I had decided I wanted to change schools. There was a 4th-grade position available, and I got an interview.

The principal asked me, "Why do you want this job?"

"I just need a change. I don't want to change husbands. I don't want to change kids. I don't want to change houses. So changing jobs seemed like the logical choice." She laughed and offered me the job.

I was enjoying a new working environment. The kids were more mature, and the teachers were supportive and fun. The curriculum was more interesting, so I had finally found the right balance between work and home. Both were manageable.

Diane and I talked every weekend to share our experiences in our classrooms. She was a kindergarten teacher in Florida, and we kept each other going through some tough years. We often questioned our decisions not to follow our father's advice to go into the medical field rather than education. Teaching was draining. We both struggled with the demands.

Alex was also going through a change since he had started high school. He was continuing to do well both personally and academically. Considering what our family had been through in the last few years, he was well adjusted. He was playing on his high school soccer team and also on the select traveling team. It kept all three of us busy with practice, games, and tournaments.

We were still bringing Jordan home for the weekends and holidays, but I often felt guilty about not seeing him more often. He was still living in the group home, which had gone through several house managers since he moved in. There was always some kind of drama going on.

One of Jordan's roommates sometimes had episodes of violently acting out. One Sunday, when they were all home, his roommate became agitated and started turning over furniture, throwing lamps, yelling, and screaming. The house manager called the police to the house. She was required to call all the parents to tell them about the incident. When she called me, she said, "It really upset Jordan. He went to his room and brought us his shoes." It was his way of saying, "Get me out of here."

This broke my heart in so many ways. But I was thankful we had never experienced that kind of rage from Jordan. For the most part, he was always cooperative and endearing to the staff who worked with him. After this incident, I brought him home to spend the night, and he seemed happy to be here.

There were sometimes issues with either the house managers, the support staff, or one of the other clients in his home. The situation was not always as idyllic as I would have liked. But I was still grateful for Orange Grove and the support we were receiving from them.

Jordan was incredibly vulnerable to all kinds of child abuse. He could be very stubborn if he wanted to be, and you couldn't reason with him. He was entirely dependent on someone else's care. He could be unusually strong. It required a lot of patience to work with him. There were three shifts of people working at his home.

Jordan had endeared himself to many of them, and they had a true calling for this kind of work. I read a quote that could have come from Jordan. "Non-verbal doesn't mean I have nothing to say. It means you will need to listen to me with more than just your ears." (Anonymous) Some people were better at that than others.

Luke had been back in Chattanooga for three months, and although I had rented the apartment for Luke, I didn't go out of my way to make it comfortable. He was sleeping on a bad mattress on the floor. For Christmas, I bought him a new mattress and bed frame. I called his landlord, so he could open Luke's apartment for the delivery to be made while Luke was at work. I wanted to surprise him. I looked around his place, finding it neat and clean. I cautiously opened the refrigerator and felt my heart drop. There was a six-pack of beer and not much else. *Oh no, oh no, please no.*

I sat on this information for a few days, trying to think of other reasons why there was beer in the fridge. *Maybe his friends left it there. Maybe he is giving it to a friend as a gift. This can't be happening.* Gathering my courage, I confronted Luke later in the week.

"Are you drinking again? I saw the beer in your refrigerator."

"Well, only a little, Mom. I think I can handle it now," he assured me.

"What do you mean you think you can handle it? We just spent thousands of dollars to get you to understand you can't handle it. You can't start hanging out with your old friends, or you're going to be right back where you started. Don't you realize this?" Panic was setting in.

"Well, it's not out of control. I can have a beer or two. You're making a big deal of nothing. I was going to tell you soon."

Well, here we were, back in denial. I was sick with anxiety and hopelessness. There was no reasoning with him. I knew he couldn't handle it now. But he had to find this out on his own.

Soon after this shattering news, I started getting phone calls from the teacher at Orange Grove, who Luke was working under as an assistant. He wasn't showing up on time. He was calling in sick and wasn't reliable. She followed this with good comments about Luke when he was there, saying the clients loved him, and he was great with them, but he had to show up. I asked her to share her concerns with him rather than him hearing it from me. He was sick of hearing my lectures, and I was tired of giving them.

I could barely keep up with where Luke lived or what he was doing during the following years. I had to remove myself from his life as much as I could. He didn't need me enabling him. He spiraled again into major drug and alcohol issues. I didn't know what to do anymore. I had done all I knew to do. The worry felt like a huge weight on my heart. Like the grief of losing Robert, but the grief was ongoing, like losing a son who was still alive.

Since my parents still lived in Ducktown, it was easy to keep them from knowing the truth about Luke's alcoholism. They were still under the impression he was doing well since returning from rehab. I didn't want to worry them anymore. "Yeah, he seems to be doing okay," was all I would say.

I wasn't spending as much time with my aging parents as I wanted. I talked to them often but found it increasingly difficult to make the trip to see them. My weekends were spent preparing the next week's lesson plans, grading papers, keeping up with Alex, visiting Jordan, and keeping the house in order.

I was trying to keep my head above the water as best I could, but I couldn't help but feel a sense of doom about my life. As if I didn't have enough to worry about going on right now, I was worried about what was going to happen next. I was about to go through menopause (my grandmother was going home!); Simon, my dog, was twelve and would be gone soon; my baby would be leaving for college, and both my parents were having health issues.

So I knew my life was going to be changing. But until that happened, I distracted myself with some amazing summer trips abroad. Margie, my roommate from college, was an art teacher in Knoxville and organized tours for her students.

She asked if I might want to join her on a trip to Italy. It was just what I needed to pull me out of my worry about the future. I joined her a year later in Greece. Being immersed in a different culture, being with different people, seeing a diverse landscape helped me keep myself together so I could continue to deal with all that was going on at home.

But soon, all the things I worried about happened. My mother had gone through breast cancer when she was sixty-one. She had a mastectomy followed by radiation treatments, and she recovered. But now, at eighty-one, she had swelling in one arm and other health issues. She was diagnosed with non-Hodgkin's lymphoma and started chemotherapy. She had completed two sessions, three weeks apart, and my father was taking care of her at home.

I was still teaching fourth grade and was taking time off from work to accompany her to treatments. I had been out of my classroom so often, and my students were taking advantage of the situation by misbehaving for all the substitute teachers. I knew I wasn't the best teacher when I was there since I was so preoccupied with worry over my mother. I was feeling overwhelmed with both situations.

To distract me from all these worries, I went shopping on an early spring Sunday afternoon. I bought a new pair of sandals at Target to usher in the beginning of warmer weather. When I got home, I heard the familiar beep of my answering machine. I clicked it before I even put my packages down.

My father's voice was quivering, "Karen, your mother collapsed as I was getting her out of bed to go for a ride. I called for the ambulance, and they tried to resuscitate her. They've taken her in an ambulance to Erlanger Hospital in Cattanooga, and Larry and JoAnn are going to drive me down there. I'll see you there."

He was having trouble getting the words out. He was realizing the seriousness of what had just happened. After listening to his message, I immediately felt the weight in my chest – the heaviness of fear and anxiety. I could hardly breathe.

I went into the kitchen to tell Dan and Alex what had happened and left for to the hospital, only ten minutes away. As I approached the building, I could hear the whirling of a helicopter overhead. It was lowering down to land on the roof. I pictured my mother inside, and a wave of panic washed over me. I knew this would not end well. I called Dan, "I need you to come down here."

Before he arrived, a nurse took me to Mother's room, where she lay on a gurney. She was alive but unconscious. The doctor came in and explained to my father and me what happened. A sudden brain embolism had caused a stroke. She had no chance of recovery. Her brain had been without oxygen too long. My father left the room because he didn't want to watch the nurse take off the breathing machine. I was in shock.

I didn't want to leave the room. I held her hand and didn't want to let go. I thought of a funny story she had told me years earlier when Aunt Lula died. Mother had insisted they put socks on Lula in the casket because she didn't want her feet to be cold. Mother was always cold-natured, so I asked the nurse, "I know this is going to sound crazy, but is there any way you could find some socks for my mother?"

She looked at me like *you've got to be kidding me* and left to find socks. While she was gone, I was alone with my mother. I looked at her hands and thought of all the ways she had used her hands throughout her life. I later wrote a poem called "Mother's Hands"… *hands that changed the diapers of three babies, hands that always planted petunias on our back porch, hands that played hymns on the piano.*

When the nurse returned with the socks, I put them on her. I kissed her and told her how much I loved her. Dan had come in and had his hand on my shoulder. He told me it was time to leave. It took everything I had to walk out of the room and into the lobby where everyone was going about their normal lives. My life had changed forever.

This had all happened so quickly. I had just talked to mother the day before. Her voice was strong, and she sounded upbeat when she asked, "How are the boys?" Only one day later and I was saying goodbye. I was so thankful there were no unresolved issues with my mother. Our relationship was not problematic in any way. She was always supportive and loving. She was a gift, and I felt lucky to have been her daughter.

My parents were a devoted couple and set a beautiful example of a long and loving relationship. But I had always been much closer to my mother than my father. Whenever I called home, it was my mother who I always talked to, giving details of my life. She would ask questions, and I would fill her in on all the antics of the kids. She would usually ask, "Do you want to say hello to your father?" I would say "yes," and there would be a short conversation with my father. But these would be brief awkward conversations. He didn't seem to know what to say or ask.

As I was adjusting to life without my mother, I was worried about how my father was going to go on with his life without his wife. He had never lived alone. He had never done any housework. He had never done any cooking. I had only seen him in the kitchen to get food out of the refrigerator or from the cabinets. I started calling him regularly, and it felt awkward since we had never spent much time talking on the phone.

We were talking several times a week, and it was becoming more comfortable. About six weeks after Mother died, he called me.

"I think I've figured out how to work the toaster." He was trying to put a little humor into his situation, but it was true that my poor Daddy was lost without my mother. He would often call me crying, one time after finding one of her Kleenexes in a coat pocket and another time after running across pictures of her as a young girl. I never knew what to say to him, but I would try. "I know you miss her, Daddy. I miss her, too." My heart was breaking as I tried to console him.

Before getting so sick, she wanted new kitchen flooring, but Daddy talked her out of it, telling her she didn't need it. After she died, he insisted we look at kitchen flooring and asked me to make a choice. After having it instilled, he would call to tell me how guilty he felt about not getting her the kitchen floor. Every time he walked across it, he cried. As much as I missed my mother and was grieving this loss, I felt terrible for my father. They were married 61 years, and he was lost and lonely.

Now I was back at work trying to concentrate on my career. But I was still dwelling on Luke's problems, which had gone from bad to worse. His addiction was getting the best of him, and he was continuing to make bad decisions. I would try to stay in touch with him the best I could. When he didn't have a car, he rode a bicycle around town. When he didn't have a place to live, he would couch surf with his many friends. When he didn't have a job, he would sleep in and drink or smoke pot.

I was familiar with the advice everyone kept giving, "they have to hit bottom." I kept waiting for this to happen, but the bottom just kept going further and further down. Nothing seemed to bother him. I thought hitting bottom would have occurred when he flunked out of college. That seemed a long time ago, and much had happened since then.

Luke was arrested twice during this period, both for public intoxication and disorderly conduct. He was getting a record that would follow him for years. I constantly worried about his drinking and driving. He had already gone through rehab, so there was nothing left to try. I was not in favor of him going again. He knew what he had to do.

I was going to have to do what Dan had said years before. I was going to have to let this play itself out. Dan had also said, "If we can just keep him alive until that happens." This was, of course, my most pressing fear. Images of an overdose or a car accident played out in my head daily.

I knew Luke was depressed. He seemed to have repressed emotions and expressed them by writing poems. He had left them on the computer or printed on small pieces of paper that he left around the house. Lyrics that I didn't understand and always had a depressing tone. Scary, like he was in a constant state of hallucination. I found one about suicide.

I'm Gonna Commit Suicide (In This Century)
> *All I do is eat and sleep*
> *Occasionally drink for a week*
> *Do everything one human would do for free*
> *So I'm gonna commit suicide,*
> *In this century.*

This made me physically sick – a knot in my stomach; the weight of fear and sadness was overpowering. I understood this poem, and it left me feeling completely helpless. There was nowhere to turn, and I knew it was out of my control. I knew it logically and practically, but in my heart, I still wanted to save him. I was his mother, and mothers protect their children. But he had to do this himself.

Occasionally, Luke would show up unexpectedly and eat dinner with us. I wondered if it was his only food for the day. We would sit around and watch TV, trying to make conversation away from *the elephant in the room*. Eventually, it would be time for Dan and me to go to bed. Luke would tell me he didn't have anywhere to go. It would break my heart and make me furious at the same time. My emotions were all over the place. It was tearing me apart to see him in this depressing state.

Sometimes I would let him move back in until he had more going for himself, but it never worked out. Dan and I were on different pages with Luke and his problems. I felt Dan had given up on him. He felt I was the enabler. There was truth in both opinions. But because I held out hope for his future, I kept trying to fix his life.

It was soon time for Alex to make college plans. *Where has the time gone?* When he was looking at colleges, I told him, "You can go anywhere but UT." I didn't want to relive any of the experiences we had when Luke attended UT. But it had nothing to do with the school and everything to do with Luke. Alex didn't consider any other schools. He had started dating a girl in his junior year of high school who was now a student at UT, so he wanted to be there with her.

So in August of 2004, he headed to Knoxville. Luke rode with us, making it feel like *déjà vu* since eight years earlier Alex went with us to take Luke to college. After Luke flunked out of college, I told him, "Alex will have a college education before you do if you don't go back to school." It looked like this was going to happen.

Alex adjusted quickly to college life. His girlfriend, Melissa, was a year older and had already been there a year. This contributed to his smooth transition from high school. Alex and Melissa were both sports fans and enjoyed the fall football season together. They were compatible in many areas and supported each other. Alex's grades were good, and he had made new friends. Dan and I were grateful.

Now we were empty nesters, without kids for the first time in twenty-six years. This felt weird. I was still a mother but not mothering anymore, at least on a day-to-day basis. I didn't sink into a depression since I was enjoying this new freedom with my time. But my school responsibilities were feeling more burdensome. I started thinking about retirement. I needed to get out from under some of the weight. I had never learned how to leave my job at work, although, in reality, I wasn't sure this was possible. I always had a stack of papers to grade, lesson plans to work on, or materials to gather for a project.

In 2006, I turned in my resignation letter. I was 55 and felt there was a lot of life left to enjoy. Financially, I knew this wasn't the best decision, but I was burned out with my career. I found it rewarding on many levels. I enjoyed developing a creative curriculum where the students became engaged and thrived academically. But in recent years, so many expectations were placed on teachers for their students to perform well on the yearly achievement tests. We had to start preparing them from day one.

Also, many parents were not supportive of the teachers, nor the principals, in many cases. I was over it all. I couldn't walk away from my family's problems, but I could walk away from these. It felt great. I would look for some type of work that didn't demand so much of my time.

Several months later, I got a job evaluating pre-school children with developmental delays. It was a perfect part-time job. I made an appointment with the parents and did a series of activities with the baby to determine problem areas. After doing the evaluation, I submitted a report with scores in different developmental areas, with the child having to score below a certain percentile to qualify for special education services.

Having gone through this with Jordan, I developed a particular interest in early childhood intervention programming. I enjoyed both the interaction with the babies and the mothers and found this work fulfilling. Unfortunately, after two years, the program changed to only full-time work. I didn't want to commit again to a forty-hour workweek.

I wasn't sure unstructured time would be good for me. With-out as many distractions in my life and free time to think about life and my life, in particular, I became introspective. With no previous writing experience, I started expressing myself through poems. Strong feelings were coming out of me, flowing onto the paper with little effort. They were free verse, with the first one being about Jordan. I submitted it to a publication that promotes advocacy for people with disabilities, with submissions from both those with limitations and parents with special needs children. My first poem was published.

For the Joy of Jordan

Silence
Green eyes talking
Walking, pacing
Smiling
Twirling, touching
Staring, smelling, searching
Exploring the world with limitations

Multi-Handicapped ...
Mentally challenged
Language impaired
Autistic
Hard words used to describe his condition
Stick in my throat and my mind.

Perhaps seeing the world through rose-colored glasses
A different perspective
Known only to him.

Through the stages of my life ...
A gift
A burden
A challenge
A lesson

How do you express such deep mixed emotions?
For the joy of Jordan

I later completed thirty-two poems, going back to childhood memories of *Big Daddy's Camp, My Great Aunt Lula, Yesterday* (the Beatles concert), *From Hot Pants to Hot Flashes, The Vacation* (about my childhood vacation to Florida), *Rise and Shine* (a saying my mother used to wake us in the mornings.) It was cathartic. It helped me purge a lot of feelings I was holding inside.

In 2007, Luke got his act together and decided on his own that he needed to stop drinking. He was finding it harder and harder to function when he drank. I was cautiously hopeful. He needed a job to start making money. I suggested he apply to a CNA (certified nursing assistant) program so he could pursue a caretaking position. He completed the course and began working with a severely handicapped young man, who was Luke's age, living at home with his parents. Luke was being responsible, and the young man and his parents praised him for his patience and compassion. It was great to hear the positive comments.

Since he was sober, we were allowing Luke to live with us again. But this put a lot of pressure on everyone. *Is he getting up on time? Is he coming home tonight? Is he going to be able to stay sober?* Many of Luke's friends had moved on in life, getting married and having children, so he was spending much of his time with us. I was beginning to think he was starting to see the light out of the dark tunnel he had been in for eleven years.

There were positive signs that maybe he was ready to change his life. I wanted him to consider trade school to acquire some specific skills, leading to a job and possibly a career. He applied to our local community college and was accepted. He enrolled in general courses and a drama class. After receiving his schedule, the drama class wasn't listed.

He went to the drama department the next day. The heads of the department, Sherry Landrum and Rex Knowles, a husband and wife team just happened to be in the office.

"I was just wondering if you could tell me why the drama class I signed up for isn't on my schedule."

"Well, unfortunately, we didn't have enough people interested, so we canceled it," Sherry responded.

Rex added, "We do have a two-year professional acting program here at Chatt State that you might be interested in. You would get a certificate when you finish."

"That sounds interesting," Luke replied.

Sherry then said the words that hooked him, "You're tall, good looking, and you have a good strong voice. You'd be great."

That's all he needed to hear. He dropped his other courses and signed on for the two years Professional Actors Training Program. I was dismayed with what I thought was his latest bad decision.

The program enrolled thirteen students, many of whom were much younger than Luke. He was in class daily with assignments and tests. He was more motivated than I had seen him in a long time. It was good to see the light and sparkle in his eyes again. *Maybe this isn't such a bad thing.* He got a part in a local community theatre play called *The Dead Guy*. Dan questioned him, "What part did you get, the dead guy?"

He was in several productions with his classmates throughout the year. It was great to see him being productive. I was trying to be supportive, but where was this all going to lead. At least he was staying clean, as far as I knew. He finished his first year and seemed more like himself. He applied for student loan money and used it to pay the rent for an apartment near downtown. I bought various necessities to help him, shopping at Goodwill to buy pots and pans, plates, glasses, and a few pieces of furniture.

Once again, he was on his own. Fingers were crossed, breath was held. Each time this happened, my hopes were high. *Maybe this is the time when it all clicks.*

Finally, life was going well for all of us. Luke had been sober for almost two years. I was proud and happy for him. He seemed more alive, and we enjoyed his company again. Jordan was healthy and staying busy at Orange Grove, and Alex was finishing up his junior year in college. Dan and I were enjoying being under less parenting pressure.

I decided it would be fun for the four of us to go on a family vacation and stay at our neighbor's house in Florida. I was excited about the trip, knowing we needed time together in a relaxed setting. There hadn't been any drama for a while. I pictured us relaxing together by the ocean and having dinners on the deck of the beach house. I bought new beach towels, plenty of sunscreens, and everyone's favorite foods. I couldn't wait to get there.

The car was packed and ready to go. Alex was already home for spring break, and I asked Luke to stay at our house the night before since we were leaving early the next morning. I didn't want to start the vacation with him possibly being late or not showing up at all. His car wasn't there when I went to bed. I kept waking throughout the night. *Where is he? Is that him coming in? Is he already asleep downstairs? Will he be here when we're ready to leave in the morning?*

After waking from a restless night, I looked out the window. His car wasn't here. *Oh, no.* I went downstairs to the boy's bedroom, and he was sound asleep in his bed. I was momentarily relieved. Alex was in the twin bed beside him. *Well, this is weird.*

"Where is your car?"

He rolled over, looking disheveled and disoriented, "Uhh, I'm not sure."

"What do you mean, you don't know where your car is?" I asked, my voice rising, not believing what I was hearing.

He was still half asleep. He kept closing his eyes as if he just wanted to go back to sleep. I could smell alcohol on him.

I felt light-headed and sat down on the bed beside him.

"Are you drinking again?" I asked, fearing his answer.

"No, why would you think that?"

"Well, maybe because you don't remember where your car is."

By this time, I was lecturing and carrying on like the crazed mother that I was. I went upstairs and told Dan what was going on. He was livid. He went downstairs and jerked Luke out of bed. He pulled him into the bathroom.

He shoved his face into the mirror and shouted, "Look at yourself in the mirror. Look what you're doing to this family."

We were both at our wit's end. But I also felt like this kind of behavior only made situations worse. I hated any sort of negative family drama. But nothing I was doing was working, so maybe it was just what Luke needed. A good wake up call. Alex was crying as he watched this interaction between Luke and Dan.

Luke eventually pieced together the night before and remembered where his car was located. Alex took him to get it. Now it was time for us to leave on our family vacation. *Oh, this is going to be fun.* We drove in complete silence for eight hours, stopped to eat lunch and never said a word to each other. Dan told me later that Luke went behind the Subway to throw up.

When we got to the beach house, we were all glad to have some space to ourselves and our thoughts. *Maybe this wasn't such a good idea after all.* I busied myself by putting away things in the refrigerator. I noticed the cup Luke had been sipping from on the trip down was sitting on the shelf. I had assumed it was water since he obviously had a hangover. I was suspicious and checked it out. *Oh my God ... this is beer.*

After this happened, I told everyone that we needed to talk in the living room. This was impacting all of us. I was going to clear the air.

"Were you drinking beer on the way here?" I asked.

"No, why would you think that?"

"Because the drink you sipped on all the way down here is in the refrigerator, and it has beer in it."

"Well, yeah, I guess, I was," he responded nonchalantly.

I hated his lack of emotion, which appeared to be a lack of concern for anyone but himself. I was full of emotions – frustration and anger.

"I'm paying for this vacation for you, and you're not going to drink while we're here. If you want to continue to drink, you can go home. I'll take you to the bus station here, and you can go back to Chattanooga tonight."

He stared back at me, considering his options.

"So what do you want to do? I'm not paying for this trip to Florida for you to come down here and drink. It's not going to happen."

"Oh, ok, I won't drink if that'll make you happy."

Dan and Alex sat calmly while I talked to Luke. I did most of the talking. I wasn't calm. I couldn't believe Luke would do this after the altercation with Dan before we left. I couldn't believe he would throw away the two years of sobriety that he had worked so hard to attain. I couldn't believe how enraged I felt.

Luke was an alcoholic and needed our sympathy and compassion, but I couldn't see beyond my anger and frustration. This time I was the one who was fed up. He wasn't going to ruin this vacation for me.

We carried on with the vacation. All of our heightened emotions settled down, and we spent time at the beach together. We had brought our dog, Sadie, and she was a good distraction as the boys played with her in the sand. Luke got his usual sunburn. Alex went out of his way not to drink in front of Luke. He didn't want to cause any resentment.

We went to dinner and tried to act like that happy family that lived down the street. We watched the summer Olympics when Michael Phelps won all his gold medals. I couldn't imagine being his mother and the pride she must have felt watching his performance. I wanted to feel something other than disappointment in Luke.

The hope I had felt during the past two years when Luke was sober now seemed gone. We had already sent Luke to rehab, and he was back in denial. I was losing hope that he could ever change. I loved him more than ever. I knew he was struggling with addiction and its consequences. I knew I wasn't always saying or doing the right thing. I knew I couldn't shame him into sobriety. I was slowly learning that he had to do this on his own, at his own pace. I just didn't have much patience at this point.

We all survived the vacation, and now it was fall, so Alex was going back to school in Knoxville. I was trying not to dwell on what was happening with Luke. He was starting his second year in the acting program, but I didn't have much confidence he could finish if he was drinking. I didn't want to lose contact with him altogether, but

I was better off not knowing what was going on. A constant knot in the pit of my stomach left me waiting for the next inevitable event to happen. Knowing was terrible, and not knowing was just as bad.

Alex was doing well in school and still dating his high school sweetheart Melissa. He continued to be responsible and active in sports. I was grateful it seemed he was not going to go in the same direction as Luke. Having this important relationship with Melissa seemed to have a stabilizing effect. She was always included in our family gatherings, and I felt their relationship was getting more serious.

Christmas was soon approaching and a big distraction for me. As always, I spent days creating a Christmas wonderland inside our home. I could live inside the perfect holiday dioramas for a few weeks. I called Luke about his plans for Christmas Eve and morning, telling him I was planning a family meal for Christmas Eve after we attended mass. He said he would join us at church, spend the night, and be there for Christmas morning. Perfect.

I kept waiting and waiting throughout the mass. *Where is he?* He never showed. Alex went to a different church with Melissa and her mother, and they joined us for the meal afterward. I was trying not to show my concern and worry. *He'll come in later and be downstairs in the morning when it's time for us to open presents.*

On Christmas morning, I slowly walked downstairs to the boys' bedroom, full of trepidation. Luke's bed was empty. My heart sunk. I could have sat down on his bed and cried, but I didn't. There were other important people in my family.

Dan, Alex and I carried on with all the festivities, each of us opening our presents and having a big breakfast. *There is nothing you can do about it now, so don't ruin Christmas for Alex.* We brought Jordan home later in the day to join us. It was good to be around his innocence and joyfulness. He smiled and laughed and enjoyed all the food. He loved dancing to the Christmas music. Jordan was the lucky one in our family since he was not capable of understanding the turmoil we were going through with Luke.

I took all of Luke's presents from under the tree and put them in the hallway, trying to forget. Luke showed up later in the morning with a massive hangover and full of excuses. I didn't want to hear any of it. I didn't ask questions. I was tired of trying to talk to him about what he should and shouldn't be doing. I took a nap later in the day. Dan found an excuse to leave.

It was a depressing day for the LaGraffs. Later that night we pulled out our old family videos, which made me even more depressed. It showed a time when we didn't know how severe Jordan's disabilities were; Luke was still a fun-loving, little red-haired kid making faces at the camera, and Alex a precious baby. Dan and I looked so happy. *Who are these people?* I wanted to stay there for a while. I wanted to change the future. I wanted us all to be happy again.

Dan and I were both feeling the impact of all this stress. We couldn't discuss Luke without an argument. It was a problem we shared with no solution. Dan was coping by spending more and more time away and seemed unusually distant. He kept busy with various projects around our house and doing odd jobs for other people. We had sold the Sandbar restaurant after owning it for ten years, so he didn't have this to take up his time. He was involved in several civic organizations through the years and on the board of Jordan's school, Orange Grove, since he had enrolled at age six.

Although I was always proud of Dan's achievements, his involvement had left me alone to handle the kids at night when he was at meetings. Now there were no kids, so I was often at home alone.

But I didn't mind the time alone now that the kids were gone. It was nice to have a quiet and peaceful house. Dan was usually involved in some worthwhile cause, but he still enjoyed hanging with his buddies to "have a couple of beers."

I was thankful that Dan's drinking hadn't escalated. I had worried when he was younger that it might become more of an issue, but he had become more responsible about not driving when he drank too much. He gave up alcohol for Lent every year and had done so for thirty or more years. It gave him more perspective on his use and appreciation for drinking in moderation. But it seemed lately, with all the stress, he had been frequenting his favorite neighborhood bar, The North Chatt Cat, a little too often.

Just the year before, Dan had been in a serious accident, thankfully nothing involving alcohol. But it brought our lives to a temporary halt. He fell twelve feet onto a concrete sidewalk while trimming limbs away from a woman's house. We had plans to go to a friend's wedding later that night.

Dan was still away finishing the job. I was starting to get ready for the fun evening ahead of us when the phone rang. "Well, I don't think we'll be going to the wedding."

"What? Why not? What's wrong? Where are you?"

Without any emotion in his voice, he said, "I'm in the back of an ambulance."

I met the ambulance at the hospital, thinking since he was talking so clearly and being humorous that it couldn't be too serious.

"Your husband has some severe injuries. He has a broken pelvis. He has two broken vertebrae and two broken ribs," the doctor informed me.

He was pointing all this out on the x-ray.

"He will be non-weight bearing for three months. He will be going to rehab for ten days and will be confined at home for a while in a wheelchair."

I was getting light-headed listening to all this. *What does this mean for Dan's future? Is this a life-changing accident?*

"Will he be able to walk again?" I asked, feeling myself getting nauseous.

"I feel sure he will. He seems physically fit, and with therapy and following our orders, he should do fine."

I wanted to ask if we could take one of the nurses home with us. I knew I had a job ahead of me.

Dan spent two weeks in the hospital, three weeks at a rehab facility, and two months recovering at home. He was in a lot of pain but adamant about not taking much pain medication. Luke and Alex had never seen their father "down," as Alex put it. Dan didn't like being in a vulnerable position and was determined to get back on his feet. He worked out every day to keep his upper body strength intact. He pushed himself to regain some semblance of his old life.

We spent all our time together, with me taking him to all his appointments. I completely put my life on hold. *Do I even have a life anymore?* It seemed all I did was worry about my husband and kids.

Dan was out of work for three months doing what he could to work from home on the computer. With Dan being so well-liked, there were lots of cards and visitors. Everyone was concerned for him. I was there for him twenty-four hours a day, bringing his meals on a tray and attending to all of his needs. *And we didn't even say "In sickness and in health" in our wedding vows.* When we first found out how extensive the damage was, he remarked, "This will only make us closer." If that happened, it would at least be one positive outcome.

But a little over a year after his accident, we had never felt so far apart. I felt he was becoming more and more distant and spending more and more time away. Through the years, when I felt our relationship didn't feel right, and we weren't connecting, I would write my feelings down or ask to talk. I thought it was time to talk. It was January, and Dan always went on a winter camping trip with friends the weekend before the Super Bowl. We sat down a few nights before he left.

PART SIX

"It's impossible," said pride.
"It's risky," said experience.
"It's pointless," said reason.
"Give it a try," said the heart.
                    -Anonymous

Chapter 12

January 2009

As much as I needed to share my feelings with Dan, I dreaded it. We weren't good at open communication. When there was a conflict between us, we were more likely to say a few biting or sarcastic remarks, with one of us walking away, followed by several days of silence between us. I was good at just letting it go, not saying anything to rock the boat. But I knew it was time to clear the air. I planned a romantic dinner with candles, hoping to set the mood for openness and thoughtful dialogue between us.

"I haven't been feeling so good about our relationship lately. I know there's been a lot of stress around here, but we need to try to keep our relationship together. I haven't felt close to you in a long time."

"Yeah, I've been feeling it too. I don't know, Karen."

"You seem to find more and more reasons to go somewhere without me. And you don't seem interested in sex anymore, and that's the only time I feel important to you. I need more affection, more than just our good-bye kiss in the morning. I'm feeling lonely. We both need to be putting more effort into our marriage. Things just don't feel right."

I said what I needed to say, but he was non-committal. I was a little taken back by his response, "I don't want to hurt you, I don't know what I want."

"You don't know what you want. What does that mean?"

"Can we just talk about this when I get back from the camping trip? I've got a lot on my mind right now. I need time to think."

"Well, I've already had time to think, but yeah, it can wait."

While he was gone on his camping trip, I spent a lot of time thinking about what was said and what wasn't said. Valentine's Day was a few weeks away, so I picked out a unique card, one I thought was reflective of our relationship, and a box of candy. I was thinking of ways to make this Valentines' special. If I was asking Dan to put more effort into our marriage, I needed to do the same.

While Dan was gone, I needed something to occupy my mind rather than mulling over what our conversation meant. I decided to pick up my interest in making collages. It was time to pursue my creative side again. I wanted to honor my great aunt Lula, so I needed some pictures. I went to our attic and looked for an old trunk I had covered in flowered contact paper when I was fourteen. It held all my mementos from childhood.

When I opened it, the smell of my parents' house was overpowering, as strong as if it still sat in my old bedroom. I was overcome with nostalgia as I looked through my scrapbooks filled with keepsakes from my life with Robert. I found an envelope tucked away with two pictures of us kissing, selfies way back in 1969. I stared at them for a long time. This was over forty years ago, and I looked like a child, with my hair in dog tails.

Even after all the years, I still felt some strong emotions. I loved the part of my life I had shared with Robert. I still thought of our relationship as a gift I would have forever. But ours was a relationship not tested by time and life's ups and downs. I had put my feelings for Robert away years ago, tucked into a little box inside me, which I kept closed. The box cracked open that day, reminding me of my other life. But this was my life now, and I wanted it to be more. I would do all I could to make it better.

When Dan got home from his trip, I greeted him with a kiss and reached to hug him. He rolled his eyes as if to say, "Do we have to do this?" I felt rejected. I thought maybe the time away from each other would help. *Maybe he's just tired from his trip.* I let it go without saying anything, but it didn't go unnoticed. We avoided any more discussion until several days later when our situation seemed even more severe. The tension between us was palpable.

I insisted we sit down to talk again. I could tell he wasn't ready to do this again so soon. As soon as we sat down, he announced emphatically, as if he had thought this out ahead of time.

"I've been thinking about this, and we've been married thirty-five years; maybe that's long enough."

I was dumbfounded.

"What? Are you serious?" I wasn't sure I wanted to hear anymore. *So does he want a divorce?*

"I think I might like just to have the freedom to do whatever I want. You know, just go to Jamaica or someplace and raise some hell," he continued.

"You have a lot of freedom to be a married man. You go on trips with your friends, and you hang out at bars with your friends. You don't have to ask for my permission. You've never had to answer to me. You can go to Jamaica or anywhere else, and that's fine with me."

None of this was making sense. I was starting to feel panicky and knew I had to ask.

"What kind of freedom are you talking about? Is this about another woman? If it is, I don't want to find out about this from someone else."

"No," he assured me.

"Well, if this isn't about another woman, I don't know what it could be about. But if this is how you feel, I'll make a deal with you. I'll give you six weeks to be a free man without any obligation to me. You can come and go as you please. I'll move downstairs. I won't be cooking, buying groceries, or doing laundry. It's all yours. After six weeks, we'll see how you feel."

This arrangement suddenly felt like the right thing to do. I thought he was taking our relationship for granted. Maybe if I stopped doing everything I usually did, he would think twice about wanting out of the marriage. This would at least give us some time before doing anything we might regret later. He was off the hook. I went downstairs and cried myself to sleep. *What am I thinking? He should be the one moving downstairs.*

The next day was Friday, the 13th of February. I had never been superstitious, but I sure felt unlucky, and life was suddenly full of gloom and doom. I never imagined us going through this. After everything we had been through, he wanted to walk out.

I waited until he left for work before coming upstairs. I was stunned by all the sudden changes in Dan's feelings and how quickly my life was turned upside down. I walked around the house in a daze.

I called my sister. I needed to talk to someone to help me sort out my feelings. I told her what had happened the night before. Her son was also going through a divorce, so I hated to burden her with my problems.

"Do you think he could be having an affair?" she asked.

"I asked him, and he said no."

This level of trust was what I thought our relationship was about. He had said "no," and I believed him. We had no history of lying to each other, that I was aware of. I had always valued this aspect of our relationship. Dan seemed trustworthy.

After talking with Diane, I decided it wouldn't hurt to check our computer for suspicious emails, not expecting to find anything. Initially, all his mail looked innocent, but after checking in old deleted files, I kept seeing the same female name. There were no emails from her, but several Dan had sent to her. It was soon evident it was true. He was having an affair.

My heart lurched. I could feel it pounding against my chest. The adrenaline was pouring in as if I had just received a shot. My reality had just changed. The before and the after. *Why haven't I been more observant? How long has this been going on? Who is this woman?* I found her profile online and stared at her picture. I was dizzy with panic. This just didn't make sense.

The emails were not personal, but enough that I knew what was going on. Dan's fraternity brothers sometimes shared risque pictures or jokes from the internet, and he was forwarding them to her. He also referred to meeting her "at home," meaning her house. This comment tore at my heart. It was breaking.

I called him at work without any emotion in my voice.

"Do you think you could come back to the house this afternoon? I need to talk to you again."

"Sure, I'll come by after lunch," he said. He had no idea what he was about to face.

I was amazingly calm. I wasn't letting this information get past just being facts. The emotional tsunami was yet to come. I showered, got dressed, and put on make-up, waiting for Dan to arrive. There was plenty of time to think about the best way to approach this. I decided I would give him the opportunity to be forthright and come clean. But after he denied there being another woman the night before, I wasn't sure if he would be brave enough to do this.

I met him at the door, and we sat down in our sunroom where just the night before, we had discussed our relationship. A clipboard was in my hands with all the printed emails and pictures he sent to her. He didn't seem to notice.

"Do you have anything else you'd like to say about what's happening, anything from our discussion last night?"

"No, not really."

I stared at him. He was expressionless.

"Well, I need to ask you some questions. What is your relationship with Ella Cadswill?"

A slight hint of seriousness crossed his face. "She's just a friend."

He wasn't going to admit anything.

"And do you send female friends pictures like these?" I asked, showing him the stack of colorful lurid pictures. My sense of calm was disappearing.

"Well, sometimes, it depends on the friend."

"Well, what about this email stating you'll see her "at home?""

It sounded like they had made plans to meet "at home," meaning her house, for an afternoon tryst.

By this time, I was yelling. I'd never been so angry in my life. He continued to lie as far as he could take it, but there was no denying this. He said there was no reason to be yelling. I felt possessed.

"How long has this been going on?"

"A couple of months."

"How did you meet her?"

"She's the daughter of a friend of mine, a younger woman in her mid-forties. She's divorced with a couple of kids." He gave the familiar excuse, "It just happened."

No, it didn't just happen. You made a decision, and that's how it happened. Remember, love is a decision, and you chose not to love. You chose to lie and cheat.

Last night's discussion was now making much more sense. He was trying to end our relationship without me finding out so he could be with her. So this was the reason to "maybe not be married anymore, maybe thirty-five years is long enough." I was enraged.

"You think you're divorcing me? I haven't done anything wrong. You're not divorcing me. I'm divorcing you!" I shouted. This comment alone changed the course of what happened next. Now I was the one wanting the divorce.

He sat and stared. I could tell his mind was racing. He seemed to be looking through me.

"This is not about you. This is about me," he said. "You deserve someone better than me. I'm not a good person."

I had always thought of him as a good person. I never thought this was something he could do. I wanted to hear his pleas for forgiveness, his remorse for being such a jerk, him admitting this huge mistake, that he didn't want a divorce. But I heard none of this.

I asked a few questions.

"So, is this woman a big sports fan?"

"No," he replied. Dan had never understood my lack of interest in sports.

"So is she a big party girl?" I asked, since I'm not known to be a big partier like Dan.

"No."

After seeing the pictures he was forwarding to her, I was pretty sure what the big attraction was.

I couldn't take it anymore. I stood and grabbed my car keys. I didn't even know where I was going. I went into our bedroom and got the Valentine's card I had carefully chosen for our romantic Valentine's Day celebration. I took it to him and sarcastically said. "Here's your Valentine's Day card." It was full of sentimental statements about our love and how special it was to me.

We always displayed birthday and anniversary cards on our fireplace mantel. He read the Valentine's sentiments, then took the card and put it on the mantel, as if all was right with the world. This infuriated me. He certainly didn't break down and ask how he could make this up to me. Or ask how he could earn back my love and trust. Would I please just give him a second chance? This would cost him his dignity, and he wasn't giving up on that. His ego was at stake.

Who is this person? Not the person I thought he was. He had become someone I didn't recognize. He wasn't the guy who made me feel safe so many years ago. Suddenly I felt an immediate urge to get out of the house as if it was closing in on me. I went to Lee Ann's office, calling her in my car to tell her I was coming but didn't tell her why. I walked right into the bank and her office.

She knew something was wrong.

"What's wrong? What's going on?"

"Dan has been having an affair and wants a divorce," I said.

I shouldn't have been unloading on her, especially while she was working. Her eyes widened and a look of shock fell across her face. She helped me to a chair and closed the door. "Oh, Karen, I'm so, so sorry."

Skip and Lee Ann had gotten divorced four years earlier. Dan and I were sad and shocked their marriage ended. We often reminisced about our fun times together. Now, my marriage was falling apart.

The circumstances around their divorce were disturbing. Skip had been out of work for a while, and his father was very ill in Florida. He decided to go and help his mother care for his father and look for a job. Lee Ann was working as a bank branch manager here and was going to look into transferring there. Their two daughters were both grown. We had stayed close through the years, but since they had daughters and we had sons, we became involved in different circles of friends.

While in Florida, Skip got involved with one of his father's caregivers. They had an affair, and she got pregnant. She was in her late forties and already had a grandchild. It was devastating for Lee Ann and both girls. He stayed in Florida with her and their child, but they never married.

I had said to Dan when we discussed him wanting out of the marriage.

"I hope you aren't going to do what Skip did."

"No, that's not my style."

But he almost had, except for a baby.

So Lee Ann was furious to hear this news about Dan. I was shaking and talked non-stop, telling her what was going on.

"I can't believe this. I didn't think Dan would ever do something like this. I'm so mad at him. What was he thinking? Do the boys know yet?"

"I don't know how I'll ever tell them. I don't think I can do this."

"I remember how hard it was to tell my girls. Oh, Karen, I hate that this is happening."

I left her office, not knowing where I was going, certainly not home. I was completely disoriented. I didn't know what to do with myself. I drove to our friends, Dennis and Shelly, and went through the whole story again. They knew us before we married and were shocked at this news. They encouraged me not to divorce, saying it would be financially devastating. But was that a reason to stay?

I eventually went home to an empty house. It felt like someone had died. Life had given me another "gift," another life experience I thought, at my age, I had avoided. Dan was sixty, and I was fifty-eight. I wasn't sure I could mentally and emotionally handle another loss. As my counselor told me later, your response was a cumulative effect from the trauma you've experienced. Even suggesting I was going through a form of PTSD. I sure felt like I was going through a war.

Later that evening, Debra, a friend from my college days, stopped by to show her support. I was already reaching out to friends because I knew I'd never make it without some support. We sat on the couch and talked. The anxiety was coming in waves and taking my breath away, as if I was drowning. We heard a car outside, and I realized it was Dan. He came bounding into the living room as if nothing was wrong.

"Are you helping her out?" he asked Debra, and continued through the house.

"I don't need any help," I lied.

She quickly decided it was time to leave, and I was alone with Dan. He wasn't feeling how I was feeling. We didn't say another word to each other. He stayed at the house and slept in our guest bedroom. He was snoring so loudly that I wanted to go in there and put a pillow over his head, for so many reasons.

My immediate concern was how and what to tell Luke and Alex. Jordan was the lucky one again since he wouldn't have to deal with any of this mess. I thought about it a long time and decided it was Dan's job to tell them. I told him I wanted him to tell the boys he had been having an affair, and we were getting a divorce, and I wanted us to be together as a family when he did this. He agreed.

For the next few days, my mind was going over, again and again, all that was said and done, trying to make sense of any of it. I felt like I was at the top of a roller coaster waiting for the drop, except this went on for days, even weeks. I couldn't eat or sleep. I walked around in a daze. I was jittery and would jump every time my phone rang. During the day, I would try to escape by watching TV or reading, but I couldn't concentrate.

At night, I would finally go to sleep on the couch and wake up in the middle of the night and go to our bedroom. I would wake up early after a fitful night's sleep, and all the thoughts would start again. I had to get up and start moving. I felt that if I didn't keep moving, the weight of my thoughts would suffocate me. They were heavy and pulled me down to a place I didn't want to be. Nothing was the same.

Dan and I had experienced troubled times dealing with Jordan's autism and Luke's alcoholism. Our marriage had been tested going through these circumstances, and I thought we had come through intact. Many marriages wouldn't survive one of these family circumstances, much less both of them. I felt like I had been left behind, and he had turned toward another woman. I felt abandoned. Just like you might feel if your parents suddenly told you they didn't love you anymore and adopted another child to replace you. I had been replaced.

After several days, I told Dan it was time for him to move out. He moved temporarily in with a single friend, a neighbor, one street away. I was surprised he didn't move in with the new woman in his life. We arranged to have a family meeting at our house the following Sunday afternoon at one.

Now it was time to involve the boys in all this. I called Alex at college. Our conversation started with our usual chit chat. My heart was breaking over having to break any of this news to him. I knew this was the beginning of a change in his world.

"Alex, I was wondering if there's any way you could come home this weekend?" Knowing I was going to be giving him life-shattering news, it was hard to make my voice sound normal.

"Why? I've got some plans and a lot of school work to catch up on."

"Well, I hate to have to ask you to change your plans, but it's pretty important. There are some family issues we need to discuss with you and Luke. I don't want to discuss it over the phone."

"Could it wait until next weekend?"

"It's important you come as soon as possible."

"Well, okay, I'll be down sometime on Saturday," he said, without asking any more questions. I could feel his suspicion over the phone. He told me later he thought one of us possibly was dealing with a serious health problem. He was suspicious and called Luke to see if he knew what was going on.

Luke knew exactly what was going on. He had run into Dan at the North Chatt Cat the day after our confrontation at the house. It was Valentine's Day. Dan was in his car, and Luke was sitting on an outside deck. Dan told him to come out to his car so he could talk to him. Luke thought Dan was going to take him to rehab again, so Dan had to give Luke the keys to his car to persuade him to get in the car.

Dan came right out with the devastating words.

"I need to tell you something. I don't want you to hear it from someone else. I've been having an affair, and your mother and I are getting a divorce."

Luke told me later that he felt his life change – his own before and after. He said he just wanted out of the car as fast as he could. He didn't ask questions. He hardly remembers anything that he said or did after this shocking revelation. He said he woke up the next morning in his apartment and found broken glass where he had thrown things around in his rage.

So when Alex called Luke several days later to see if he knew anything about what was going on, why he needed to come home so suddenly, Luke told him the reason. Just what I was hoping to avoid. I wanted the boys to hear it from Dan, and I sure didn't want Alex to find out over the phone. Alex immediately drove home instead of waiting until the weekend. And I was furious with Dan.

The family meeting was as hard as I was expecting it to be. We all took our places in the living room. The places we all sat when we watched TV together. But everything was different today. The anger I was feeling made me feel strong. I spoke first.

"First of all, I didn't appreciate you telling Luke about this at a bar. I told you I wanted you to tell the boys with us together. When I called Alex to ask him to come home, he called Luke, and he told him everything. Why couldn't you have at least done what we agreed on?"

"Well, I just ran into Luke at the bar and thought I'd tell him. What difference does it make?"

"It was important to me, but I guess that's not important to you anymore."

The boys had never witnessed us having any big arguments, and now we were telling them we were divorcing. Dan and I didn't have a relationship that involved fighting or insulting one another, so this kind of confrontation was new to us all. Neither of us was yelling, but there was obvious tension and anger between us. I wanted to keep things calm, but our voices were full of emotion.

Dan told the boys, "Your mother and I don't have much in common anymore."

I stared at him, thinking, *Oh yeah, only thirty-five years of shared experiences.*

"I guess you could say we've grown apart."

I told the boys how I discovered what was going on. We discussed some of the contents of the emails.

He had sent Ella an email, "Happy Anniversary Baby."

I questioned him about this, "What does that mean?"

"We'd been dating a couple of months, and I just sent it for fun. It's from a song,"

"So you remember the exact date you first met her? That's strange since you can't even remember your sons' birthdates." I questioned him, "When is Luke's birthday? And Jordan's? And Alex's?"

He couldn't tell me any of the boys' birthdates. Alex got up and left the room. He was crying. We all sat in silence as we waited for him to rejoin us.

"That's what it feels like to be deeply hurt," I said to Dan. He had no idea the pain this was causing the three of us. Now he was the one in denial.

Before ending the family meeting, Dan asked the boys if they had any questions.

"Is the affair over?" Luke asked.

"Yes, it's over."

"Was this your first affair?"

"Yes, this was my first affair," Dan said.

I wasn't so sure he was telling the truth.

The boy's friends had always admired Dan as a gregarious life of the party kind of guy. Alex asked him, "What are my friends going to think?"

Before leaving, Dan told the boys, "Your mother and I are going to become business partners. I'll continue to do my part financially and help out however I can."

So I'm a business partner now. This is how you end a thirty-five-year marriage. So neat and tidy.

The meeting ended with Luke announcing, "I'm hungry. I'm going to fix a sandwich." He showed no real emotion like Alex. Luke's feelings had become even more repressed since becoming dependent on drugs and alcohol. But I knew he was deeply hurt by what his father had done.

After the boys left the room, Dan told me he would be in touch concerning our finances. I was still feeling surprisingly strong. I thought I stood up for myself during the meeting and didn't appear to be falling apart. I didn't shed one tear. That didn't last long.

After the family meeting, Luke left to go to his apartment, leaving just Alex and me alone in the house. He told me he was also having trouble sleeping, so we headed to the pharmacy to get some type of sleep medication. We came home to watch a movie, trying to distract us from what we were both experiencing. Suddenly, the front door flew open.

"Hey, you got any beer here, Mom?" It was Luke, all wild-eyed and staggering. I jumped up. He was drunk.

I couldn't face any more drama. I was emotionally drained.

"Oh, Luke. Please no. There's no beer here. What are you doing?" I asked as he made his way into the kitchen.

"I'm here to get beer." Alex started pulling on Luke, trying to get him back out the door. They struggled, pulling a six-pack back and forth between them.

"Man, leave me alone. I need this beer."

I was trying to reason with him.

"Luke, just stay here, and please don't drink any more beer. You're only making things worse."

Alex and Luke were yelling, shoving each other out through the door and into the yard.

"You idiot, leave it here," Alex yelled.

I should have known this was how Luke would handle this shocking news. He left without the beer. And Alex and I were left with our frustration and anger.

Later that night, I sat down and wrote Ella another email. I had sent one shortly after finding out about the affair. I wanted her to know I knew what was going on. I didn't know what she knew about Dan and me and our relationship.

"I have known Dan since I was 19 and he was 21. We have been married for thirty-five years. We have three sons, Luke, 31; Jordan, 28; and Alex, 23. I hope the thrill you and Dan are getting out of this affair will be worth tearing apart our family."

I got no response.

I sent another one after our family meeting, "I wish you could have been here to see our youngest son, Alex, crying over what has happened to his family."

She sent an email back, "Leave me alone."

I knew how Luke would cope with all this, but what about Alex? When he left to go back to school on Monday, he told me he would start counseling. I was worried about him. He was a sensitive person, just like Luke. He was just as upset over what was happening with Luke as he was about what was happening between Dan and me. I was so happy he had Melissa with him in Knoxville. He was going to need her support.

I was fifty-eight years old and had never lived alone. I didn't want to start now. It wasn't because of the fear of a robbery or intruders. It was the emptiness I felt that scared me. I had stayed home alone many times when Dan traveled or was on a trip with friends or family. It never bothered me. I had always enjoyed my time alone. But this time, there was a different feeling of being alone. It was the same emptiness I experienced many years before when I lost Robert so suddenly.

I was relying on several close friends to help me cope at home by myself. They would try to get me to relax with a glass of wine. I was barely holding myself together. It was hard just getting up, eating, getting dressed, and showering. I knew if I had any alcohol, I would lose myself. Maybe start crying and not be able to stop.

Every night loomed ahead of me. I stayed up late, trying to get sleepy but had trouble falling asleep. I felt like someone had given me amphetamines. My thoughts raced, and my heart felt truly broken. The single pillow on our bed haunted me. The smell of Dan's clothes still in the air made me long for him. The room felt diminished. The silence in the house was loud. I would curl up in a fetal position trying to protect myself from this new reality. I finally asked Luke if he would mind staying with me until I could get a handle on my emotions. I thought maybe this might help him, too.

After several more days, as reality sank in, I was despondent. My whole sense of safety and continuity in life felt disrupted. Even my dog, Sadie, seemed to know something was not right as she stood in front of me staring while I fell apart. I felt so broken. I didn't want to go through this. I cried inconsolably. Deep sobs were coming from me that I hadn't experienced in forty years.

Death had a finality to it, but this kind of grief was different. I found myself in a panic every time I considered another question about my future: *Will I need to go back to work? Will I have to move into an apartment? How will we divide all our assets? Do I need to get a lawyer? What is this going to do to Luke? Will the boys still have a relationship with their father? Will Dan marry Ella and the boys have a step-mother?*

One morning, about a week later, it was all too much. My body started responding physically to this flood of emotions. I started shaking uncontrollably, my fingers tingling, and feeling light-headed. I couldn't catch my breath and started hyperventilating. *What's happening to me?* I couldn't calm down. I was scared. I called my doctor, and he recommended I go to the emergency room.

I was in no condition to drive myself. Luke was downstairs asleep, but I didn't want him to see me like this. I called three friends, but none of them answered their phone. No one was around to help. This only increased my panic. I certainly couldn't call Dan. *Now, what do I do?* Out of fear and desperation, I called Ross, my friend Melissa's husband, describing my situation, and he came to the house. He was at a loss as to what to do.

Just after he arrived, my friends showed up after receiving my desperate messages on their phones. Suddenly Ross, Lee Ann, Melissa, and Debra were standing over me trying to decide what to do. I felt like a wimpy, broken-hearted, rejected wife. I wasn't feeling strong anymore. I was feeling helpless and hopeless.

Lee Ann drove me to the hospital with my other friends following. I found myself in the emergency room, rattling on to the staff about my husband and his affair.

"Are you married?" I asked the male nurse taking my blood pressure. "I hope you never do what my husband did. He had an affair. This is what happens to people when they find out," I managed to say. I was still crying hysterically.

He didn't know what to say. I felt like my body, and now my mind had been taken over by a strange person I didn't recognize.

My blood pressure was high, so they kept me and planned to run other tests to be on the safe side. I knew this was all a result of the week of hell I had been through. After giving me medicine to help me relax, and a warm weighted blanket, I calmed down. I finally got relief from the panic attack, although no one ever called it that. I was drained.

Lee Ann was upset with Dan over all that had happened, and now this. She called him to tell him I was in the hospital and let him know she felt it was his fault.

I had finally regained some control and stopped crying. I was waiting for the doctor to release me if all the tests were negative. I was breathing normally again, dozing on and off when I looked up and saw Dan standing beside my bed. I imagined him saying,

"Honey, I'm so sorry for all this pain I've caused you. I hate seeing you like this. You didn't deserve any of this. I'm willing to do whatever to keep our marriage together. How can I ever make up for what I've done?"

He said, "Do you know the results from the tests yet?"

"There's nothing wrong with my heart. It's just broken." I managed to reply. An appropriate cliché for what was going on at the time. I knew there was a condition called "broken heart syndrome," so maybe this was my diagnosis. It sure felt broken. Dan stood and stared at me.

"Do you want me to stay?"

"No."

He turned around and walked out.

That afternoon I was home with a prescription for anti-anxiety medication. I knew I needed someone other than a friend to talk to, so I called our priest and made an appointment. I called Diane in Florida, and she suggested I leave town and fly down for a few days to get away. This sounded like a good idea. I was ready for whatever might give me a different perspective on what was happening. The night before the trip, I went to the priest and unloaded lots of thoughts and feelings. I went home and packed. I left my wedding ring at home.

Diane wasn't prepared for my state of mind. As soon as I walked into her house, I broke down crying. It felt so strange not having Dan to call to say, "The flight was great. Diane picked me up, and we're at the house now. I'll call you later in the week." This is what I normally would have done. But nothing felt normal now. Later, Diane told me I had an aura of sadness surrounding me. She could feel my despair from the way I walked and talked.

Before I left for Florida, I searched several online websites looking for information to read. *How do I get through this? Does everyone who goes through infidelity feel like I do?* I ordered books with titles I thought might help. One book caught my attention, *My Husband's Affair Became the Best Thing That Ever Happened to Me,* by Anne Bercht. I didn't know if this might mean she moved on with her life and found happiness as a single woman, or it helped her to have a better marriage. I spent much of my time at Diane's reading, hoping to gain more insight, more perspective to give me enough strength to survive.

My sister and I walked every day. The movement and talk seemed to help. She was sure we could work this out and get back together. I wasn't so sure. I didn't tell Dan I was going to Florida, so I decided I should send an email letting him know Luke was staying at our house. I started sharing my feelings with him through emails.

After talking with Diane and learning more about affairs from several of the books, I let Dan know I was willing to look again at our relationship. I wasn't sure I wanted a divorce after all. I knew I still loved him despite all that had happened. I sent long heartfelt emails, and I would get a couple of lines from him without much feeling. He said he wasn't sure what he wanted. He was confused. He made an appointment to see the same priest I consulted.

My sister and I usually find time to shop when we are together. I was not the least bit interested. I was so preoccupied I couldn't even watch TV or movies. I was not a fun house guest.

Early on Sunday, before I was flying back home on Tuesday, I checked my email to see if I had gotten a response from Dan after sending him another email. I saw an address that was Ella's, with an email sent to Dan, forwarded to me. *Now how did this happen?*

I was curious and could immediately feel the anxiety building as I read what she wrote. It was titled Our Final Sweet Goodbye. *I will be here for you if it takes five days, five months, or five years. I have never been as happy as I have been in the last 13 months. If you go back to her, you will regret it.*

There was more, at least a half-page love letter to Dan. He had told her he needed time to think things through and wouldn't be seeing her for a while. He went to her house for their "sweet goodbye" and one last intimate evening. This was a much more serious relationship than I had thought. She was not going to let go of him easily, calling him her soulmate.

It was brutal reading what she wrote to Dan. He was my husband. I printed the email. I staggered down the stairs to show my sister.

"What's wrong? What happened?" she asked, wondering why I was suddenly so distraught.

It was hard to talk. I felt like I had been punched in the stomach, my heart racing. "I just got this email. It's what Ella wrote to Dan. It's all about their relationship. He lied. He told me it was only going on for a couple of months. They've been seeing each other for thirteen months. Just read this, you won't believe it."

I sat on the steps, my head in my hands, feeling the blood drain out of me. I was once again in panic mode. My sister and her husband didn't know what to do.

I called Dan. I hadn't stopped crying yet.

"Why did you send her email to me?" I wailed.

"What email?" he asked.

"The Final Sweet Goodbye email."

"I didn't send it to you. I wouldn't do that. She must have forwarded it to you."

"So you went back to say goodbye? Why did you do that? You told the boys and me the affair was over."

"I felt like I owed her that."

Later, I thought of so much I wish I had said. "What about your wife? What do you owe her? The truth?"

"Karen, it's over now with her. I'm so sorry you had to read that. I didn't send it. I'm looking forward to you coming home so we can talk," he said.

I didn't know what to think. This complicated everything. I had extended an olive branch by telling him I wanted to reconsider getting a divorce, but that was before reading this email.

I was soon on my flight home to see what could be done to our damaged relationship. This was the first flight I ever remembered not having trip anxiety. I was hoping maybe the plane might go down. It would be easier dying than facing what was waiting for me at home. The grief and depression seemed to be radiating from me, permeating the entire plane. I sat and stared ahead for two hours.

I had made arrangements with Luke to pick me up at the airport. But he called Dan after we talked and told him he thought it was a better idea for him to pick me up. He told his father, "I think the sooner you guys talk, the better."

I came out of the terminal thinking Luke was late to pick me up since I didn't see my car anywhere. Then I saw Dan standing beside his car. He looked unsure of himself, very unlike Dan. I stopped on the sidewalk and couldn't go any further. He came toward me and opened his arms. I leaned into him and started crying on his shoulder.

We both just stood there, not knowing what to do next. Finally, Dan said, "Luke wanted me to pick you up. We'll talk when we get back to the house." He loaded my suitcase, and I got in. *After thirty-five years of marriage, how can it feel so uncomfortable sitting next to him?* We drove back to our house in complete silence. I couldn't stop shaking.

~

It was early March, and there was a beautiful, lone, yellow daffodil in full bloom along our sidewalk when we arrived home. It seemed to be standing strong among the dormant grass and the dead leaves. I took this as a sign of possible renewal for our marriage.

We sat and talked for several hours. There was no yelling, some crying, some apologies, and more open communication than ever before. Dan took full responsibility for what he did. He never put any blame on me as far as the reason why this happened.

"I thought I was just having a fling, and I couldn't find a way out. I didn't want to hurt you. She was going to tell you if I broke it off. She wanted to get married. I always loved you."

I always loved you … I needed to hear those words. But how could he do all this to someone he loved?

I didn't immediately start questioning myself as to what I did to contribute to this situation. I was not the guilty party, but did I share part of the blame? We decided to go slowly and see how it went between us. He was still living with our neighbor.

We went out to eat that night. It felt strangely odd to be out in public together. I feared running into people who knew what had happened between us. *What if we run into her?* He picked me up like we were on a date and dropped me off after dinner.

"Do you want to come in?" I asked awkwardly.

"It's probably not a good idea. You go in and get a good night's sleep. I'll call you tomorrow." Once again, the world felt different.

We continued this way for several weeks. I was anxious when we were apart. But I felt a sense of relief when we got together at night after Dan finished work. We regressed to our dating days. We drank wine every night and rekindled our sexual relationship. I had read in several books and articles that women usually either go one way or the other when it comes to sex again after infidelity. They either don't want to have anything to do with their husband, or they can't get enough. I couldn't get enough.

I was trying to fill the huge hole this left inside me. Something had been taken from me. This was the only time I felt complete and safe. But it didn't make any sense. *Why am I acting like this?* I felt I was rewarding him for his bad behavior, but I couldn't help myself. I was shopping regularly, buying new sexy underwear and lingerie. We were reconnecting but weren't dealing with what had happened.

I was hyper-sensitive to everything Dan said or did. I was continually judging all his words and actions. We were having dinner together one night at the house, and afterward, he got himself a bowl of strawberry ice cream. I sat and stared at him and him back at me.

"Why didn't you ask if I wanted any?" I asked.

"I just didn't think about it," he replied.

"You only think about yourself, don't you?" I shouted. I didn't give him time to come up with any more reasons. The anger I felt was coming out.

"Why are you so selfish? It's all about you, isn't it? So I have to go get my own ice cream, or do I just sit here and watch you eat yours?"

By this time, I was crying, and he had taken his ice cream back to the kitchen, *How can he be so insensitive? Why does he only think of himself? Doesn't he ever consider how this makes me feel?* Everything was different now, even eating ice cream.

After two weeks of reuniting and a lot of tears, Dan said, "You're never going to get over this."

Two weeks and I was supposed to be "over it." I knew we needed couples therapy, and Dan agreed. I happen to see a well-known relationship therapist, Terry Real, on TV, working with a couple using a specific technique after the husband's affair. I found a therapist in Atlanta with experience using this method.

We scheduled an appointment in Atlanta for a three-hour initial evaluation. Three other two hours sessions followed this. *Oh, man, this is going to be intense.* Dan would often get defensive. He told the therapist and me, "I'm about 99% back into this relationship." He was worried about what I was going to require him to do to stay in the marriage.

The therapist said we shouldn't be living apart if we were going to work on staying married. She felt living separately regresses to a dating situation, and that is not real life. I was happy to hear this since I was not entirely comfortable with letting Dan back in my life so quickly.

It was painful to hear some of the details about the affair.

"She had a big king-sized bed, and we would just go there and hang out."

"She replaced pictures of her kids in her bedroom to pictures of us."

"Sometimes, I would mow her lawn just to help her out since she was a single mom."

Over and over, I heard words that made my heart break. This was brutal.

We later decided traveling to Atlanta was going to be too much. We told the therapist we were going to continue back in Chattanooga. I think Dan was relieved.

After going through another therapist who wasn't a good fit, I finally found one I connected with. She heard it all. I went back to my relationship with Robert, all the issues with Jordan, and the continuing saga with Luke. I liked going by myself, but I also liked it when Dan would come, and we could focus on our relationship. He was more comfortable opening up to this therapist. He felt safe with her.

Within two months, we were back living together. Alex and Luke were bewildered at us getting back together so quickly. I told them, "I'm just following my heart. I know I still love him." I felt deep inside that we belonged together, and I wanted to give our marriage another chance.

I didn't want to give up on our shared history of thirty-five years. *Do these feelings come from being replaced by another woman?*

No way is she going to take my man away. I can be just as sexy as she is. I can please him in any way she did. He is mine, and she is not going to take him away. Those insane feelings of jealousy I felt in high school had reared their ugly heads. I was too old for all this, but I felt it just as strongly as if I was sixteen again.

Ella texted Dan several times after we got back together. He showed them to me, which made me feel he was being open since he didn't respond. This proved to be too much for her. Now she thought she was being ignored.

I was trying to take care of myself, both physically and mentally, to cope with my new reality. One morning, I asked my friend Debra to walk. She was a good listener, and I had a lot to say. It was a beautiful spring day, and I was doing a pretty good job of taking one day at a time. I was beginning to have some hope for our continuing relationship and marriage. The exercise had kicked in some endorphins, and I was feeling more optimistic. When I returned home, I was still in my workout clothes when my phone rang,

"Is this Karen?"

"Yes."

"This is Ella Cadswill." There was a long pause on my part. Suddenly my heart was pounding. She could probably hear it.

All I could think to say was, "I don't know what to say."

"There are some things Dan hasn't told you about that I think you need to know."

The first words out of her mouth were, "Dan and I are deeply in love." *Oh my God, do I want to listen to this?* I didn't know if I was going to throw up or pass out. I got a pencil and a piece of paper and sat down. She spent the next forty-five minutes telling me all about their thirteen months together. I knew I would never remember it all, so I sat there, as if I was her secretary, writing it all down. She began when they first met and went through all their time together, every single thing she could think of. I sat there, stunned, and listened to it all.

At one point, I asked, "Didn't you know he was married?" As if she cared.

"Well, I didn't know at first, and when I found out, it was too late. I was already in love."

He had on a wedding ring. *How could you miss that?* I could feel myself getting lightheaded and knew this was not going to be good for me. I should have hung up, but I was too curious and wanted to find out exactly what went on between them. Dan would have never told me what she was telling me.

"We went on trips together." *How could this be? They took trips together. When? How could all this have gone on?* Dan and I had gone to a bed and breakfast in a small quaint town in Tennessee for one of our anniversary trips years before. I remembered the new lingerie I bought for the occasion and us eating breakfast in front of a cozy fire in mid-October. When I was out of town visiting Diane for her birthday, he took Ella to the same place one weekend in February, only one month after meeting her. I wonder if she bought new lingerie, too.

I was focused on writing everything down. I could have said to her, *"Yes, Ella, is there anything else you would like to add to your account of what happened? Do you have more incriminating evidence he is guilty? Could you give us more details to enhance the story? And what was he doing the night of September 17th, the day of his wife's birthday?"* But I said nothing. And she just kept going.

"We took a trip to Dan's hometown and Niagara Falls in September when Dan went to one of his class reunions," she continued. *What the hell?* I was dumbfounded. It was the same weekend as my fifty-seventh birthday. I was home alone.

"We stayed one night on the American side and one on the Canadian side. Our room overlooked the falls. He called it our honeymoon," she told me. *Honeymoon? … oh, my God.* It seemed every event she told me was a little worse than the last.

"He took me to his home town and showed me his old house, and we went to the cemetery to see his parents' graves." *… to Jack and Rita's gravesite. What was he thinking?*

It all sounded so intimate, worse than if he had taken her on a trip to Paris. I didn't react on the phone. I was speechless. But this didn't stop her from continuing to assault me with more crushing information.

Dan had planned a 60th birthday for himself the previous June. It was at a local barbeque restaurant, and he arranged to have two bands outside to celebrate. He handed out invitations for months, so the place swarmed with family and friends.

"Remember the night of his party? I stayed with him at the hotel that night," she said.

What the ... Holy shit ... don't tell me you were there? How much worse is this going to get?

This was the hotel where many of Dan's family and friends were staying. We had also rented a room and planned to spend the night after the party. But after it was over, I decided to go home because I had planned a brunch the following morning for the visitors from out of town. I needed to be home early to prepare the food. How perfect for the two of them.

As she went on and on, I could feel myself starting to panic. My hands were shaking so much I could hardly hold onto the pencil or the phone. It was all more information that I could begin to process. I knew I needed to hang up. I couldn't take much more. Every new revelation felt like being stabbed with a knife, again, and again, and again. With this much pain, how could I not be bleeding?

I told her I was going to have to hang up. She had a final question to ask.

"How could you not know he was having an affair when he came home with my smell?"

What do you possibly say to that? This was cruel. I couldn't speak anymore.

She finished by saying, "If he comes back to you, he'll be thinking about me." *Well, now, how am I going to live with this?*

By this time, Dan was in the driveway. Ella had called him at work to tell him she was going to call and tell me everything. He pleaded with her not to, but she wanted revenge. It was over between them, and she was not happy. He arrived just after I told her I had to go. I couldn't listen to anything else.

I could feel another panic attack coming on. I could barely catch my breath. Dan watched this all happening and didn't know what to do or say to me.

I couldn't discuss any of it. I had to rely once again on my anti-anxiety meds. *How many more times will I need these?* At least now, after two previous episodes, I knew what was happening. I went to bed, leaving Dan to watch TV. All this new information was heart-wrenching to me.

I lay in bed, waiting for the medicine to kick in. I wanted to be numb. I wanted to sleep. I wanted to believe that none of it was true.

We didn't talk until the next day.

I was still in a mental fog, but I had to know the truth.

I pulled out the list I had made.

"I wrote down everything Ella told me. It was horrible listening to her tell me all this stuff. It was … crushing. I just … I can't believe all this happened without me finding out about it."

I went through each thing she told me.

"Is this true?

"Yes."

"Is this true?"

"Yes."

I paused after everything I said to get my courage up to ask again. Everything was true. All this had gone on over thirteen months. My marriage would never be the same.

"Karen, I'm sorry about all of this. I did some terrible things. I was selfish. I hoped you wouldn't have to find out about any of it. I didn't know how to tell you. I thought it would be better if you didn't find out. I knew it was going to hurt you. This is all a mess, and I caused it all."

For several days afterward, I was in a deep depression. I tried to sleep, but when I would lie down, all the details played out like a record that was stuck. I went over and over all the information in my mind, not able to think about anything else. I heard her voice, saying the same things over and over.

Tossing and turning, night after night, I often got up and went to our living room where I could distract myself. Realizing I had gotten up, Dan would come in to find me stretched out on the sofa with a blanket, a book or magazine, and a box of Kleenex.

"Karen, come back to bed. You need to sleep."

"I can't sleep. That's why I got up. I'm going to try to read until I get sleepy. Go back to bed."

I just wanted to be alone.

I needed him to say words he was unable to say. He would try to console me but had trouble knowing how, since he was the one who had caused this pain. This kind of emotional rawness felt uncomfortable for both of us. What good would yelling, blaming, and accusing do at this point? We were going to need some serious counseling if we were going to get through this together,

Nothing was worse than trying to sleep next to Dan snoring when I was dying inside. I was tormented by all the intimate details Ella told me. Thoughts bounced around my head like balls in a pinball game, going from one event to another ... over and over, around and around. There was no way for them to escape.

I needed to be distracted from the intrusive thoughts, but when you're trying to sleep, all you have are your thoughts. It was impossible to think about anything else. I found myself silently repeating the *Lord's Prayer* and even, *Now I Lay Me Down to Sleep,* over and over, trying to get relief from hearing her voice in my mind. Anything to keep from obsessively ruminating over her phone call. This was torture.

A few weeks later, I remembered a couple of older women dancing with Alex and his friends beside Dan and me at his birthday party. The party that Ella came to before I knew what was going on. One of the women was dressed very seductively in an off-white, crocheted dress. You could clearly see her underwear through the dress. I had wondered who she was.

Several months after the party, I had given Dan a photo album of pictures I gathered from family and friends from the night of the birthday celebration. It was time to pull out the album. There she was, in her revealing dress, with the smuggest look on her face, as if to say, "I know something you don't know."

Chapter 13

May 2009

My life felt out of control. All I could do was ask God for help getting through this mess. *Give me hope.* I wasn't much of a believer in God's plans. Everything happens for a reason wasn't working for me. It didn't work when I was nineteen, and it wasn't going to work now. For many people, this gives great comfort, but I wasn't one of them. I felt God had nothing to do with all I had gone through. I wasn't questioning my faith or asking, "Why me?"

I identified with a quote by Anais Nin, "We don't see things as they are, we see them as we are." And I was a real mess at this point. Nothing was clear. I had come to terms with my struggles in my own way, through the filter of my personal experiences. So far, I had found ways to accept it all without bitterness or giving up on life. I thought I had gained strength and courage from it all, but this latest challenge had thrown me for a loop. It was unexpected, and the feelings were unfamiliar.

Our counselor suggested Dan and I arrange a day and a time to talk at home and limit the discussion to an hour. This advice was to prevent us from talking about it constantly and letting it drag on for hours. This was perfect for Dan because it prevented long, drawn-out sessions. Still, he would dread every Wednesday. I, on the other hand, would be spilling over with what I needed to say, but had to wait until Wednesday. I was always left with unresolved feelings all week.

When Ella called telling me all about her relationship with Dan, she also shared that she had pictures of the two of them.

"If you want to see them, I can send them to you."

I didn't have to think twice, "No, I don't need to see any pictures."

I had plenty of pictures in my head. I didn't need to see any real ones. I imagine she thought pictures would be more harmful than words.

But she found a way for me to see the pictures. Checking my email messages one morning, I noticed an email from my ex-sister-in-law with a message, "Sure was strange seeing a picture of your husband online with another woman."

What? This is strange. Why would Jan be sending this to me? I went to Ella's Facebook page, and there were pictures of them. Several from their trip to Niagara Falls kissing at a bar and one of "their romantic room over-looking the falls," as she described it. I found out later my ex-sister-in-law didn't know anything about the pictures nor did she have a gmail account where the message came from. Because my curiosity got the best of me, I ended up seeing the pictures.

Now I not only had words to try to forget, but pictures. There he was, kissing her at the end of a bar, probably after he told the bartender they were on their honeymoon. A picture of him standing in front of the falls with his light blue sweater draped around his shoulders. How happy he looked, smiling back at her.

Spring arrived, and we felt the need to get away. Get out of the city, away from people we knew. Maybe we could pretend we were other people, not people trying to mend a broken marriage. We agreed there wouldn't be any discussions during our week away.

Our neighbor offered his beach house in Florida. It was rather like our honeymoon, as we frolicked like newlyweds. We spent our days on the beach drinking "summer delights," the drink we fixed when we pretended to be newlyweds many years ago. We shared romantic dinners out or at the house and would head to the beach to watch the sunset. I took my sexy lingerie and used it all.

Back at home, I found it hard going out in public because I felt we were being judged. The news of Dan's affair had spread like crazy – some juicy gossip for everyone. When I thought we were getting divorced, I told everyone I didn't care who knew, except for my father. He was becoming more frail and didn't need to know and worry about me.

When I first learned about the affair and was so distraught, I also made phone calls to Dan's brothers and told them what was happening. I loved them as if they were my own brothers. It was hard to consider them not being a part of my life. I shared more than I should have but reasoned maybe they could talk some sense into Dan.

Dan's sister lived in Chattanooga, so when I called to tell her about the affair and gave her the name, she yelled, "Oh my God, I know her. I talked to her today." *What?* Susie was working as one of the receptionists where Ella worked, and since Ella had attended Dan's sixtieth birthday party, they had talked frequently since then. After my phone call, Susie never talked to her again.

Our boys dealt with our drama in their own way. Alex was finishing his undergraduate degree and going to counseling on campus. He was conflicted by all this family turmoil. I was grateful Melissa was there giving emotional support. He distanced himself from the family for a while and asked me not to mention Luke and his problems to him anymore. He was unsure about my decision to stay with Dan. Jordan was oblivious to it all, the lucky one.

Luke, on the other hand, was continuing to struggle with his demons. All that had happened between Dan and me had given him more reasons to escape with drugs and alcohol. Out with a friend one night, he was drunk and did something he regretted. He came to the house days later with an incredibly swollen and bruised hand and wrist. His middle finger was raised and crooked, and he couldn't straighten it.

"Oh, my God, Luke. What happened to your hand and your finger?"

"I hit a side mirror on a car."

"How'd that happen? Were you driving?"

"No, Chuck was driving, and I was waving at a friend and leaning out the passenger window. Chuck got too close to the car, and I nailed the mirror."

"Did you go to the doctor? It looks terrible."

"Naw, I don't have any insurance. But it hurts pretty bad. Do you think it could be broken?"

"Well, yeah, look at it. Something is wrong, or it wouldn't look like that." I replied, wondering how he waited this long without medical treatment.

I got him an appointment with my general practitioner, who determined his wrist was broken and referred him to a hand specialist. Surgery was required to straighten the finger.

As we left the hospital, the doctor gave me two prescriptions, one for pain and the other for infection. I decided since I was paying, I wouldn't fill the pain medicine.

"I didn't fill the pain medication. I decided since you waited so long to see the doctor, you could take a little pain. You can take Tylenol." I knew he didn't need to get addicted to opioids in addition to everything else.

"What? But the doctor prescribed it. He must have thought I needed them. Even if I don't take them, I could sell them."

"What? Are you serious?" I asked, trying to process what he said. He not only was admitting he thought this was reasonable but didn't seem the least bit hesitant to be suggesting it. *Who is this person?* Even though I was paying, he was mad I hadn't gotten it so he could resell it. I was baffled by his immature reasoning at age thirty-one.

～

In late May, both sons were graduating. We pulled ourselves together to be there for them. Alex was finishing his degree in recreational therapy, and Luke completed his coursework, earning his certificate in the acting program. Their graduations were one day apart.

There were finally positive events going on in our lives, and we wanted to celebrate their accomplishments. Luke dressed in a sport coat and looked extremely handsome at his little brother's college graduation. His finger was still in a brace but continuing to heal. Alex was finishing college before him, just as I had predicted.

We all attended Luke's graduation the next day and went out to eat afterward. It was a nice reprieve from all the negative energy. The following weekend we had a graduation party at our home and invited many of their friends and ours. I hadn't seen many of them since finding out about the affair, and I thought this would be a happy occasion to clear the air. Everything went smoothly – good food, good friends, good conversation, and good music. It felt wonderful to be celebrating something. Everyone was on their best behavior.

Dan and I were continuing to get out and have as much fun as possible. We always attended an annual riverfront music festival, so we decided to rent a hotel room near the event, go out for dinner, and make it a special occasion. We were seeing friends we hadn't seen in a while and enjoying ourselves.

We decided to check out a new bar near the event. We walked in, and the place was empty except for two people, Ella, and another man. I knew this would happen at some point.

"Well, there she is," Dan said.

That's all he had to say. I knew who he was talking about.

My pulse quickened, my whole body tensing. I wasn't going to be intimidated by her. I suddenly felt confident and empowered. We sat at the bar and ordered a drink. She was all over this man and seemed to be checking to see if we were watching. Ella was showing Dan she had moved on. I couldn't keep from staring at her. She had long brown hair, dark brown eyes, and big boobs. Very much the opposite of how I look.

So this is the woman who slept with my husband, I kept telling myself. Four months had passed since their affair ended. Dan kept wanting to leave, looking for the back door so we could slip out unnoticed. I was sort of enjoying this because I was with him and she wasn't. I insisted we finish our drinks and when I was ready to leave, I said, "We're going to walk out the front door with our arms around each other."

So we stood up, and he put his arm around my waist, and I put mine around his. We walked right past them and out the front door. I was back in high school again.

We saw Ella several more times during that summer, usually at an outdoor music concert. I remember what she wore every time. Seeing her caused a physical reaction in me ... racing heart, light-headed, a tightening in my chest, and nausea. It would take me several days to get over the feeling. It was as if the whole affair was a massive fire, and as time was moving forward, the fire was slowly burning down. But every time I saw her, it added fuel to the fire, and I was back at square one again.

Now that Luke was free from his school responsibilities, he had lots of unstructured time, which was not good for him. He was working as a waiter at a local restaurant, making ends meet as best he could. After completing the acting program, he and a classmate decided they wanted to go to LA to check out the acting scene. Luke had no money, but this didn't keep him from quitting his job and heading off on a wild and crazy trip to Hollywood. A decision made without thinking it through, which was typical for Luke.

With his friend driving, they left for California, stopping briefly in Dallas, where they stayed with my cousin, Kay. His friend was stunned at how far away it was and how long it took to get there, probably never having been out of the state of Tennessee. After several days of bumming around, his friend became disillusioned and decided he would fly home and ditch his car there. This left Luke with no way back. Two close childhood friends were living in LA, so he borrowed money from one of them, and after borrowing from another friend from home, he pulled enough together to fly back home.

Now he was back in Chattanooga without much going for himself. I continued to try to include him in our family get-togethers. That summer, one of Dan's brothers, Kevin, called to say he, and his wife, Susan, would be coming through for a visit. It was going to be awkward after the long email I sent him about Dan's affair. I'm sure he didn't want to know any details. I attributed this to me not being myself at the time. *Will I ever be my old self again?* I planned a nice meal, and even with some apprehension, I was looking forward to their visit. Alex was in town, so I also invited Luke.

Since Luke didn't have a car, Alex agreed to pick him up. They arrived at the house, and as soon as I saw Alex, I knew something was wrong. He had such a look of disgust. Luke was drunk.

Alex was upset, and I was furious. I made a decision he wasn't going to stay, driving him back to his apartment myself. We went on with dinner and tried to pretend all was well. We told Kevin Luke couldn't make it, he had other plans.

Later, as we sat on our back porch enjoying our guests and the beautiful summer weather, Luke showed up again. We heard him before we saw him. Now he was in worse shape than before, since he had had several more hours to drink. Dan got up from the porch and confronted him in our front yard. I came inside and was watching from the living room. I could hear everything that was said.

"I wanted to be here to hear what Uncle Kevin had to say to you about the affair," Luke told him.

"We aren't discussing that this evening. You need to leave," Dan said.

Luke got as close to Dan as he could.

"You're a fucking loser for fucking that fat bitch," Luke shouted at him.

Luke wasn't holding anything back tonight. I felt my heart sinking. Dan pushed Luke toward the gate and into the road.

"Go on, get out of here."

Kevin, his wife, Susan, and Alex and I peered out the window, watching this face-off between father and son. I wanted to cover my ears and eyes and pretend this wasn't happening. Luke stumbled away, mumbling words into the air. This quickly put an end to our relaxing summer evening.

With so many ongoing family issues, I needed to find ways to engage my mind again. I needed to be completely immersed in something so there wouldn't be room for any other thoughts. I was sick of all the negativity in my life.

The year before finding out about the affair, I had gotten involved in making mixed-media collages. I bought various art supplies and was continually thinking of new ideas. I was more excited about this than anything I had done in a long time. I applied and got accepted into a weekly community event, the Chattanooga Market. I displayed my work on Sundays and loved interacting with the public. Dan would go with me and help set up my booth. The profits from my sales were minimal, but money wasn't as important as expressing my creativity.

I was spending all my free time downstairs. The playroom was now a sort of art studio. I was in the middle of a piece depicting my mother as a child when I learned about the affair. From that point on, I lost all interest. The collage was still sitting there a year later. I couldn't finish it. My mind was so preoccupied that all my creativity had disappeared. I wasn't myself in so many ways.

Although I knew I needed to stay involved in an engaging mental activity, my body was refusing to cooperate. I began to experience the stress more physically, having recurring urinary tract infections and stomach issues. Although I had an appetite, I got full quickly. I didn't have room for both the stress and the food. I was as thin as I was in high school.

I found myself headed to the emergency room in the middle of the night after experiencing unusual pain in my abdomen. This resulted in having surgery to repair a hernia pressing against my intestines. I began to have morning headaches leading to repeated trips to various doctors, having a sleep study, and several brain scans. The headaches were determined to be tension related. I was going back and forth from the ENT doctor, the allergist, and the neurologist. I felt all I was doing was seeing doctors and started feeling despondent. When I broke down in my gynecologist's office, she encouraged me to start an anti-depressant. I was ready for help.

This was helpful in many ways. I started sleeping better, and it took the edge off the constant anxiety. I started feeling more positive. Dan and I were doing most of our social activities together but still enjoyed getting together with friends. As a young married couple, we began a tradition of having an annual Halloween party, but it ended when we celebrated Halloween with our kids. So we decided it was time to send out invitations and again go all out with costumes and decorations. We both love a party, especially at our home. I had nearly as many Halloween decorations as Christmas decorations.

I had an over-sized bra … about a 40DD, that I padded with fiberfill. It was always part of all my Halloween costumes. I had been Mother Nature, a motorcycle mama, a waitress, Dolly Parton, and other well-endowed women. When I was twelve and got my first bra, little did I know I wouldn't get much bigger than that 28AA. So every Halloween, I could pretend to be well-endowed.

This year I dressed as a policewoman, complete with handcuffs and a baton, long blonde wig, thigh-high black boots, and black leather mini skirt. Dan dressed as the devil, with a red bodysuit and horns, with a sign on his back, "The devil made me do it." We were attempting a little humor over our situation. Friends laughed, slightly uneasy.

It was a fun evening. Some friends came that we hadn't seen in years. I didn't want it to end. We were able to forget everything temporarily. A pause in all the drama. We laughed at our friend's hilarious costumes and danced on the screened porch. We weren't too old to have a good time.

Back in the real world, we were continuing counseling and working to restore trust in our relationship. I asked Dan to call me if he visited any bars. I had always given him the freedom to have a few beers with his friends. He was a man's man and thrived on the camaraderie of his friends. He usually asked if I wanted to join him. Sometimes I would, but most of the time he went without me. I knew our marriage would never make it if I forbid him to hang with his friends. Either he was going to have the integrity to do the right thing, or he wasn't. I wasn't going to be his mother or his babysitter.

If I had taken a piece of paper and written positives on one side and negatives on the other, it might have read like this. The positive side would start with Dan's great work ethic. He had worked his way up in the financial planning profession, selling retirement plans to small companies. He now ran his own business, LaGraff Retirement Systems.

He was always responsible with our money, never buying frivolous items, and making good decisions about saving money. He was generous with his money, always a good tipper, and treating people in service positions with respect.

He gave his time generously to Jordan's school, serving on the board for thirty years, one year as president, going to monthly meetings without complaint. He was always eager to help anyone in need.

Dan had a wonderful sense of humor. He took pride in our home and yard, working endlessly to keep everything in shape and working order. He was the most productive person I knew. I could barely write down a chore on a to-do list, and he had it done.

He had been a good father in many, many ways. He was always involved in their sporting activities and willing to drive them around town for social events. He didn't use his physical strength to intimidate them. He only had to use his voice. He didn't belittle them but encouraged them to do their best.

I asked the boys how they felt about their father growing up.

Alex said, "He always stood up for me. When I was being made fun of because I was so short, he always took up for me in front of my friends."

Luke said, "He always tried to make me accountable. He wouldn't let me get by with stuff."

Dan didn't have a lot of rules the boys had to follow, but two they remember well, "Don't use the word hate. That's a strong word. You don't hate anything. You just dislike it." And anytime they said words sounding like, "Oh, God," they were reprimanded. "Unless you are praying, you should never use God's name in vain."

Also, on the positive side, Dan never complained about what I cooked and complimented any of my attempts at fixing something new. He was always open to going out to eat when I didn't feel like cooking. He never questioned me when I spent money on myself, the boys, or the house. He helped around the house, often doing the laundry and always the dishes. He kept himself in great physical shape by finding time to work out to enhance his vitality. He was not critical of me in any way.

Dan was a good person. A good person who had made some terribly selfish decisions. The positives outweighed 'the negatives. There was only one negative but it was a biggie. He cheated. *Can I live with this ultimate betrayal, infidelity, and its ramifications? Am I selling my soul for my marriage?* I was in a constant battle with myself.

The list of good attributes was long. Dan was recognized at Jordan's school for being board member of the year. I was asked to send in pictures of Dan through the years, and a slide show was compiled. On the night of the presentation, the director of Orange Grove was full of compliments ... hard-working, responsible, reliable, loyal, motivated. The room was full of people who only knew this side of Dan.

As I sat and listened to all that was said, it was all true of Dan. This only made me more confused. He was a dichotomy. I couldn't imagine the person he was talking about doing the things Dan had done. I was holding onto a secret that no one knew. He was given a large pewter platter engraved with *Man of the Year*. Dan put it on our mantel. It made me furious every time I looked at it. He may have been *Man of the Year*, but he sure wasn't *Husband of the Year*.

PART SEVEN

The world breaks everyone
And afterward many are
Strong at the broken places

- Ernest Hemingway

Chapter 14

December 2009

I was still struggling and made plans to help myself move forward with the healing process. I had been inspired after reading the book, *My Husband's Affair Became the Best Thing to Ever Happen to Me,* just after finding out about the affair. It helped me decide to give my marriage another chance.

The author, Anne Bercht, turned her marriage into all she wanted it to be. She and her husband, Brian, made it through their marriage crisis and developed careers helping other couples trying to restore trust and love in their relationship. On their web site, Beyond Affairs, there was information about every aspect of affairs. I was determined to stay in my marriage if I only knew how. The web site included a list of seminars available for anyone who wanted a more in-depth healing experience. I felt hopeful that this would help me work through many of my reservations about staying in my marriage.

Although I was apprehensive and anxious about this commitment, I flew to Florida in early December for the weekend seminar. *Is this a hokey useless weekend more about taking my money?* It was expensive, but I hoped it would be a worthwhile experience. I was told to look for a specific van that would take me to the venue. In the van were five other women in the same situation. We quickly bonded over our shared experience – our husbands had all had an affair.

As the weekend unfolded, we were each given a chance to tell our story, "D-Day," as they called it, was Discovery Day. I felt an immediate connection to one other woman since she also found out about her husband's affair on the same Valentine's Day weekend. She was also working to maintain her marriage, but many other women felt their marriages were over, sharing their anger, resentment, and bitterness.

Several women shared stories about cutting up their husband's suits and attacking their husband's car with a screwdriver. They wanted revenge. I couldn't see how anything like this would do anything but make the situation worse. Some women wanted a new expensive diamond ring or a lavish vacation as payback for what they had been through. Or they even considered having their own affair. None of this appealed to me. I learned that everyone has their own way of coping. All I wanted was for Dan to be genuinely sorry for what he had done and never do it again.

Throughout the weekend, many questions were rolling around my head. *What if I had gone through with the divorce right after finding out? What would it be like to be single again? What would it be like to date again? Would I even want to date again? Would Dan go back to Ella? Would the kids be alright if we divorced? Would I regret letting Dan come back into my life? Could I be happy letting go of my marriage? Will Dan ever do this again?* As much as I wanted answers to all my questions, there wasn't anyone who could give me any. I would have to figure this out all on my own,

The weekend turned out to be positive, but also emotional and draining. It was designed to make us feel strong if we stayed in our marriage and strong if we decided not to stay in our marriage. There were written assignments and group activities to help us realize we could get through the trauma and learn from the experience. There were over twenty women and several leaders who shared their personal stories. The retreat began Friday night and ended Sunday afternoon, and I left feeling I gained insight and knew I wasn't alone. Anne Bercht autographed my book.

When I flew home, I spent time between flights browsing in the bookstore. I was still searching for advice on how to get through this. I wasn't interested in fiction of any kind. I needed inspiration. One title caught my attention, *Broken Open: How Difficult Times Can Help Us Grow* by Elizabeth Lesser. This was precisely how I felt, broken open.

Elizabeth Lesser, I found out later, is the co-founder and senior adviser of the Omega Institute, an organization conducting workshops in holistic health, psychology, cross-cultural arts, and spirituality. In her book, she writes about her own experience of being broken open after going through a divorce.

After buying the book, I started writing down passages that spoke to me. When I finished reading, I immediately turned around and reread it. I had never done this before. I felt like the book was written for me. She wrote, "If we do not suffer a loss all the way to the end, it will wait for us. It won't just dissipate and disappear. Rather, it will fester, and we will experience its sorrow later, in stranger forms."

I wasn't sure I had processed the pain from previous losses. I often felt like I was trying to run from the pain, always pushing it away. I hated the way it made me feel both mentally and physically. Her advice was to "descend all the way down to the bottom of a loss and dwell patiently, with an open heart, in the darkness and pain, then we can bring back up with us the sweetness of life and the exhilaration of inner growth." I wondered where I was in this process.

Elizabeth says, "I have seen people crumble in times of trouble, lose their spirit, and never fully recover. I have seen others protect themselves fiercely from any kind of change, until they are living a half-life, safe, yet stunted." She says there is another way to deal with a fearful change called the Phoenix Process, named for the mythical phoenix bird who remains awake through the fires of change, rises from the ashes of death, and is reborn into a more vibrant and enlightened self.

I had already been broken open several times, with the death of Robert, the heartbreak of having a profoundly handicapped child, Luke's alcoholism, and now Dan's affair. My life had provided many opportunities to become "vibrant and enlightened," but was I? I wanted to be. I didn't want to be a martyr and feel sorry for myself. Should I feel thankful for the "growth opportunities?"

Was it all in my attitude toward what had happened to me? I remembered reading a quote from Hugh Downs, "A happy person is not a person in a certain set of circumstances, but rather a person with a certain set of attitudes." I wanted to be a happy person. I was still capable of having happy moments, maybe hours or even days, but a happy life, I was learning, didn't seem possible. *Does anyone have a happy life?*

~

During this time of questioning myself and my marriage, I read an article in our local paper about a young photographer who had started a new business called *El Mariposa* (Spanish, for The Butterfly). She was focusing on women and their need to come out of the dark and be confident in themselves. She scheduled appointments for women to be photographed, exposing themselves becoming butterflies, so to speak. It sounded like just what I needed. I called and made an appointment. She interviewed me before the photo session. I was the oldest client she had booked for this experience. *Can't fifty-eight-year-olds become butterflies, too?* I was nervous, so she told me to bring along a bottle of wine if I thought it would help me relax.

We spent three hours in her studio. I took five different outfits, several quite seductive, and she was terrific at making me feel comfortable. The bottle of wine helped. As she gave instructions, I slowly changed positions as she continually took pictures. The clicking of the camera made me feel like a model. It felt exhilarating. I had never felt so free and uninhibited.

She asked me what made me decide to do this. "My husband had an affair," I explained.

"Well, you're beautiful, and I'm glad you did this for yourself," she offered. She gave me a copy of a poem about not letting another person diminish you. I did feel like a butterfly. For our 36th wedding anniversary, I gave Dan the album of pictures as a gift. He looked at them uneasily.

"Wow, these are beautiful. You look beautiful. But this isn't really you." Well, it was, for one fabulous day.

As time went on, Dan and I were always looking for ways to have fun together. We planned a trip to Las Vegas for our wedding anniversary. We tried to keep up with the pace of the city, but it was hard at our age. Neither of us liked gambling, but we did enjoy getting dressed up, going to shows, and having nice dinners out. The energy of the city was invigorating. We didn't let what had happened take away from our fun. We always enjoyed being together.

I was excited because we had gotten tickets for the Beatles *Love* Cirque du Soleil performance. We planned a romantic dinner before the eight o'clock show. After we finished our delicious steak dinners, Dan brought out a small box.

"I got you something. I wanted to surprise you. I think you'll like it 'cause I heard you mention one time that you'd like one."

"Wow, thanks, dear. This is a surprise. Can I open it now?"

I opened the box, and there was a small white CVS bag inside. *What could this be?* Inside the bag was a silver circle of love necklace, still with the $4.95 price tag on it. The rhinestones almost looked real.

I wasn't sure how to react. It was a circle of love necklace that I had always wanted, a circle of diamonds to represent our continuing love. But a fake one? I didn't want to seem ungrateful. I could tell by his face that he was excited about giving me this gift. I put it on, and Dan started laughing. *What's so funny?*

He then handed me a small white jewelry box. I opened it, and there was the one I had always wanted, with real diamonds. I started crying – finally some tears of happiness.

"I love you, Honey. I always will. You're the best. Happy Anniversary." he said.

He helped me put the gorgeous diamond circle around my neck. We made a toast to our love and then left to go see *Love*.

⤳

We finished the first year of our attempts at reconciling by planning another trip together, this time to Memphis. We were at our best when we were out of town, spending time together and relaxing, away from the mundane day-to-day routine of life.

Dan had made a bid at a golf tournament auction for a stay at the Heartbreak Hotel, on the grounds of Elvis Presley's estate, Graceland. We drove to Memphis and enjoyed touring this popular tourist destination. We went out for Memphis' famous barbecue ribs and had a few drinks. We toured Graceland and learned all about the history behind Elvis' fame and fortune. I couldn't help but think about how much Robert would have loved this shrine to his favorite performer.

It was Valentine's weekend, and Dan had picked out a beautiful card and candy. I did everything I could not to think about what was going on last Valentines' Day when I learned about his affair. It seemed fitting that we were staying at the Heartbreak Hotel. My heart still felt pretty broken.

❦

Back at home, I still had to need to stay busy. As long as I had something to do with my hands, I didn't seem to dwell on what was in my head. I decided to repaint our hall, but that meant all the pictures that lined the walls had to be taken down. Our hallway is a tribute to all the good times our family has shared – bringing Alex home from the hospital, Luke holding his soccer team's state championship trophy, Jordan fully clothed sitting in our blow-up swimming pool, all of us in Halloween costumes, over ninety pictures in all, all events that had held us together for more than four decades.

Alex had said the day after he found out about the affair, "I can't even look at the pictures in the hall." The walls also included pictures from Dan and me and our families and friends before we had kids – Jack and Rita, my parents and brother and sister, Big Mama and Big Daddy, Aunt Lula, Skip and Lee Ann. I was known in my family as the most sentimental, so I liked being surrounded by those I loved.

To paint the walls, all these pictures had to be taken down. I reframed some of them and rehung them. The only picture that fell and broke during this whole process was our wedding picture. This seemed to provide the impetus for me to once again put my feelings down on paper in the form of a poem.

Heavy Heart

The weight
Fills my chest
As though
I carry something
Upon it
....holding me back
....holding me down
....holding onto unresolved
issues and emotions

Yearning for lightness
....joy
....freedom of spirit
Loss came early
Changing my world
Challenging my faith
Drowning my dreams

With every other loss
....devastation
....despair
....disappointment
....disillusionment

My heart feels
....fragile
....inflated with sadness
Like pieces of stained glass
Carefully and sparingly
Soldered together
With faith and hope
Ready to crack and break
Into a million pieces

As if I need a sign
Across my chest
HANDLE WITH CARE

Longing for release
I search for peace
Looking for inspiration
....reasons to forget
....reasons to forgive
....reasons to forge ahead
I struggle
I read
I pray
I look for lessons learned from adversity
Have I been a good student?
Or is my heavy heart
Holding me hostage?

I continued to search for insight to deal with all the feelings I was experiencing. Online, I discovered Celeste Roberge, a sculpture artist who created a unique image out of welded steel in the form of a human, kneeling on one knee with the head bowed. It is made of 4,000 pounds of open welded steel, and the structure is full of river rocks. It was meant to depict the Cairns of Europe, which are piles of stones used to mark a specific site, a burial, a road, or a boundary.

Although her intent was not to depict grief, many people identify with this sculpture as showing the weight of grief. It visually embodies what it does to a human to grieve. The weight is heavy, close to unbearable. I identified with this image.

I hated the way my grief made me feel. I wanted to crawl out from under it. *Why am I having such a hard time moving on?* I wished at times that I hadn't found out everything – all the places they went, all the things she told me, the words she used, the pictures. And I had even had to see her in person. I was overwhelmed with it all.

For most people, infidelity is the one unforgivable act, but I wanted to forgive. We had invested decades in our relationship. I didn't want to give up on it. But infidelity strips away the trust, the unspoken bond which is the basis of marriage. There was an agreed-upon monogamous bond that Dan violated. I was taken advantage of in the most serious way. Our marriage was tainted. *Is it even possible to try to make it healthy again? Do I even want to try?* I knew grief well, but there was a difference in the grief this time because the person I loved caused the pain.

But I still wanted the marriage. And Dan still wanted the marriage. So we had more work to do. He said he wanted to do whatever he could to make things work between us. Dan committed to weekly counseling to get to the bottom of his selfish and irresponsible behavior. He was able to compartmentalize his actions and justify that as long as no one was getting hurt, it was alright. But as one counselor asked him, "Weren't you hurting yourself?" *Where was his integrity? Where was his conscience? His morals?*

He rationalized his choices and wasn't able to set personal boundaries for himself. Cheryl Strayed mentioned in her book, *Tiny Beautiful Things*, that when she found out about her husband's affair she felt he was good at looking at short-term fun rather than long term fallout from his infidelity. This was true of Dan. I also identified with her comment that when she found out about her husband's affair she staggered around the room as if she had been shot. My wound was healing but still there.

During this tumultuous time, Dan and I often took walks together. It seemed more comfortable talking when we were moving. One afternoon we stumbled upon a small animal, probably a squirrel that had been run over, lying on the road with guts and blood splattered everywhere. It was almost unrecognizable.

"That's exactly how I feel," I told him.

He shook his head, "I'm so sorry for all this, Karen. I know you're hurting. I don't know what I can do to make this any easier for you. I'm just thankful you're giving me another chance."

"I'm trying."

We were still living together and working on understanding and improving our relationship. I was still trying to give reconciliation a chance.

~

The only advantage to all of our drama was there was less time to worry about Luke. He had continued drinking since our family vacation in Florida, so I had to put it out of my mind as best as I could. Jordan was being cared for, and I felt confident in his situation at the time. Alex had been accepted into a graduate program for occupational therapy and would be starting in the fall. My father was now 93, and his health was declining. We had hired full-time caregivers. I was thankful he hadn't found out about Dan's affair.

I was still reading books and often visiting the web site, Beyond Affairs, trying to make my way through our changed marriage. I learned that Beyond Affairs offered a seminar for couples that I felt would be beneficial. I didn't give Dan a choice but told him if he wanted our marriage to continue, we were going. I was hoping this would help him be more open and not be defensive.

We flew to Florida and spent a weekend exploring our relationship. The couple leading the seminar stated that affairs aren't necessarily because you have a terrible marriage. Men and women have affairs for various reasons. All this time, I had struggled coming to terms with how I could not have known how bad our marriage was, for my husband to be seeking out another woman.

Dan was still not able to come up with a reason as to why he had done what he did. Other than it was exciting and a little addictive. I wasn't so naïve that I couldn't understand being attracted to another person or that getting attention from someone else might feel invigorating at our age. I liked to think I would never be unfaithful, but my fidelity had never been tested. Dan had always been somewhat of a flirt and was very comfortable around women. I just never thought he would cross that line.

Throughout the weekend, there were written assignments we shared with each other. We completed a timeline of our marriage and looked at what was happening in our lives together, compared to our level of happiness. We completed personality inventories to look at how we might view and live life differently. We were one of the older couples attending. It was emotional and brought us much closer as a couple.

I was able to realize the value of learning about everything that had happened between Dan and Ella. Our relationship didn't have a chance if there were secrets. Following the weekend experience, we participated in six phone seminars. We were again moving in a positive direction.

The following spring, we made plans to attend a family wedding in Chicago. Dan's niece, Mary, was having a large formal wedding, and this would be the first time seeing most of Dan's family since everything that had happened between us. Now weddings made me feel cheated and full of melancholy. But I knew we should attend. I wanted all of our family to be there, but because of Luke's recent behavior, I refused to pay his expenses. He would be the only cousin not there. I told him not to go to our house while we were gone.

I enjoyed myself the entire wedding weekend. It was good being with family again. I love all of Dan's siblings, and they were there with their spouses and all the nieces and nephews. We ate, drank, and partied like Dan's family has always known how to do. They all like to dance, so we enjoyed the live music. A family tradition was started years earlier with everyone doing the gator. It was quite a sight watching both the young and the old moving around the floor.

But before we knew it, we were on the road back home. The eight-hour drive home from Chicago was in a horrendous rainstorm. After dodging flooding in several cities, we arrived home late on Sunday night to find Luke passed out on our couch – a half-full beer can sitting on the end table beside him. *Oh, shit.*

We were both tired from the trip. Dan exploded in anger. He pulled Luke off the couch.

"What the hell are you doing here?"

Luke was disoriented and drunk, so his answers weren't making sense. Dan pulled him into the hall and downstairs to his old bedroom.

As they stumbled down the steps, Dan yelled, "We told you not to come to the house. Didn't you understand that? We don't want you here like this."

I felt sick. I was mad at both of them. *How much more can we take?*

Dan went to bed, and I sat in the dark in our sunroom, watching the lightning and pondering my life. Luke came stumbling back upstairs. I was hoping I wouldn't see him again until the next day.

"I'm leaving," Luke said.

"You're leaving? Where are you going tonight? It's pouring down, and you don't even have a car. Please don't go." I pleaded.

"I don't know where I'm going. I'm just leaving here; that's all I know."

"Just go back downstairs. We can talk about this tomorrow."

Now it was raining even harder. Lightning strikes were raging across the sky, giving everything an eerie appearance. The sound of thunder filled the house.

I looked at Luke. I was looking at a stranger. *I don't know who you are.* I just wanted this all to end.

"It doesn't make sense to leave tonight. You can figure things out tomorrow."

"Naw, I'm going."

He was still drunk, so there was no reasoning with him. Nothing I said made any difference. I watched as he walked away in the driving rain. He had no car and no place to go home to. *Where is he going?*

I was at my rock bottom. I was tired of this endless gut-wrenching journey. I had never felt such a complicated mix of feelings. I was mad at him for coming to the house. I was disappointed he was drinking again. I was scared for him to be going out into the storm. I was mad at Dan for his angry response.

I sat alone for a while, trying to let go of my anxiety. I closed my eyes and focused on my breathing. *There is nothing you can do. You have done all you can do.* I took a sleeping pill and went to bed. *Maybe I won't wake up in the morning.*

I thought this was possibly as bad as it was going to get, so I was not ready for the phone call I received the following Tuesday.

"Do you have a son named Luke?" he asked.

Oh, no, my God. It was a man's voice. He identified himself as a Chattanooga police officer. My heart lurched. I instinctively sat down, afraid of what was coming next.

"Yes, I do. What's happened?" I asked.

All the fears about Luke were coming to mind. *Overdose? Hit by a car? Murdered?* I was bracing myself for what the police officer was going to say next. *Can there possibly be more bad news?*

"There is a warrant out for his arrest. Do you know where we can find him?"

"What did he do?" I asked.

"A woman named Ella Cadswill has filed an assault charge against him for throwing a beer on her."

I didn't know what to say. *What the ... what was he thinking? Why did he do this?* On Sunday, as we drove home from the wedding,

Luke had gone to the North Chatt Cat, the favorite local bar. Ella was on the outside deck with her new boyfriend. Luke was high on pain medication he found at our house, combined with the alcohol he had been drinking all afternoon. Ella was with a small group of people. He confronted her.

"So you're her, huh? You fucked my dad and tried to ruin my mom by calling her and telling her all about it. Way to go. You're a real winner."

Then even louder to the whole deck, "Hey, ya'll. Hey everybody, see this chick. She's a homewrecker."

He told me later he felt the resentment leave and felt justified in this public humiliation. No sooner had he finished with this discourse when he felt the owner of the bar, Dennis, pull him away.

"Ok, Luke, that's enough."

Dennis sat Luke down at the bar inside to cool off and hopefully come to his senses. It began to rain, which brought Ella and her friends inside. Luke was hoping to get more of a reaction from her, like maybe her running out of the bar in tears. So he wasn't finished with her yet. He was still feeling spiteful. She didn't seem to be upset enough about what had just occurred, so it was time for more action.

Luke got up from the bar. He took his beer, and as he walked toward the door, he threw it on Ella. Now he might get a reaction. This brought Dennis to his feet.

"Okay, Luke, get the hell out of here. You gotta go."

Luke said he felt great as he walked out into the rain. He later told me, "I did it for you."

Did this for me? Oh my God, he just made everything much worse, for him and for me. This was going to complicate everything if we saw her again.

The policeman pulled me into the mess when he said, "Ma'am, you just need to encourage him to turn himself in as soon as possible."

I started calling his friends, driving around town, frantic to find him. Luke was nowhere. I felt responsible. He was in hiding. The longer he went without turning himself in, the worse the consequences might be. Here I was again, trying to save him from himself.

He told me later he often wanted to trade places with Jordan when life seemed too overwhelming, and this was one of those times. He managed to convince a childhood friend, Scott, who was married with a child, to let him spend a few days at their house. I finally thought to call Scott, thinking he might have heard from Luke. He was there.

"Luke, I've been trying to get in touch with you for days. I got a phone call from the police. Ella has filed an assault charge against you. The police have a warrant out for your arrest."

He laughed. "No way. For throwing a beer? I hope you're kidding."

"No, I'm not kidding. You have to go down to the police station as soon as possible. Do you understand? This is serious stuff."

"Yeah, sure. I'll go right down."

He was skeptical about my advice, sounding unconcerned as he said he would talk to me later. He had more important things to do, like going to a Widespread Panic concert in Knoxville.

I was frantic to find out if he had turned himself in. The next day I got a phone call from Alex, who was working in Knoxville.

"Mom, Luke just showed up here at my job. He's high on something. He was loud and obnoxious. I don't know what to do." He sounded frustrated and scared.

"Oh no! All I can think of is to tell your boss there's a warrant out for his arrest and to call the police if he comes back. I'm sorry you have to deal with this. Just try not to let it get to you. Call me when you get off work."

I could tell Alex didn't want to embarrass himself by letting his boss know his brother was a mess. I was furious Luke had involved Alex in his latest bad decision. Alex was tired of all our family drama.

Dan and I decided we weren't going to get any more involved. Luke needed to learn there were consequences for his irresponsible behavior. Luke called Ted, one of his roommates from his aftercare program, now living in Minneapolis, who was a lawyer and asked for advice.

"Turn yourself in."

There was a ten-day time frame from when the assault charge was filed and Luke turning himself in. Time for a lot of worrying.

After he turned himself in, we didn't post bail for him. So Luke spent ten days in jail, ten days for throwing a beer on Ella. She had gotten her revenge. I passed by the jail several times during the ten days. I was envisioning him getting himself together, feeling remorse, and making a commitment to turning himself around. I thought this might be his hitting rock bottom.

Luke was released after he went before the court and pleaded guilty to a simple assault charge. Ella was there with a friend, the bar owner, Dennis, her boyfriend, Fred, and another man. They were all at the bar when the "assault" occurred. We did not attend. Luke was now a free man but not a changed one.

⤳

Because of all that had now happened between Ella and Luke, I decided to send her a letter of apology. What Luke did was going to stir up lots of emotions for her. It certainly did for me. It was going to make me feel more stressed if we saw her again. I reasoned she might think we thought this was great.

We are writing to let you know we don't condone Luke's behavior. We were out of town, and Luke spent the weekend drinking. Luke has serious drug and alcohol issues and would never do this had he not been high. But this does not excuse his behavior. We apologize on his behalf. We both signed the letter. I felt we were doing the right thing.

Several weeks later, when things had settled down once again, I saw a *Just Busted* newspaper lying in Luke's bedroom. It was a local paper that posted mug shots of people who had been arrested for various offenses in our county and other local counties. It was only a dollar, but the people distributing it were making a fortune since most everyone loved to see who the most recent screw-ups were and what they did. I was mortified when there was Luke's picture under "Assaults."

I couldn't believe it. Who would have ever imagined this could happen? I thought of the nursery school teacher who was worried about Luke being so passive and wanted him to stand up for himself. Well, here he was, in color, for the world to see. Not passive anymore. When I asked about his picture in *Just Busted*, he said, "Oh, well, it's no big deal. I've been in there before when I was arrested for public intoxication." Nothing was a big deal to him anymore.

I was once again searching for books to help me cope with another of life's challenges – an addicted family member. Luke was doing things wrong, but I was doing things wrong, too. I was drawn to Glennon Doyle's book, *Love Warrior*, and what she wrote about her own addiction. She feels that addiction is a place sensitive people go to numb themselves from life. Luke was always a sensitive child. He was gentle, calm, and always compliant. He was a happy-go-lucky kid. But now he didn't seem happy or lucky.

He was struggling as an adult to overcome his fears, self-doubt, and pain. Alcoholism was also in the family tree on both sides of our families. He was going to have to be able to step back from his addictions and see what it was doing to him. I couldn't do this for him. I just wanted it to happen sooner rather than later.

After suffering herself from both food and alcohol addictions, Glennon Doyle wrote that addictions are safe little deadly hiding places where sensitive people retreat from love and pain. But since love and pain are the only things that help people grow, people start dying as soon as they hide. Luke had been in hiding for a long time. He was now thirty-two, and this started when he was eighteen. He was back to no job, no money, no car, and no place to live.

Once again, we allowed Luke to come back to our house after he was released from jail. My only requirement for him to stay with us was that he go to AA meetings. I would drive him and wait on him. I was afraid he would leave the meeting, so I sat in my car and watched as the people filed into the building. Many of the people looked like they had lived a very rough life.

I envisioned him inside, as he said, "Hi, my name is Luke, and I am an alcoholic." Like maybe what he would have said at summer camp years earlier, "Hi, my name is Luke, and I'm a soccer player." I knew Luke belonged there, but my heart ached for the sensitive, athletic, innocent young boy I proudly called my son. I was seeing less and less of the old Luke I once knew and loved. Where had he gone?

Luke was at a loss as to what to do next with his life. But just as we were getting more and more worried about his situation, his friend, Ted, who advised him to turn himself in, called Luke. He offered him the opportunity to live with him in Minnesota to get his life back together. Ted was now a father, a lawyer, single, and living alone, so we thought he might be a good influence on Luke. His only condition was Luke had to stay sober.

Luke thought it was a good idea. We thought it was a great idea. We decided to put him on a plane to snow country. If nothing else, maybe he could shovel snow. We were just relieved that Luke had a new start somewhere other than in Chattanooga. We had just had as much as we could stand.

Of course, we kept in touch, and Luke always said everything was going well. He told us he was actively looking for a job but hadn't gotten a call back yet. This was what we heard week after week. Finally, after almost three months, a job at a fast-food restaurant came through, and we were cautiously excited for him.

A week after learning this good news, I got a phone call from Luke. He didn't sound like himself. His voice sounded distant and flat.

"Mom, I guess I've got some bad news. Ted asked me to leave his house. I'm in a motel and don't have anywhere to go. I don't know what to do. He just brought me here and left. I don't have any money."

What?? Should I just hang up?

I sat down, feeling the familiar panic. "What did you do? Why would he ask you to leave?"

"Oh, it was stupid. Ted has a change jar he keeps by the door, and I took some of the change to buy some candy and stuff at the store."

I couldn't believe what I was hearing. That spark of hope had already disappeared.

"Why would you do this, Luke? It wasn't your money. It was his. He has been kind enough to let you stay with him, and this is what you do?"

"I was bored. There's nothing to do here. I was going to pay him back when I got paid."

Ted's daughter put her spare change in the jar, saving money for college. Ted was livid. He was tired of Luke sitting around, not doing much. Luke was riding Ted's bicycle and going to the store to buy candy.

Holy shit ... when is he going to grow up?

Another dead end. Luke was dealing with the dilemma that Glennon Doyle described in her book. She says in the beginning, as alcoholics try to stay sober, they face feeling bored, or drink and ruin everything.

We wired money to pay for a bus ticket home. *Are we doing the right thing? Should we have just left him in the motel room to figure this out on his own.?*

No, I couldn't just leave him there. I couldn't. I remembered the poem he had written about suicide. I had to get him home. Two days later we met him at the bus station at midnight. We rode home in silence. What was the point of giving a speech or advice?

What now? He asked again to go the LA to pursue his acting dreams. Thinking about him being in LA, many thousands of miles away, was undoubtedly appealing. I was tired of being involved in all his drama. He had completed the two-year acting program for what it was worth, and he was full of lofty ideas.

We checked on sober living facilities in LA. The pricing started at $6,000 a month – *Yeah, I don't think so.* We found one at the end of the scale for $500 a month. We just didn't know what else to do. Dan agreed to give him three months to get on his feet to start paying his rent. He packed and flew to LA in September.

∽

By this time, Dan and I were more than ready for a vacation. My 60th birthday was in mid-September, so Dan and I decided to go to Mexico to an all-inclusive resort. I envisioned us relaxing with drinks and a good book beside the sapphire blue waters of the Gulf of Mexico every day. At night we would have quiet romantic dinners with good wine and a view of the ocean. We wouldn't mention any of our kids' names or what happened between us for the past two years. We might even pretend we were on our honeymoon.

Before we left, there were hurricane alerts for parts of Mexico. We considered canceling but decided against it even though we were apprehensive. We ventured on, and from the day we arrived, I started feeling sick.

Our room was right beside a pool with lots of wild and crazy twenty-year-olds, playing loud music all day and into the night. I was feeling my age and on edge. I was frustrated that I was feeling this way since I was supposed to be relaxing and enjoying myself.

We watched several beautiful weddings on the beach. The brides in their beautiful white gowns were staring lovingly into the eyes of the man who was promising her his undying love. This left me feeling sad and angry, bringing me to tears a few times. There was no getting away from all that had happened. Reminders were everywhere.

I thought back to the words Dan said at our wedding, *Karen, I take you as my wife. I pledge to share my life openly with you and to speak the truth to you in love. I promise to honor and tenderly care for you, to cherish and encourage your fulfillment as an individual throughout all the changes of our lives.* And as Dan gave me my ring, *Karen, take this ring as a sign of my love and fidelity, in the name of the Father, and of the Son, and the Holy Ghost.*

Dan had broken these vows. He didn't do what he promised. *Are we even married anymore? I am still married to him. I haven't broken my vows. But is he still married to me?* All this left me feeling light-headed, bursts of adrenaline filling my chest, like fireworks inside me. The rest of the time, at least for a while, I tried to put it all in the back of my mind. But it just wouldn't stay there.

We made dinner plans for the night of my birthday. I had brought a short brown V-necked jersey dress with high heeled sandals and dangling gold earrings. *Is this appropriate for a sixty-year-old? How can I be sixty?* Sixty sounded old.

I took a shower, washed my hair, put on make-up, stopping and starting all the while trying to stop a panic attack. It felt like the waves we watched at the beach all day. They would subside and come again, getting stronger all the time. I was not doing well.

But I was determined I wasn't going to miss my birthday celebration. Dan was dressed and looking handsome. I put on the outfit I had planned to wear. I looked in the mirror and was fashionably dressed, thin, tan, and blonde. He snapped a quick picture of me before we were planning to leave for the evening. I looked like I was having the time of my life.

When another wave hit, I reluctantly said to Dan, "I'm not going to be able to do this. You go on and get something to eat. I feel terrible."

He looked at me sympathetically and seemed disappointed.

" Oh, Karen. I hate this. I wish you felt better. What can I do?"

"Just go on without me. I just want to go to bed."

"Do you want me to bring you some food back to the room?"

"No, I'm not going to be able to eat."

"Will you be okay by yourself? I don't have to go."

"No, go on. I just want to be by myself."

I took off the outfit and put on my pajamas. I crawled into bed and turned on the TV. Dr. Phil was having his 60th birthday party. I guess this would have to substitute for my own party. *So happy for you, Dr. Phil, your life looks perfect.*

Dan brought back a small cake he ordered, inscribed with "Happy Birthday, Karen." I couldn't eat any of it. I couldn't remember the last time I felt happy.

My problems only got worse. But I pushed through for the rest of the week. We spent more time at the beach, thinking just lying around would help me to relax, but nothing seemed to help much.

Here we were with fabulous restaurants all around us, lavish buffets of exquisite food, and I had no appetite. The thought of food made me nauseous. I was so mad at this turn of events. I had been stuffing so many feelings, and all of them caught up with me. I was so glad to be going home.

As we waited on our plane at the airport, I decided to check out the souvenirs to kill time. When I walked through the terminal, the panic returned, and I was faint and nauseous again. Rushing into the restroom, I chose the last stall in case I passed out; maybe no one would notice. I was sweating and repeatedly wiping my face down with a wet paper towel.

I gave myself a lecture, "*You are on your way home. You will be fine when you get home. There is no reason for so much panic. You will be home in a few hours. You aren't going to pass out. You aren't going to pass out. You aren't going to pass out. You aren't going to throw up. You have to get up and find Dan.*"

Finally, pulling myself together, I went out into the bathroom and approached the attendant.

"I need help. I'm sick and need you to find my husband." She shook her head and shrugged her shoulders. She couldn't understand English.

Another attendant walked over. "Can I help?"

I gave her my flight number and gate, and wrote a note to Dan, "I almost passed out in the bathroom. I need you to come get me." I wrote his name down and sat down outside the restroom to wait.

Dan followed the attendant.

"I was getting worried about you. You were gone a long time. I thought we were going to miss our flight." He brought me a bottled water, and I stayed there until I felt more stable.

He kept asking me, "Are you going to be okay? You don't look so good. You need anything else besides water?"

"Yeah, I'm okay, I guess." I didn't want to make a scene.

But everything wasn't okay. Physically I was not okay. Emotionally I was not okay.

Could this be one of the causes of my anxiety and panic – always being diplomatic, never wanting to rock the boat, afraid of confrontation, never saying what I want to say. I was good at holding in feelings that would be better off expressed, holding in feelings until I made myself sick.

I was going to have to pull myself together to get home. I was facing a three-hour flight to Atlanta and a two-hour drive to Chattanooga. *If I can just get home, I'll be fine.* The waves of anxiety would wash over me, completely out of my ability to control. I laid my head down on the food tray and tried deep breathing to calm myself. Dan gave me a back and neck massage. I just wanted to go to sleep to escape all this for a while, but I couldn't relax enough for that.

We managed to get back to Atlanta and finally Chattanooga. I was still fighting the waves. I gave myself a couple of days of bed rest to try to get over these episodes.

Dan was getting more and more concerned.

"I'm worried about you. You aren't getting any better. You've got to start eating. I think you should call your doctor."

I just kept thinking I would wake up the next day and would be better. I tried going to the grocery store and took Dan with me, just in case I needed him. I didn't feel like I could drive or go anywhere, not knowing when these attacks were going to happen. I was feeling out of control of my body.

I tried relaxing all day, lying around on the couch reading. This was the opposite of what I had been doing. I had previously stayed as busy as possible, trying not to think about any of it. Neither approach was working.

Just as all this was happening, Margie was coming through town on her way from an art show and asked to stay over on her way home. Having her with me was comforting. She sat on the side of my bed and knew just what to say and what not to say. She gave me hope I could get through this. But soon she was back on the road.

At the end of a very rough day, Dan insisted it was time for me to go to the emergency room. It was the same hospital where I went after just finding out about the affair. They must have remembered me as the crazy lady whose husband had an affair because they didn't get too excited about my condition. They left me on an examining room table for several hours. I was cold, shaking, and crying.

I finally called Dan who was still in the waiting room on my cell phone.

"Come back here. I'm freezing. I need a blanket. They haven't even seen me yet." I was miserable. Finally, a nurse gave me a shot of Ativan. A wave of relief washed over me just as the anxiety had at the airport. No one even mentioned panic attacks. *Aren't there supposed to be doctors at this hospital?*

Because of my stomach issues, they decided to admit me. I spent two nights in the hospital where they ran tests to rule out several conditions. Nothing was showing positive, so I was released. By this time, I was so thin the doctor wrote on my chart "anorexic." I wasn't intentionally trying not to eat. I just couldn't.

Over the next two weeks, I weaned myself off the Ativan. I knew it wasn't good to get dependent on those. I was determined to focus on myself and getting healthy again. I was working out and regaining a sense of calm. I was still seeing my therapist, who helped me sort out my feelings.

There was also a very good reason to get better. Alex and Melissa had gotten engaged and were planning a wedding in June. This was such happy news, and Dan and I were excited to have hope for the future. Alex had started his graduate program in occupational therapy and was focused on getting his degree. We went to parents' day at the school and felt such pride and optimism for him.

That fall also brought a huge surprise after checking my email one morning – a letter of apology from Ella. I was shocked. She stated she always felt guilty after making the phone call to me. She said she felt nothing when she saw Dan now but felt bad for me. She didn't apologize for the affair, just the phone call. It was only a few sentences long, but it did make me feel better. I wrote back to tell her I appreciated it, and shared the email with Luke and Alex. It was another step in healing.

〜

While we were in Mexico, Luke had started his life in LA. His trip had not gone smoothly. He left Chattanooga a few weeks earlier and I was still full of anxiety over the decision we had made. *This is crazy. How can we expect this to work when nothing else has worked?*

Alex had sent us a letter telling us he felt we were making a big mistake by once again helping Luke out.

"Why would you be sending him to sunny California after everything he has done?" he wrote. This was true. He sure didn't deserve this chance, but we had run out of options. We thought this might work for him since he initiated it. I still had hope.

I had waited an entire day after he should have arrived in LA before he called to tell me he was safe. There was plenty of time for me to imagine various scenarios as to why I hadn't heard from him. He had another wild story about how he fell asleep at one of his connections and missed his flight. I was already beginning to regret our decision to send him to California. *How is he ever going to manage?*

I found out months later that he had been drinking at the airport. He missed his flight and was rerouted to Santa Barbara. A friend of his had a brother living there, and Luke called to see if he could crash at his place. When he finally arrived in LA, he was dealing with a hangover. Not such a great way to start a new beginning at a sober living facility. He lugged his two suitcases all over LA, getting on and off buses until he arrived at his place around midnight, quickly learning he was in a different environment.

I was worried about this new arrangement for him. There were men at this sober living house just released from prison, men of all nationalities, gay and straight men, and men with mental illnesses. Since it was the lowest on the price scale for sober living, many were using it as a place to live, whether they needed it to stay sober not. I didn't know any of this at the time. It was a sober living facility but without much structure. He would have to want this for himself to stick it out.

He was attending AA meetings and sounding hopeful on the phone. He called to tell me he had gotten a job working at a school for disabled students. Luke had years of on the job training having a brother like Jordan. He was patient and kind and was not intimidated by any kind of unusual behavior. We were thrilled something was working out for him.

Our excitement didn't last long. Several weeks later, Luke was released from this job. After doing a background check, the school found the simple assault charge. I don't know who was more disappointed, him or me. He was always going to have a criminal record. He could never be a certified nursing assistant again. This was all he had going for himself beyond his high school diploma. His future looked bleak.

Luke had only been in LA for three months, so we decided he should stay there for Christmas. I still longed for him to be with us but knew it wasn't in his best interest. I sent his Christmas gifts, and he opened them alone in his room.

That year Chattanooga had its first white Christmas since 1969. And Luke was missing it. Both boys love snow, so Alex was running down the hall at 7:30 am with his snow clothes on, ready to play outside. He was full of excitement, so I wasn't going to show any sadness to ruin his Christmas. The three of us opened presents together. Jordan joined us later in the day. He always gave us things to smile and laugh about. He knew nothing about what the rest of us were going through. And that was refreshing.

We were excited to open the family Christmas package Luke had sent. He wrapped individual gifts for all of us. He didn't have much money, so I couldn't imagine how he had managed to do this. He sent Jordan a package of dinner rolls. Jordan had a reputation for grabbing everyone's roll at dinner when they weren't looking, so now he could enjoy his own dozen rolls. The perfect gift! He sent me calming tea and a lint roller for the accumulating dog hair. Alex received a bag of sunflower seeds and Dan a Rolling Stone CD. I was impressed with the amount of thought he put into buying such personal gifts. Maybe he was starting to realize the importance of his family.

Chapter 15

March 2011

Luke had been living in LA for seven months. It was a break from all the tension leading up to his move. But I did miss him, just not all the drama. As far as we knew, all was going well – no phone calls from the police.

Instead of imagining his life there, I decided to schedule a trip to LA by myself. I needed to see him, wanted to see his house, and possibly meet a few of his friends. He had gotten an internship at a performing venue doing the sound and lights. He was meeting new people and attending AA meetings regularly.

We hugged a long time in the airport terminal. It was good to see him again in person. His blue eyes were bright and clear, his red hair was trimmed, his body still lanky, but he looked healthy again – so much better than when he left in September. I kept staring at him. *Do I have my son back?*

I rented a car and was apprehensive about driving in LA, but Luke knew his way around well. We ate at a few cool restaurants and stayed in a room near the beach. We went to several comedy shows and did some sight-seeing.

"You don't have much of a safety net living in LA," I told him.

"Yeah, I know, it's been good for me."

He was learning he had to depend on himself. He wasn't going to be calling his friends or us to get him out of trouble. We were relating like adults, having some discussions over all that had happened in our family. He sounded more positive, and I was optimistic about his new frame of mind. I was full of hope, the one virtue that had gotten me through to this point. When I got back home, I felt a sense of relief from the worry and the uncertainness, the anger, and the fear.

While I was in LA, Luke received his wedding invitation from Alex and Melissa. I hadn't seen it yet. I teared up. I felt a mix of happiness and sadness. Time was moving on. My baby was getting married.

The wedding was planned for June in Knoxville. And before I knew it, Luke was back home for the wedding weekend. I wanted to be involved, so I volunteered to make the floral centerpieces for the rehearsal dinner and decorate the outside entrance of the wedding venue. I thought this would be a fun way to show my support. We rented a van to get the flowers and all of us to Knoxville. Luke was helping with all the errands to make everything happen smoothly.

The wedding would be held outdoors under a magnificent elm tree on the grounds of a historic school building. The day of the wedding was predicted to be one hundred degrees. Many family and friends were coming and staying at the same hotel. Jordan was coming to the reception with his caretaker and staying in the hotel with all of us.

After we got to Knoxville, I began to realize this commitment I thought would be fun was a huge mistake. Our hotel room was filled with bouquets of various flowers I was trying to keep from wilting. *Why did I do this to myself?* While everyone was sitting by the pool socializing and enjoying time with family, I was frantically arranging flowers. I was feeling anxious and had to keep stopping to close my eyes and take deep breaths.

The rehearsal dinner was perfect. The sunflowers, gerbera daisies, roses, carnations, and baby's breath all looked beautiful against the white table cloths. It was wonderful having so many people you love together in one room. I gave a toast.

"I just want to say how happy I am for Alex and Melissa. It seems like only yesterday I was picking out Melissa's corsage when they were going to her senior prom. After living with four men, I am so happy to finally be getting a girl in the family. Alex has always made good decisions, and I am so thankful he has chosen Melissa for his wife." We all dined at a restaurant in Market Square. The food and wine were delicious.

The wedding day had finally arrived and we were on a hectic schedule. We had to take the flowers to the wedding venue in the early afternoon and arrange them all. Then we had to drive back to the hotel and get dressed. And then drive back to the venue for early wedding pictures. The timing needed to be perfect.

After we loaded the van with all the flowers, we got on the road. But soon we found ourselves in a dead stop on the interstate. There was a wreck, and the traffic was going nowhere. *Oh my God, what if we are here for hours? What if someone from the wedding party is in the wreck? How will anyone get to the wedding? Will they have to postpone the wedding? How much longer will we have to sit here?* My stomach was churning.

We waited and waited, losing an hour of our already limited time. We eventually made our way along the narrow country road to the wedding site. But by this time, I was feeling symptoms of a panic attack, which I knew all too well. Dan helped me arrange the flowers in the sweltering heat.

We frantically rushed back to our hotel with exactly 20 minutes to get ready for Alex's wedding. It was not the way you want to start an evening of such importance. I started giving myself a lecture again, *Karen, calm down. Breathe. Breathe. Calm down. You cannot panic. You will go to Alex's wedding. Calm down. Breathe.* I sat and closed my eyes for a few minutes, even though we didn't have any to spare. I was trying to talk myself out of being so panicky, but I was sweating and feeling short of breath. *I can't miss Alex's wedding.*

I managed to get dressed, glad I had showered earlier in the day. We got in the car, and I had a thirty-minute ride to pull myself together. Dan turned the air conditioning on high as I closed my eyes, started deep breathing, laid the seat back, and I asked him not to turn on the music. I tried to take full advantage of this downtime.

By the time we arrived, I was feeling more like myself. We took all the necessary pictures and greeted family and friends as they gathered for the ceremony. Just before Luke escorted me down the aisle, I rushed into the bathroom for one last swipe of my face with a cold paper towel. Hopefully, this would be enough to get me through the service. I said a quick prayer as we headed out the door and outside to the beautiful wedding taking place – Alex's wedding.

Once I was seated, I started to relax. I wasn't going to ruin this important day for Alex. I wanted to focus on his marriage and not mine. The ceremony was conducted by my niece's husband and was meaningful in many ways. Melissa looked stunning in her elegant sat-in dress with a simple Queen Anne's lace flower in her hair, carrying a bouquet of wildflowers. Alex and Melissa seemed incredibly happy, and I was happy for them.

My father owned a beautiful silver Thunderbird convertible, and Alex asked permission to drive it away from the wedding to the reception. We decorated it with cans and signs but were given strict instructions from Daddy not to write on the car. By this time, my father was too frail to attend the wedding, but this gesture made everyone aware of his presence.

The reception was held in an art gallery in Knoxville. Now it was time to relax and have a good time. Aside from all the joy I felt for Alex and Melissa, there was also joy at seeing Jordan enjoying himself so much. There was a smile on his face the entire evening, and he loved the music. His brothers took him on the dance floor, joining him as he did his *Rain Man* dance. The evening was full of excitement and happiness. It was a beautiful time for our family. We had struggled with so much in recent years. But we were one big happy family, at least for that night.

I was slightly worried about how Jordan would handle being around all the food and drink. He was fast and could grab a drink without you even noticing. I warned his caregiver to keep him away from the wedding cake. He had a reputation at our house for digging into birthday cakes before the birthday person could blow out the candles. Most of our cakes had huge gaping holes in them.

Alex and Melissa cut the cake, and we were trying to get the five of us in a picture. Luke sat his cake down on a table near us to be in the picture. Jordan grabbed it, and it was in his mouth before anyone could stop him. The photographer captured our entire family laughing together. *We're all smiling at the same time.* It had been a while since that had happened

I noticed a change in Luke when he was home for the wedding. He looked better than I had seen him in years. He had been sober for only ten months, but it was making a difference. He seemed more alert and not so withdrawn. He was helpful throughout the wedding weekend. I worried about how he would handle the reception, with most everyone drinking. But he didn't seem bothered and was interacting socially with all the guests. I was still queasy from the panic attack and didn't have any alcohol. The guests were all commenting on the delicious food and wedding cake. I couldn't eat anything.

It seemed the weekend flew by, and Luke was now back in LA. He continued to pursue his acting ambitions. He was cast as William Shakespeare in a play and had to dye his red hair black. He was taking acting lessons and trying to do stand-up comedy. He was doing part-time work when he could find it. We wanted this to work for him. Even though he was far away, and we didn't see him as often as we liked, he was where he wanted to be, and so far things were going smoothly.

Dan and I went together to see Luke the following spring. Dan had plans to attend a conference in LA, so we decided to make it a vacation. We were thankful to see Luke doing so well. By this time, he had gotten a sponsor in AA who we met for dinner. He was an older man also doing acting work, and we liked him a lot. He complimented Luke on his dedication to the program and pointed out his positive attributes. It was both comforting and refreshing to hear his words.

"Luke's a great guy. He's worked hard to get where he is now. You should be proud of him." My chest filled with pride at hearing these words. Dan and I looked at each other and smiled. The kind of smile we hadn't shared in a long time.

Luke's success was primarily due to his involvement in AA. One of the steps involves being of service to others. So Luke had started tutoring an older man at the downtown library. I went with him while he worked with him. I was touched by Luke's patience. He interacted easily with him and encouraged his attempts at learning to read. I was a proud mother again.

Luke had moved out of the sober living facility and was now living in a small room located outside a house where he had access to the kitchen and bathroom facilities. He told us he felt it was time to try to live on his own. I was apprehensive, but I knew this was the next step for him. There was barely room to turn around, but it was his, and Luke never required much in the way of luxuries to be content.

We went shopping at Goodwill and bought him a few items. We came home with renewed optimism for Luke and his future.

Life was going smoothly for a change. But that didn't last long. With three children, there was always something going on. I had just had lunch with a friend when my phone rang. It was Jordan's male caregiver.

"Karen, this is Antwane. Jordan has fallen and won't stand up. He collapsed while he was standing behind a chair. We're taking him to the emergency room."

My hands started shaking, along with my voice, "Does he seem to be in any pain? Did he hit his head? Did he have a seizure?"

"We're not sure what happened exactly. You know Jordan. It's hard to tell what's going on. We're going to get him checked out. Can you meet us at the hospital?"

Dan and I arrived as quickly as possible. From looking at Jordan, it didn't appear to be serious, but with Jordan being non-verbal, we didn't know what he was experiencing. The emergency room was full of people. Because he didn't come in an ambulance, we had to sit in the crowded waiting room for several hours. I was livid.

I tried walking around the parking lot to relieve some anxiety. I had a knot in my stomach that was making me nauseous. I needed some fresh air. Jordan sat patiently in his chair, which was a good indication there was something seriously wrong because he rarely sits down, except to eat. Three and a half hours later, the doctor gave us the news.

"Jordan's pelvis is fine. His feet and legs are fine."

I felt a sense of relief as he said these words.

He followed this news with, "But he has a broken hip."

Oh, my God. My heart dropped. The doctor determined Jordan's seizure medication had lowered his bone density, and this caused his hip to break. I fell back into a chair beside his hospital bed.

"He will have to be in a wheelchair for six weeks with no weight-bearing for it to heal," the doctor explained.

"How is this ever going to work?" I asked. "Jordan paces all day. With his autism, I don't know how we'll be able to keep him in a wheelchair."

"You'll have to find a way," the doctor stated.

This sounded like a complete impossibility. I started crying, knowing it wouldn't help anything. I was angry. That wasn't going to help either. *Dear God, calling on you again. Just help Jordan get through this. And me, too.*

The hospital admitted him, and it was late when we got to his room. Jordan's surgery was scheduled for the next day. They were going to put a plate and pins to secure his broken hip. Since Jordan lives in a group home, they have staff with him 24 hours a day. I was never as thankful for this as I was that night. I was mentally exhausted. Dan and I left to try to get some rest to face this new challenge.

I got to the hospital early the next day, and his surgery had been postponed until later in the day. He was restless and in pain. I was restless and in a different kind of pain. I sat with him all day. The surgeon had already performed six surgeries when they finally took Jordan to the operating room. It wasn't until 1 am that the doctor came to tell us the surgery went well, and Jordan was doing fine. We waited until he returned to his room to leave. My heart broke to see him like this. I sobbed all the way home.

Jordan handled this whole situation better than I anticipated. You can explain what is happening, but you never know how much, if any, he understands. The time sitting by his beside seemed endless. After five days, he was released to go back to his group home, which was a significant ordeal since one-on-one care was needed twenty-four hours a day. All the new staff was trained by the physical therapist as to how to safely position and move him. He got limited physical therapy.

It was going to be a long six weeks. I circled this on our calendar, and I marked off every day. He wasn't used to being immobile, and the caregivers were constantly looking for ways to entertain him, mainly watching music videos non-stop. I visited him every day to break his routine and give him something to look forward to. It broke my heart all over again every time I saw him.

We anticipated Jordan would be walking as soon as the six weeks ended. *Finally, this is over.* I went to his house, thinking what a joy it was going to be to watch him get out of the wheelchair. Unfortunately, this was not what happened. He was hesitant to put weight on his leg. They would help him stand, and he would sit right back down. It required months and months of therapy to try to get him mobile again. The physical therapist did water therapy in the pool, which he loved, but still, he wouldn't take that first step.

The progress seemed slow, so after six months, the surgeon decided to do an x-ray again. The two previous x-rays showed the pin and screws in place and no other issues. This one showed necrosis, the one complication the doctor told me could happen but was rare. There was a failure of blood supply to the bone, and it was dying.

This meant we were back to square one with Jordan's recovery. He had to go back into surgery for a total hip replacement. *This isn't fair.* I was so angry but what good was that going to do? *How can it be that after all Jordan has been through, we are now starting over?* It had always been one step forward and two steps back with Jordan, but this was our worst nightmare.

Seeing all these doctors and spending so much time in the hospital was reminding me of our early years with Jordan. Only now, we knew what was wrong. But this didn't make it any easier. With all these complicating issues, I didn't know what his future might hold. *Will he ever walk again? Surely, his luck won't be so bad that he can't talk or walk?*

The possibility of taking this away from Jordan was more than I could comprehend. It took a full two years before he was walking independently, and even then with a significant limp. He often seemed to be in pain, but it didn't slow him down much since he loved to move.

Hoping to keep him off his feet as much as possible, we installed both an outside and inside swing at his house. Although swinging wouldn't be considered age-appropriate for Jordan since he was thirty-one, he loved it. It gave him the stimulation his autism demanded. I was grateful he was walking again, which we had pretty much taken for granted until now. Jordan was good at providing opportunities for learning all kinds of gratitude.

PART EIGHT

I wanted a perfect ending. Now, I've learned the hard way that some poems don't rhyme, and some storms don't have a clear beginning, middle, and end. Life is about not knowing, having to change, taking the moment and making the best of it, without knowing what's going to happen next. Delicious ambiguity.

- Gilda Radner

Chapter 16

February 2013

So Dan and I were back on track with our marriage; Jordan was walking again; Luke was continuing to stay sober, and Alex and Melissa were enjoying married life. My biggest concern now was my father. He was still alive, but his physical condition was deteriorating. He had turned ninety-five in November and had lived a long and productive life. He was mentally sharp but bedridden.

We hired caregivers to care for him and his beloved dog, Gizmo. My father loved his dogs and especially little white, fluffy Lhasa Apsos, calling them his "fuzzy buddies." Through the years, he had four and named three Gizmo. Every time one of them died, he would get another dog who looked exactly the same and name it Gizmo. That way he could pretend his dog hadn't died. I rarely saw my father cry, but when he lost one of his dogs, he always took it unusually hard. Since he was now alone, he especially valued the companionship of Gizmo.

Since my father now required care at home, I was thankful that my brother, Kimmy, and his wife, Linda, also lived in Ducktown. They were there to oversee the caregivers for my father, and since they were both pharmacists, they made sure his medicines were given appropriately.

My brother had recently been diagnosed with prostate cancer, so he and Linda had to go out of town to attend to his medical issues. They asked me to come and stay with my father while they were gone. I knew he couldn't live much longer, so I was happy to spend time with him, especially under these circumstances. He had lost his appetite, and he was sleeping more and more during the day. He made little conversation, and he knew he was nearing the end. He had stopped watching TV, even the nightly news which had always held his interest.

While I sat and looked at magazines or read a book by his bedside, he enjoyed listening to a CD one of his caregivers gave him of 1940's Big Band music. He was a young man then, and I could tell by the stare in his eyes he was back in his youth reminiscing. I wish he had shared his thoughts with me. He had never shared much about his youth, other than stories about his interest in airplanes and his exploits during the war. Now, he seemed too tired to recall much.

After I had been there a few days, he started having a terrible cough and a low fever. I was afraid it was pneumonia, so the home health nurse evaluated the situation. After listening to his lungs, she insisted we go to the hospital. But I didn't want him to die in the hospital. I had hoped he could stay home until the end. I struggled with the decision.

I busied myself the remainder of the day with mopping, dusting, vacuuming, anything to take my mind away from what I knew was happening. My concerns were overruled by my brother, his wife, and the nurse. I waited all day to make the call for an ambulance to take him to the hospital.

Outside the front of my parents' house, there is a large mountain called Big Frog. It can be seen in the distance and is majestic. It towers over all the other mountains, and depending on the sunlight, turns various shades of blue and green. My father used to fly over it on his many trips away and knew he was near home when he saw it on the horizon.

When the ambulance came for my father, the sun was starting to set behind Big Frog. The sunlight spread across all the rolling hills, giving them a beautiful glow. I watched the sun sink behind the mountain. This was a poignant reminder that maybe my father's time here was over.

It was a cold February night, so I put a little black beanie on my father's head and watched out the window as they maneuvered the stretcher out the front door. He looked much younger than his ninety-five years, with hardly a wrinkle on his face. He hadn't been outside in months. I knew he would never be home again.

I spent the next ten days at my father's bedside. He continued to decline and eventually was given morphine. He was retaining fluid, and it was seeping out of his skin. He quit eating and wasn't tolerating liquids. It was immensely painful to watch, but I was determined he was not going to die alone in the hospital.

Diane came from Florida, and we shared the responsibility of staying with him during the day, and I stayed at night. I took Gizmo the III to see him one last time. My father's face lit up as I put Gizmo on his bed. They locked eyes as Daddy gently gave him a back rub. They laid there quietly for close to an hour.

Suddenly several staff members barged into the room, "You have to take the dog out of here. We could lose our license for having an animal in the hospital."

"Well, we got permission from his doctor. He needed to see his dog."

I picked up Gizmo, and Daddy said a final goodbye to his last "fuzzy buddy."

I had been at the hospital every night for a week and was feeling weary. I was allowed to sleep in the bed next to him in the Hospice room he was assigned. The bed was uncomfortable, and I wasn't getting much sleep. This experience, along with all that had happened with Jordan, Luke, and Dan and me, left me feeling like I wasn't sure I could take much more. I had thought that so many times before. But I really didn't have a choice.

My senses were assaulted with the constant beeping of the morphine machine, the unappetizing taste of the hospital food, and the antiseptic smell of the hospital itself. And the sight of my Daddy so debilitated was heart-wrenching.

Daddy had been restless all day and hadn't spoken in several days. I was trying to distract myself by reading, but it wasn't helping much. I finally turned off the lights to try to sleep. It was 11:30 pm, and my phone rang. It was Jordan's house manager sounding slightly frantic.

"Miss Karen, I hate to bother you this late, but there's been an incident with Jordan here at the house. We're taking Jordan to the hospital because he drank some cleaning fluid that was left out by the third shift cleaning crew. He seems to be okay, but we've got to find out if it's toxic."

Standing there in the dark, I was light-headed and panicky. I couldn't believe what I was hearing. *No way ... how could this have happened?* She didn't know I was out of town attending to my dying father.

"What? Oh, my God. Dan and I are both out of town. My father isn't expected to live much longer, and I'm here with him at the hospital in Ducktown. It's an hour and a half away from Chattanooga. How did this happen at 11:30 at night without someone watching Jordan? Where was the staff?"

I could hear the fear in her voice, "I don't have time right now to tell you everything, but I'll call you as soon I know something. We're leaving for the hospital."

Surely, I can't lose my son and my father on the same day.

I got the call just as I was starting to drift off to sleep. Now I was full of adrenaline. My dad had been breathing loudly and a little erratic throughout the evening. I had gotten used to it. Several nurses called it the "death rattle."

I started to pace around my bed but suddenly became aware that the room was strangely quiet. I walked over to Daddy's bed. His breathing had stopped.

I had been preparing myself for this all week and, at this point, wanted his suffering to end. … to be with my mother, his three brothers already gone, his mother and father. I had said these words to him several times during the week. I desperately wanted to believe them.

We were in the room alone. It was just after midnight, and the hospital was eerily quiet. So many thoughts were rushing through my mind. He saw me into the world, and I saw him out. I hesitated to tell the nurses. It would be official then.

I knew he was gone, but I held his hand. It was swollen with fluid; his fingers were thin, and the tops bruised. His hands had served him well. I studied them as I had my mother's after she died. He had been a fighter pilot during World War II and built two different airplanes. He had done such productive work throughout his life. I was so proud to have been his daughter. I stayed with him until the end. He died exactly ten years to the day as my Mother. It took all my courage to leave him and walk down the hall to let the medical staff know what had happened.

Diane came to say goodbye, and Dan drove us back to the house. We were both relieved his suffering was over, but broken-hearted we had lost our Daddy. As we sat and talked, April finally called to tell me what Jordan had consumed was not poisonous and, after careful observation, he was released to go back to his group home. One of the workers had put cleaning liquid in a red solo cup, and Jordan drank from it, as if it was a Coke. The worker was fired.

I felt grateful for this wonderful news. It was strange suddenly feeling so happy when I was so sad. This was the epitome of living the ups and downs of life in a single day. I was relieved Jordan was okay but still felt guilty I couldn't be there with him. But I knew his autism had spared him the fear that everyone else had. I had to trust that Jordan would be okay, so I could prepare to bury my father.

His funeral was three days later, and all of his children, in-laws, and grandchildren, except Jordan, were there. At his age, there were not many friends left. However, he was well-liked and respected, and many people from Ducktown attended the service. His reputation as a flying enthusiast was well known.

Through the years, both his children and grandchildren delighted in hearing the distant sound of the roaring engine from his Beechcraft Bonanza, and later the Long EZ. When we all gathered at my parents' house for a meal, we would often be waiting for Daddy to return from a trip. At some point during the meal, one of the grandchildren would say, "I think I hear Papa." Everyone would run outside as he neared the house; his red and white plane against a bright blue sky was dramatic. We could see his silver-gray hair through his window, his headphones always on. He would fly low and buzz the house, dip a wing, wave, and quickly ascend back into the sky. He hadn't done this in a while, but to think I would never see it again was painful.

He told me years earlier he wanted the poem, *High Flight*, included in his funeral. It was written by John Magee, Jr., who was a Royal Canadian Air Force pilot killed in an accidental mid-air collision over England. My father also lost one of his brothers, Martin Campbell, Jr., during the war, in an accidental collision in Arizona. He had been especially close to Martin.

As teenagers, they ordered plans for an airplane and built it in Big Daddy's barn. They both got licenses; the plane passed inspection, and they started giving local people airplane rides for a dollar. For many people, it was their first, and sometimes only, airplane ride.

The poem Daddy requested was one my father had heard at funerals of his many friends who were pilots. I was glad he had shared this with me since I wanted a meaningful service to honor his incredible life.

Another request he made was to have a song included which had been written about him. The song was personal and written by a young woman, who, as a young girl, lived down the hill from my parents. She sang this beautiful song, accompanied by her guitar. It was called "Watch Him Fly."

Watch Him Fly

I knew him as a little child
He lived upon the hill
Friendly face always had a smile
He had a dream that took him up
High above the world
I remember thinking when I was just a girl

Watch him fly! Watch him flying way up high
Up above the mountains, soaring thru the sky
Watch him go! Watch him soar into the night
Around the world and back again
Into the arms of his favorite girl
Watch him fly! Watch him fly!

To hear him tell the stories
Of what his life has been
A local boy, a hero
A husband and a friend
His eyes light up with wonder
When people listen in
Just close your eyes you can join the ride

Through the clouds, he lives his dream
Way above the world it seems
He finds his peace and comfort there
All his troubles and his cares
Melt away just like the sun
Over the horizon
Where you can see his heart take flight
Watch him now as he flies!
Watch him fly!

The funeral concluded with Taps as several veterans presented my brother with an American flag since he had also served in the
military. Family and friends joined us at the house to reminisce about
my father. There were many funny stories. My father was a storyteller
and could remember all the details from all his flying missions he frequently shared with anyone who would listen. He had a good sense
of humor.

The house felt unbelievably empty when everyone left. As Diane and I cleaned up from the wake, I was overcome with emotion
– tears rolling down my cheeks. Now Mother and Daddy were both
gone. I felt like an orphan.

We had to decide what to do with my Dad's dog, Gizmo, the
3rd. He had gotten him only five months earlier from a shelter. Gizmo had adjusted well to life at my father's house with the caretakers
caring for both of them. He would lie quietly with my father on his
bed and seemed just as happy to be there as my father was to have him
there. I decided to take Gizmo home with me. My older dog, Sadie,
would now have a playmate, and I would still have a part of my father
with me as long as Gizmo was around.

⸾

Dan and I decided it was time to get away for some fun. We
needed something after all the recent stress and heartbreak. Paul
McCartney was scheduled to play at Bonnaroo, an annual three-day
music festival held in Manchester, Tennessee, only 45 minutes away.
This is like an annual Woodstock for the current generation.

I told Luke over the phone, "I did something a little crazy to get ready for the weekend."

"Like what, Mom?" Luke asked, thinking maybe a tattoo or a piercing.

"I painted my fingernails green." This was going to be one wild time!

I was going to see Paul McCartney again and was as excited as when I was fifteen. We bought tickets and headed out in our small camping trailer. We were among many other old hippies reliving their youth. We awoke early before the younger crowd was out and about, still in their sleeping bags and tents. There were acres and acres of grounds transformed into living headquarters for all the festival-goers. It was well organized and clean, with food and restrooms easily available. It was mid-June, and the heat was miserable. We cranked up our air conditioner and took a nap in the afternoon before going out in the evenings for the concerts.

Paul sang twenty-four Beatles classics and seven songs from his time with Wings. A *Rolling Stone* magazine reporter stated this about the evening, "It was like being able to see Abraham Lincoln deliver the Gettysburg Address in person."

Paul was fabulous and played a two and a half-hour set. He wore similar clothes as in his early days playing with the Beatles – a black jacket, white shirt, and black tie. He later took off the jacket, to much applause, and looked incredibly sexy for a seventy-year-old man. His voice was strong as he paid tribute to both John and George.

To see well, we had to watch the concert from the giant screens placed among the crowds. I got as close as I could, reminiscing about my youth with every song. But where were all the young girls screaming and crying? All I could see were quite a few older women and men with gray hair. *How did this happen?*

Dan and I were moving forward with our marriage and contemplating our old age at this point. We had lived in our house since I was twenty-five and Dan was twenty-seven, now we were sixty-three and sixty-five. *Who lives in one house their whole married life?*

We did a lot to improve and renovate it through the years. We didn't have any interest in making another house our home. I had painted every room several times, put wallpaper up and taken wallpaper down, stenciled walls, painted our picket fence twice, made curtains, and refinished furniture through the years. Dan had built a brick sidewalk, a stone planter, helped renovate the downstairs, and built the screened porch. We were here as newlyweds, and now we were looking at our twilight years. We didn't need to downsize, as many other couples were doing. Our house was a perfect size, but we decided to do some major renovations.

We started by enclosing our beloved screened porch. Many family memories were made on the porch, so it was a hard decision. Birthday celebrations, Halloween parties, graduation parties were usually held there if the weather permitted. It overlooked the beautiful wooded area, which enticed us to buy the house so many years ago, making it easy to forget we were so close to downtown. We enclosed it with glass windows, a stone floor, wood trim and ceiling, and a large stone fireplace. It turned out to be a stunning room. Perfect for just the two of us.

Our next project was renovating our bathroom. If there was anything that made me want to move to a bigger house, it was the bathroom and the closet space. Since our house was built in 1927, these areas were small. So we took a bedroom and converted part of it into a walk-in closet and part into enlarging our existing bathroom. Now we had a large open bathroom with a walk-in shower and a large jetted tub. This was a long slow process but worth it all. Dan and I handled all this disruption in our home well since we knew it would be worth the wait.

Our last project was designing a place for relaxation and entertainment in our side yard. It had been a playground area when the kids were little, with swings, slide, and a sandbox. After they outgrew these kinds of activities, we put in a hot tub, which was enjoyable for many years but now sat idle with a broken motor. We hired a gardener to design the area and another contractor to install a water garden.

It was now a picture of impressive beauty. Bushes and flowers bloomed at various times of the spring and summer, giving it color and interest, with some unique yard art; a frog doing yoga, and a gigantic metal butterfly. I used my great aunt Lula's old coal stove as a plant stand, and Big Mama's concrete birdbath was placed beside the walkway.

The pavilion had a dining table and seating for a crowd, making it fun for entertaining. Dan and I also enjoyed our time alone there for dinner, or coffee in the mornings, finding it relaxing, listening to the small waterfalls surrounding the pond. We called it our "Golden Pond." It seemed we had done renovation on our marriage and also our house. I guess we were here to stay.

During this time, I was feeling more like myself and contemplating getting involved in some type of work. I wanted it to be fun and only part-time. I always loved frequenting a business in town called The Knitting Mill; an old knitting mill factory renovated into an antique mall where I was always finding cool stuff for our house. There were over a hundred booths with a wide variety of vintage and antique items.

So I decided to rent a booth and look for items to sell. I started going to estate sales, and this was a great place to find bargains to resell. And the booth also gave me a place to sell my mixed media collages. This would be more like a hobby, but I was hoping to make a little spending money.

I spent six weeks finding inventory for the booth. I found this was a perfect creative outlet for me since I loved decorating and arranging everything in my booth. I brought my items in, arranged them, and the managers sold them, taking a 10% commission, plus monthly rent for the booth. Some months I made a few dollars, and some months I lost money.

My entire playroom, which I had recently used as an art studio, was now full of garage and estate sale items. I enjoyed this for three and a half years since it seemed to combine several of my talents. Eventually, the people who owned the historic building sold it to an investor. So The Knitting Mill Antiques closed, and I was out of business.

Dan and I were doing well again, getting out socially to see old friends and enjoying going out to dinner. We still missed the fun we use to have with Skip and Lee Ann. We had shared a mutual engagement party, lived beside each other as both newlyweds and new parents and shared ownership of the Sandbar. We were especially close, and I still grieved over their divorce.

We frequently saw Lee Ann since she still lived in Chattanooga, but Skip was living in Florida with the woman who had taken care of his father and was the mother of his five-year-old daughter.

Skip stayed in touch with Dan, and he called to confide in him about some health problems he was having.

"I can't even mow my grass anymore without getting winded. And I've been having chest pains. I don't know what's going on."

"Skip, don't fool around if you're having chest pains. You need to go see a doctor," Dan told him.

"Aww, I know, but I don't have insurance. I need to wait until November when I turn sixty-five, so I can get Medicare."

"Well, you might not be here in November. Don't let that stop you. You don't need to wait any longer."

Skip suffered from an unusual fear of hospitals. He had a hard time even visiting Lee Ann at the hospital after the birth of their children. Skip's oldest daughter, Leslie, was a nurse, and after talking with her, Skip decided he probably did need to come to Chattanooga to meet his newest granddaughter, and see a doctor.

I hadn't talked to Skip much since he left town, still holding a grudge over everything he had put his family through. I was trying to be more forgiving since Dan had also put his family through our share of grief. We invited Skip over to see all our renovations to the house. He didn't look well and was shuffling along as he walked. I could tell he was getting out of breath.

Later that week, Leslie called to invite us to join her daughters, husband, and her sister, Lindsey, along with Skip at the old Sandbar Restaurant. The actual restaurant was eventually torn down, and a new modern restaurant called The Boathouse was built.

There had been many changes in our lives since owning the Sandbar. But we could always count on the scenery from the deck to remain the same. Overlooking the Tennessee River, with mountains in the background, it was still gorgeous. It was the best place in town to watch the sun setting over the water and settling behind Signal Mountain. The three bridges crossing the river at the forefront provided an interesting contrast to the natural landscape.

It was a fun night. However, it still felt strange to me that Lee Ann wasn't with Skip. He was worried about his upcoming doctor's appointment and mentioned if anything happened to him, he wanted his obituary to say, "He led a colorful life but a wasted one." I wondered how this made his daughters feel. Skip had struggled establishing a career since his days owning the Sandbar. But he had plenty to be proud of, particularly his daughters. We all just laughed his remark off as Skip being Skip.

He brought his daughter to Tennessee with him, but his girlfriend had stayed at home. Leslie and Lindsey tried to be open and loving to their half-sister. They understood that none of what Skip had done was her fault. Skip had made many selfish decisions.

Several days later, Skip went to the doctor, and tests were done that revealed he needed open-heart surgery. He was scared. Leslie assured him he would be well taken care of at the hospital where she worked. She knew the doctor and many of the nurses who would be taking care of him.

We went to see him the day after surgery. He was talkative but had experienced an episode the night before when his heart stopped, and the nurses had to use electric paddles to bring him back. His voice was weak, but he told me when his heart stopped, he saw "the green fields of heaven, just like in the 23rd Psalm." We laughed, and I told him I thought it was "green pastures."

"You're lucky, Skip. You can have a new lease on life now. Try to start taking better care of yourself and stop smoking."

He was a smoker when he was younger, but had stopped for ten years or more, only to start again when he moved to Florida. I brought him a funny musical card since he was always into music. He seemed to be recovering fine. His girlfriend was now in town to visit and possibly take him home if he continued to improve.

Several days later, on the 4th of July, I got a call from Lee Ann to tell me Skip was having trouble again. She was at the hospital to help with Leslie's kids since she and Lindsey were at his bedside. We decided to ride over to help in any way we could.

It was a dire situation by the time we arrived in the late afternoon. His heart had been stopping all day, and they couldn't get it regulated. We went into the ICU room and found Leslie, her husband, Matt, Lindsey, and Lee Ann on one side of Skip's bed. On the other side were the girlfriend and their daughter. Dan and I were standing at the end of the bed.

It felt like a movie scene. Skip had gotten a sizeable three-leaf clover tattooed on his forearm years earlier with Lee Ann, Lindsey, and Leslie's name on each clover. It was never as noticeable as now. It made me feel uncomfortable, so I could only imagine how Lee Ann felt. There it was, for all of us to see.

Everyone was in shock as we all watched the monitor showing Skip's heart rate going all over the place. Eventually, the doctor came in and talked to Leslie, telling her there was nothing more they could do. Skip was unconscious at this point. We were all crying, even Lee Ann. She told me later all of her resentment toward Skip fell away when she saw him struggling to live. He died minutes later.

Dan was asked to give the eulogy at the funeral. He was apprehensive about doing this. Skip and Dan had been friends for forty-five years with quite a colorful past. They loved to reminisce about their college days at UTC. They both enjoyed a good time. Skip was the guy Dan had flipped a coin with to see who was going to ask me out on a date. I had known him as long as I had known Dan.

Dan wrote the eulogy to be somewhat humorous, but in the end, he had trouble getting through it. His voice cracked as he felt the emotion from what he was doing – saying goodbye to one of his oldest friends. Leslie and Lindsey, Skip's daughters, asked me to read the 23rd Psalm and I changed the verse about green pastures to green fields, since that was what Skip told me he saw. We were stunned over how fast this had happened. Our friend, neighbor, coworker, and Jordan's god-father had died.

~

Later that summer, Dan and I were sitting in our den on a beautiful sunny Saturday afternoon. There was no rain or wind anywhere around. Dan had just come in from eating lunch with friends and parked his truck along our fence, as he always did since we don't have a garage. The TV was on, and suddenly we heard a deafening noise outside. Dan looked at me, and I looked at him.

"Oh, my God. What was that?" we both said at the same time. I sounded as if it could have been an airplane crashing into our house. The sound filled the entire house, loud and violent. As we ran toward our front door, all I could see through the windows were tree branches.

"It must have been the tree," I shouted. We had recently talked about the sixty-foot oak tree, beginning to lean to one side.

Dan had said, "Well, if it falls, I think it will fall away from the house." He was right. We opened the front door and saw the hundred-year oak tree uprooted and fallen across the yard, onto the fence, and into Dan's truck. Our perfect white picket fence was demolished.

If I didn't know it already, now it was official. There was no perfect life behind a white picket fence. The tree totaled Dan's truck, which only minutes before he was sitting in. We decided not to replace the white picket fence but instead got a bronze-tinted aluminum one. Maybe we should have looked into a steel fence, possibly providing more strength when unforeseen circumstances crash into your house and your life.

~

Life continued to give us the good with the bad, with or without the picket fence. Alex and Melissa were continuing to do well. He now had a master's in Occupational Therapy. His career choice had been influenced by Jordan and his exposure to those caring for him. It taught him compassion and having a kind heart that made him well suited to his profession.

He was the kid who did everything right and in the right order. He got into minor trouble during high school, just enough to make him know he didn't want to go down the same road as Luke. He and Melissa bought a house, got a dog, and were happy and healthy. Melissa had gotten her Masters in Family and Children's Studies. I wasn't going to be giving her any advice about her family or her children. She was smart and grounded.

We were trying to see Luke at least twice a year— during the summer and at Christmas. We talked and often text, so it didn't seem so hard not seeing him as often as I would have liked. I was trusting what he was telling us was true. He was continuing to stay sober and going to AA meetings. He was doing some acting, but not getting paid for any work yet.

I started talking to him about going back to school since his boarding house was across the street from a community college, Los Angeles City College. Of course, I was again thinking of a vocation for him so he could support himself. He was thinking more about a career in the movie industry. He enrolled and started taking courses.

⌒

This gave me hope for a more positive future for Luke, but when something positive happened in my life, it was often offset by something negative. I got a phone call from Jordan's gastroenterologist telling me he had seen Jordan about his continuing issues with coughing. I knew this was happening, and it was worrisome since he often had prolonged episodes of deep coughing until he gagged.

Because he was not eating well, he had lost a lot of weight. I remembered Jordan's issues as a baby trying to coordinate his swallowing, breathing, and eating. His lack of muscle tone was now affecting his throat and swallowing more seriously.

The doctor said, "It's only a matter of time before he gets aspiration pneumonia. I'm recommending he have a permanent feeding tube." I panicked. I was driving when I got his call and should have pulled over. I gripped the steering wheel and started to cry. I didn't want to hear this. *Why? Why? Does Jordan have to go through something else? He can't talk, and now he can't eat?* I didn't know who I was even asking my questions to. Life wasn't fair. *But how many times do I have to be reminded?*

Eating was one of the few pleasures for Jordan. He loved his food and also other people's food. Dan and I were devastated by this news. I found myself crying on and off for most of every day. I just couldn't wrap my head around this, not to ever be able to eat again. This was the ultimate cruelty for Jordan. But we didn't have a choice. The doctor reminded me of the danger of getting aspiration pneumonia. Several of Jordan's classmates had succumbed to it.

We scheduled the procedure. We arrived early and met Jordan and his house manager at the hospital. Before they came to get him, I couldn't stop crying. One of the nurses tried to comfort me, assuming this was a temporary solution to a temporary problem and didn't seem to understand why I was so upset.

This was permanent. He would never be able to eat or drink normally again. Jordan had gone through so much, and now this. I was mad at the world. I could feel myself pushing against the anger, but I had to accept this was medically necessary.

I was so thankful for the care Orange Grove provided for Jordan whenever he was in the hospital and at his home. I didn't know how we would have ever managed without their help. Jordan was well known by almost everyone that worked at Orange Grove, especially the medical staff.

No situation was perfect, but he now had a caring and loving house manager and staff that loved him. They had learned to read his body language, and he had a way of communicating most of his needs. He had a life away from us that gave us some reassurance that he would continue his life when we were gone. It was hard to consider this possibility, but it was facing the reality of having a profoundly handicapped child.

After all of the time tending to this latest issue with Jordan, I needed a step forward in a positive direction. Life seemed to be weighing in on the negative side again. It was Halloween, and as always, my house was decorated with cute pumpkins, ghosts, and goblins. We were expecting Alex and Melissa and their chocolate lab, Maple, to stop by on Sunday afternoon. They had been to visit her parents and were heading back home to Knoxville. I asked Alex if Maple had a Halloween costume.

"Yeah, we got her one. I'll show it to you when we come over."

I was eager to see what kind of costume they bought for my grand dog. I loved Maple Jean, such a fun, gentle dog.

Dan and I waited for Maple to make a grand entrance. She walked in with what looked like a new sweater.

What kind of outfit is that? I glanced down to look at the words printed on the back. "I'm going to be a big sister." I reread it. *"What? Oh, wow, really?"*

"Does this mean what I think it means?" I asked as I jumped up to give Alex and Melissa a hug. I was going to be a grandmother. This was the best news I had gotten in a long time. I was thrilled. My baby was going to be a father. Where had the years gone? I was experiencing pure joy. I had forgotten what it felt like to be so happy.

The time went by fast, and we were grateful Melissa had an uneventful pregnancy, with all signs pointing to a healthy baby boy. We were so excited for this next chapter in our lives. Three weeks before the due date, Dan and I went to Knoxville for a couples baby shower for Alex and Melissa. It was an evening full of fun and games, good food, and socializing.

Melissa was glowing with anticipation. I was still adjusting to the idea of Alex being a father. So many thoughts were going through my mind as we drove back to Chattanooga after the party. Their lives were about to change in so many ways. How can anyone be prepared to become parents? We all just figure it out as we go.

The next day was Sunday, Memorial Day weekend, so Dan and I were relaxing, thinking of possible plans for the afternoon. I got a phone call from Alex.

"What are you guys doing today?" he asked.

"Oh, we don't have any plans yet."

"Well, how about coming to Knoxville to become grandparents? We are at the hospital now."

This was going to happen today. Melissa's water had broken early that morning, and they were awaiting the contractions.

I waited for a few hours and packed clothes, not knowing how long I might be there. I drove to Knoxville by myself with Dan coming later. When I got there, Melissa was walking the hallway, having some major contractions. She was in her hospital gown, holding onto the wall as her mother rubbed her back. I could practically feel them myself, as my heart went out to her in sympathy. It was painful to see the familiar look of anxiety and anticipation of the unknown on her face. Her mother and sister were there with her.

Dan and I and Melissa's parents spent the entire afternoon sitting and waiting as she labored away. Melissa's sister was helping Alex to birth the baby, sending texts to let us know what was happening. Finally, she told us Melissa had gotten an epidural and was ready to push, and we could come back to see her briefly.

She was on her side and looking apprehensive but beautiful, still full of baby. I told Melissa I loved her. I could see a combination of emotions on Alex's face – possibly fear of what this next phase of life would be like, happiness that he was about to meet his son, thankfulness that they had gotten this far in the labor process.

Around 12:45 in the morning, Alex walked out with his blue "It's a Boy" hat. We knew it was a boy, but they had kept the name a secret. Alex was smiling, and I hugged him tightly. As the emotion of what he had just experienced surfaced, he started to cry.

The baby would be named Benjamin Harold LaGraff. Benjamin was a name chosen just for him, and Harold was Melissa's grandfather's name. It was a strong, bold name. He was six pounds, four ounces, 20 inches long with dark brown hair.

We had to wait for another hour or so before we could see him. It was 2:15 a.m., and we were all tired but ready to meet our grandson. He was small and delicate, bundled in a blue blanket. Perfect in every way. His little fingers and toes were fascinating. His tiny feet were sticking out from under the blanket. His dark eyes were peering out at the world. My heart was full of gratitude.

Chapter 17

August 2016

Life had settled down, but I still found myself waiting for the next challenge. *What's going to happen next?* I was pleasantly surprised to get some exciting and positive news from Luke. Finally, good news. He had gotten a role in a popular TV show called *American Horror Story*. He had missed our family reunion in July because of the filming, but he wasn't sure he made the cut to be in the episode. It was a non-speaking part. He was The Scalped Man.

As a young boy, he loved to pretend he was a superhero by dressing in his Spiderman or Superman outfits, always putting on costumes and acting out being someone else. Now he was in a real TV show, playing alongside Sarah Paulson and Lady Gaga. The show was a horror story, so he spent two hours in makeup to make him appear scalped. It was filmed at night in Griffith Park, and he was given his own trailer with his name on the door. This was all unbelieveable.

Dan and I sat down together to watch Luke's debut. I hadn't watched a scary show in many years. However, as a kid, they were a favorite. We started to think his scene had been cut because the show was almost over when suddenly he appeared coming out of the woods in the last scene. It was frightening when he let out a scream, looking ghastly with his long red beard and scalp covered in fake blood. It was surreal to see him on screen and his name included in the credits. He had come a long way. Dan and I were able to share a proud moment for our son. It felt amazing.

Dan and I were continuing to enjoy traveling. Now that the kids were gone and I was retired, this kind of freedom was liberating. Although Dan was still working, his career was flexible since it was his own business. We planned a trip out west to Las Vegas, the Grand Canyon, Bryce, and Zion National Park with his brother, Arnie, and sister, Susie.

I spent days online booking rooms, making flight arrangements, and entertainment reservations. The trip was in early September, and the weather was perfect. Being around the amazing scenery was uplifting and gave me a new perspective I needed. We hiked the canyons in Zion, walking over rocks and water up to our knees. We saw some beautiful sunsets over the magnificent rock formations.

I felt invigorated by the sky, the clouds, the rocks, the water, and the trees. In the big picture of life and nature, my problems were small. Life was good, and I felt a lightness that came from being surrounded by all the beauty.

Following our trip out west, we had a wedding to attend. I was still uneasy about going to weddings. They were a reminder of what I had lost. But this wedding we weren't going to miss. Skip's youngest daughter, Lindsey, was getting married in the mountains of North Carolina. We both had trouble realizing Skip wouldn't be there.

Skip's daughters arranged a chair with Skip's hat and his Sandbar jacket on the front row to represent his presence. It brought tears to my eyes. I was sad that Skip had died so young, sad that he had left Lee Ann, sad that we wouldn't be making any more memories with him.

Skip's girlfriend came to the wedding because their daughter, Lindsey's half-sister, was a bridesmaid. We were all friendly and nice to them since everyone knew this event was hard for them too. Lee Ann was able to extend genuine kindness to them. The girlfriend had apologized to Lee Ann about the circumstances surrounding her and Skip getting together. Forgiveness was the right thing to do. I was still working on forgiving Dan.

Our forty-third wedding anniversary fell only a few weeks later. We went to the Boathouse, the restaurant built after the Sandbar was torn down. This place always brought on feelings of melancholy. I remembered it as it used to be when we were both young and in love, full of ambition and excitement over what life would bring.

It was a crisp fall evening as we sat on the deck overlooking the scenic Tennessee River. Anniversaries always gave me a reason to look back on all the years and be thankful for our relationship. But now, there were mixed emotions. I wished I could change the past and make it different, but I knew I couldn't. All I could do was look toward the future. Maybe even just try to enjoy the present.

The bottom line was we still loved each other. There were many things I still loved about Dan. I knew he had a sensitive side in there somewhere. I had seen him cry over sentimental movies or TV shows. He just had a hard time showing it in real life, thinking he always had to be the strong one, the stoic one, the unemotional one. I was torn between the Dan I had known for forty-six years and the Dan that had made some selfish and irresponsible decisions. He gave me a beautiful anniversary card with his words saying he loved me more than ever.

～

I was feeling stronger emotionally than I had in a long time. There wasn't much now that could make me fall apart. I was a big girl and had learned from experience that "this too shall pass." I was staying busy, exercising, reading, and spending time with friends.

I took a six-week mindfulness class, which was helping me to focus on the present, not the past or the future. On the night of the first class, we sat in a large circle and were asked to introduce ourselves and tell why we were there. I imagined myself telling them all my reasons for being there. Where would I even start? It was hard trying to concentrate on my breathing with so much crap in my head.

I attempted to put my feelings into words. "I'm here because I dwell on the past too much. I've had some rough life challenges. I don't know what the future will be, but I'm always worrying about it. So I know I need to learn just to be in the present, the right now. But it's so hard to do." I felt a sense of accomplishment after finishing the course. Like I had learned some coping skills.

I was also doing volunteer work at the local Ronald McDonald House and at the Hart Gallery, a gallery designed for people with mental limitations, giving them a chance to create art and sell it in a gallery. Both were opportunities to get outside myself and to be of service to others.

I was looking after my emotional well-being. I was hardened now and determined that whatever happened, I was strong enough to get through it and to the other side. Life was always going to be hard and unpredictable.

Even though it had been seven years since the affair, I still thought about it every day. There was always some reminder. I had followed my heart and stayed with Dan. My mind told me to be cautious. It warned me that I might not be able to heal a broken heart again. My heart told me I still l loved Dan, and I could still feel his love for me.

I took solace in words by Michele Weiner-Davis, a licensed clinical social worker, family therapist, and author. She writes, "People who've been betrayed need to know that there's no shame in staying in a marriage – they're not doormats, they're warriors. The gift they provide to their families by working through the pain is enormous."

We had ended counseling several years earlier. We had gone from once a week, to twice a month, to once a month. We had discussed all the resentments, the anger, the betrayal, the deceit, the embarrassment, and the pain. Dan said he would continue as long as I needed to go, but even I was tired of talking about it all. I was at peace with my decision to stay in our marriage. We had decided to get on with our lives together. Love is a decision, and I had chosen to love.

Now it was just Dan and me with no kids living with us, and no in-laws still alive. In some ways our world seemed to be getting smaller. My grandparents were gone; my parents were gone. At some point you realize, you are next. My sister was still in Florida and my brother in Ducktown, but I didn't see them often.

After my father's death, my brother spent four years renovating my parents' house in Ducktown, readying it to sell. My brother called to say he had finally found a buyer. My parents had lived in the house from 1961 until my father died in 2013. Most of my childhood memories revolved around this house. The one built right next to Robert's house.

I felt incredibly grateful to have had a childhood home to go back to for fifty-two years and nostalgic about never spending time there again. I asked my brother if I could come and say my goodbyes before the closing. He told me the people were moving in that weekend, but he didn't think they would mind if I stopped by.

I was hesitant since I envisioned going by myself to each room and reflecting on the past – the bedroom where I spent so many hours on the phone with Robert, the bomb shelter where slumber parties and birthday parties were held, the dining room, with the gold flowered wallpaper, where we gathered for so many Thanksgiving and Christmas dinners, and the steps I climbed the night of my first kiss. I decided I needed to go for one last visit.

The buyer and his wife met me on the steps as I introduced myself. They were overly friendly and kept telling me how happy they were to have the house. Unfortunately, the man followed me around the entire time and gave me no time by myself.

They had already moved their furniture in, and it was disorienting and confusing seeing different furniture in my parents' house. It was like a bad dream. I wanted to wake up and see everything as I remembered it.... the plaid couch in the den with the afghan mother had made lying on the back, the ladder-back chairs along the sides of our oblong maple kitchen table, the twin beds Diane and I had shared for so many years... all gone.

My mother's elegant dining room with the crystal chandelier was now a game room for their grandchildren. There was a fake fireplace in the living room with Native American pictures hanging on the walls. A bearskin rug was lying on the beautiful hardwood floor in the den. The bomb shelter room was now a room for his gun collection with an enormous gun safe. *None of this belongs here. This is not right.*

It all felt so wrong. *Oh, my God. This is my parents' house. It will never be your house. Never.* I couldn't get out of there fast enough. This saved me from the emotional goodbye I had anticipated.

∽

While I was in Ducktown, I also attended another emotional event. I had received an invitation to Mrs. Lee's 90th birthday celebration. I had stayed in touch with the Lee's through the years, stopping in to see them when I went home. They were always upbeat, asking questions about my kids and telling me about their latest global adventures.

Mrs. Lee was now living in North Carolina with her oldest daughter, Linda. Dr. Lee had died two years before from complications from Alzheimer's. I visited him in the nursing home several months before his death, but he didn't recognize me. I had always felt a connection to them and their other three children. I represented Robert to them, and they always seemed grateful I had continued a relationship with their family.

The birthday party was at the church the Lees had attended and where Robert's funeral had been held. For her gifts, I gave her flowers, a crystal butterfly, and a picture of Robert in a frame, one I knew she hadn't seen. It was from my senior prom when he wore a gold and black tuxedo, looking handsome with his playful smile.

I didn't want to make her feel sad on such a happy occasion, so I worried a little about including it. She called me several days later to thank me for coming and for the gifts. She was still mentally sharp. She especially liked the picture.

She talked a little about Robert. "He was a good kid at heart, just a little mischievous."

She caught me off guard when she said, "Yeah, we knew Robert was climbing out his window at night and coming to your house. But we just didn't say anything."

Oh my... she knew about that? There was an extended pause at my end of the phone. I never knew they were aware of our middle of the night trysts in my bedroom. Even after all these years, I could feel myself blushing.

"Well, you weren't supposed to know about that."

We both laughed.

At the party, one of Robert's cousins approached me and asked, "Are you Karen Campbell?" I had never met him.

"Well, yeah, it was my maiden name."

"Robert used to talk about you a lot," he said. For several hours afterward, I was thinking about the path my life might have taken. *Would we have gotten married? Would I be living in Ducktown with Robert? Would he be a veterinarian? Would we have children? Would he still be riding motorcycles?*

Life had taken me in a different direction. Despite all that happened in my marriage through the years, I had experienced joy and love with Dan and my sons. Life had certainly not been boring. My children and husband had provided more than enough drama.

As for Luke, he was still living in LA and had completed an associate's degree in film production from LA City College. Dan and I flew out for graduation, which was held at Griffith Park with the mayor of LA as the commencement speaker. Luke was easy to follow in the crowd of graduates, with his long red hair and beard making him stand out among the other students.

I was feeling exuberant as I thought back to all we had been through and now this. I tried to focus on enjoying every minute of his accomplishment. The announcer giving out diplomas was loud and slightly obnoxious, but when she said, "Luke John LaGraff," I felt my heart soar. He had come a long way. We had come a long way.

We wanted to celebrate Luke's graduation, so after the ceremony, we invited a few of his friends over to our rental house. Luke was now an AA sponsor to a young man, also named Luke. We included him in the celebration. Our Luke was now seven years sober. He had not had a drink or taken any drugs since the day he arrived in LA. Seven years. *Who would have ever thought this could happen?* I was just as proud or maybe more proud of this accomplishment and his commitment to sobriety as I was about his degree.

We met some of Luke's friends who were dealing with similar issues who had been an inspiration to him. He loved the diversity of the people he had met in LA. He felt the support and camaraderie of people from all walks of life. Luke attributed his success not just to going to the AA meetings but committing himself to work the steps of the program. He had learned how to take one day at a time.

His ambition to be an actor had been his motivation to go to LA in the first place. And he knew that wouldn't happen unless he was sober. But his desire to stay sober was about so much more than that now. He shared that he loved waking up without a hangover; he loved being able to think with clarity; he loved helping other people; he loved his sense of well-being, and he loved living without a constant sense of impending doom. He loved being clean and sober. He had also stopped smoking several years earlier. I was so proud of him. I smiled the entire time we were there.

We spent the next five days in sunny California. Luke stayed with us in our rental house, and we enjoyed our time with him, relating as three adults. We ate breakfast on Sunset Blvd., went to the Los Angeles County Museum of Art, and rented bikes, spending an afternoon at Venice Beach. The weather was cool but felt good after living with the high humidity in the south.

It felt slightly odd to be laughing and having fun together. The relationship between all of us had been strained for so many years that it often was difficult even to make conversation. Between all that we went through with Luke before he got sober and all that had happened between Dan and me, we had struggled with what to say and how to say it. So now the air was clearer, less oppressive. We could all breathe a little easier.

The following December, Luke flew home for Christmas. I always loved picking him up at the airport. There's something special about family members coming home for the holidays. All the hustle and bustle with Christmas music in the background always got me in the Christmas spirit. I loved watching him coming closer and closer and finally being able to give him a big hug. This year I held onto him for a long time.

I was thrilled that we would all be together for Christmas. I reminded everyone to bring their Christmas tee-shirt, pants or pajamas to wear on Christmas morning. I had given them as gifts through the years. We didn't have matching ones, but different ones, just like all of us.

When the boys were old enough to cook, we started a tradition of them cooking Christmas breakfast for everyone. We were going to have a traditional breakfast of eggs, bacon, pancakes, and sweet rolls. And coffee, although I still had a hard time realizing my boys were old enough to drink coffee.

Dan and I woke up early and settled into our new den. He finished putting the rest of the presents under the tree and turned on the tree lights. I looked over all the sentimental ornaments I had collected through the years. I looked at all the family Christmas pictures I display during the holidays. The sparkle from the lights and the shimmering of the tinsel gave the room a festive atmosphere. At this moment, there wasn't room for any negative emotions, just gratitude.

Dan brought me a cup of coffee as we sat by the fire reading the newspaper in our Christmas pajamas. The room felt cozy and warm. Gizmo the 3rd, slept in my lap, and Sadie was asleep in her bed on the floor while we waited for everyone to join us. Soon Alex came upstairs to start breakfast. Melissa and Ben were still sleeping in the downstairs bedroom and would soon join us.

"Merry Christmas, Mom. Merry Christmas, Dad. You guys hungry?" Alex asked.

"Merry Christmas, Alex. We're ready when you guys are," Dan said.

"Looks like Santa came last night. We must have all been good this year," Alex said with a laugh.

A few minutes later, Luke joined Alex in the kitchen, and they started their usual banter as they started to cook.

"Man, you're cooking those eggs too long."

"Those pancakes aren't big enough. I could eat ten of those."

"What are you doing? That's not how you cook bacon."

They loved playfully going at each other. There was lots of laughing.

Our family felt complete when Jordan's house manager brought him to the house for the day. He was dressed for the holiday with a bright red sweater and jeans. He looked so handsome. His green eyes were talking. Both boys stopped what they were doing to give Jordan a big bear hug.

"JD, you're looking good, man. Merry Christmas. Did you get to see Santa this year?" Alex asked.

"Jordan, good to see you. You ready for some Christmas music?" Luke asked.

He turned on the stereo and found a classic Christmas song.

"Up on the rooftop, reindeer pause, Out jumps good old Santa Claus, down through the chimney with lots of toys, All for the little ones, Christmas joys. Ho, ho, ho, who wouldn't go! Ho, ho, ho, who wouldn't go! Up on the rooftop, click, click, click, Down thru the chimney with good Saint Nick."

It had the perfect beat for Jordan's *Rain Man* dance. Jordan was smiling ear to ear. He loved his brothers, and they loved him.

"Ho, ho, ho Jordan, you got it, man," Luke said, as they moved to the beat.

We watched from the living room as the boys danced around the kitchen, holding onto Jordan's hands.

Dan and I looked at each other and smiled. Our family of five was still together. Our imperfect family. Love won.

Alex and Melissa are out of town for a wedding. I am staying with Ben overnight. He is now eighteen months old. His bedroom is next to mine. It's 5:10 a.m., and I wake to Ben's slightly quivering voice,

"Mommy?"

"Daddy?"

"Mommy?"

"Daddy?"

I walk into the hall and carefully open his door. His night light shines a soft yellow warmth across the room. He is standing in his crib with his large, expressive blue eyes almost glowing. I gently retrieve his pacifier and lie him down with his stuffed lamb tucked under his arm. The colorful quilt I made as a naïve expectant mother, forty years ago, hangs over his crib, "Our Baby Is Here." I comfort him with gentle pats on his back. He peacefully closes his eyes, and I slip back to my room.

I lie awake afterward feeling emotional, remembering the days when my parents could make everything right with the world. Your mother and father are the first people in your life to make you feel safe and secure or not. I feel grateful for my parents' years of dedication to their children. I miss them terribly.

I ponder Ben's future as he grows into a young man. Now he is sweetly innocent and pure, the beautiful and endearing qualities of a baby. Your instinct is to shelter them from life's harsh realities. You wish you could change the world for them. In time he will have to deal with all of life's hardships, as we all do. He will learn and grow from them, just as I have.

I can't go back to sleep. I think about the challenges I've been through. *Would I change it all? Would I be the person I am now without having gone through it all? What lessons have I learned? Do I feel stronger for having gone through the disappointments? Have I become more resilient?*

Each challenge changed me. Each challenge opened up a world with which I was unfamiliar. Each challenge taught me things about myself and about life. All I know for sure is I have survived until this point in life, not knowing what might lie ahead.

I struggle with what Gilda Radner called "delicious ambiguity." I'm not sure I could call it "delicious." I seek clarity and sureness in life, and there is none. As the cliché goes, "There are no guarantees in life." My challenge is to realize I have no control over what happens in my life – only control over how I react to what happens. This is my struggle.

I do know I am still here, enjoying life with family and friends, with many blessings for which I am thankful. I have faith in the goodness of life itself. I work at looking forward and not back.

The house is quiet. Ben has settled down and feels secure enough to trust that for now, he is alright. I choose to do the same as I drift slowly back to sleep.

What Readers Are Saying

- I rarely read books as quickly as I read *So Much for the White Picket Fence*. This memoir is a real page-turner, not merely because the author has led quite a colorful life but because the writing is clear, honest, literate, and creates pictures in my mind. The story is a powerful testament to faith in family, in humanity, in the universal puzzle known as God, and mostly to the author herself.

  Joe Ryan-PhD Clinical Psychology, English Professor, Los Angeles City College

- How do you keep moving forward with resilience, holding fast to love, faith, and forgiveness in the face of great loss and suffering? This is the story Karen LaGraff bravely shares in her inspiring memoir. She shares searingly honest details of her journey learning to accept her past, and also to live and learn from the traumas she experiences in her own family. The book will leave you with hope that "If Karen can make her way through, so can I," which is exactly the sense of hope many need, especially now.

  Cali Yost, Author of *Tweak It: Make What Matters to You Happen Every Day*

- Karen LaGraff has put into words both the pain and the joy of living in her emotional memoir that reminds us that life itself goes on through both the dark and light times. Her words are beautiful and haunting, and I found myself drawn into her journey, as if I lived it with her.

  Greg Wilkey, Principal East Side Elementary School and best-selling author of YA fiction

- You'll find parts of yourself in Karen LaGraff's captivating story of love, loss, and life. In an era when intense grief and anxiety had no outlet in the counseling office, we read her words and echo, "me too." Readers will be able to feel, experience, and resurrect their own stories. And that makes this memoir worth reading, along with great therapy.

  Judy Herman, LPC-MHSP Counselor, Speaker, and Author of *Beyond Messy Relationships*

About the Author

Karen LaGraff

Karen LaGraff has a B.S. in Education from the University of Tennessee in Knoxville and a M.ED. from the University of Tennessee at Chattanooga. She has worked for UTC as a student teacher supervisor and for the state of Tennessee under the Early Intervention program evaluating pre-school children. She taught elementary school for eighteen years before retiring.

She now does volunteer work for the Ronald McDonald House, the Hart Gallery, and Bridge Refugee Services. She enjoys reading, writing, traveling, exercising, gardening and spending time with family and friends. She has three grown sons, two grandsons, and lives in Chattanooga with her husband. She can be reached at somuchforthewhitepicketfence@gmail.com

Dan, Jordan, Alex, Luke and Karen LaGraff, June 2011. "We were all smiling at the same time."

References

Bercht, Anne. *My Husband's Affair Became the Best Thing that Ever Happened to Me*. New Bloomington, Indiana: Trafford Publishing, 2004.

Bercht, Brian and Anne. *BeyondAffairs.com*

Davis, Michelle Weiner-Davis, *Healing from Infidelity,* Colorado: Michelle Weiner Davis, 2017

Doyle, Glennon. *Love Warrior*. New York: Flatiron Books, 2016

Lesser, Elizabeth. *Broken Open*. New York: Vintage Books, 2012.

Strayed, Cheryl. *Tiny Beautiful Things*. New York: Vintage Books, 2012

Wilderness Treatment Center, Marion, Montana. *WildernessTreatmentCenter.com*

Sources of Quotations

Part 1- Vicki Harrison- Pinterest

Part 2- Sonia Ricotti- www.goodreads.com

Part 3- Linda Wooten-www.everydayparenting.com

Part 4-Bob Marley-www.lovetravelquotes.com

Part 5-Anonymous- Pinterest

Part 6-Anonymous-Pinterest

Part 7-Ernest Hemingway-www.quotesplanet.com

Part 8-Gilda Radner-www.huffpost.com

Myriad Pro and Eccentric Standard on 50# LSI Créme White
Type and Design by Karen Paul Stone